EXCHANGES IN EXOTICISM

Cross-Cultural Marriage and the Making of the Mediterranean in Old French Romance

Exchanges in Exoticism

Cross-Cultural Marriage and the Making of the Mediterranean in Old French Romance

MEGAN MOORE

UNIVERSITY OF TORONTO PRESS
Toronto Buffalo London

Toronto Buffalo London
www.utppublishing.com

ISBN 978-1-4426-4469-4

Library and Archives Canada Cataloguing in Publication

Moore, Megan, 1977–, author
Exchanges in exoticism : cross-cultural marriage and the making of the Mediterranean in Old French romance / Megan Moore.

Includes bibliographical references and index.
ISBN 978-1-4426-4469-4 (bound)

1. French literature – To 1500 – History and criticism. 2. Byzantine literature – History and criticism. 3. French literature – To 1500 – Mediterranean influences. 4. Women in literature. 5. Sex role in literature. 6. Nobility in literature. 7. National characteristics, French, in literature. I. Title.

PQ183.M66 2014 840.9'35837 C2013-905687-4

University of Toronto Press acknowledges the financial assistance to its publishing program of the Canada Council for the Arts and the Ontario Arts Council.

University of Toronto Press acknowledges the financial support of the Government of Canada through the Canada Book Fund for its publishing activities.

For Thomas, Sophie, & Gabby

Να εύχεσαι νάναι μακρύς ο δρόμος.
Πολλά τα καλοκαιρινά πρωιά να είναι
που με τι ευχαρίστησι, με τι χαρά
θα μπαίνεις σε λιμένας πρωτοειδωμένους·
να σταματήσεις σ' εμπορεία Φοινικικά,
και τες καλές πραγμάτειες ν' αποκτήσεις,
σεντέφια και κοράλλια, κεχριμπάρια κ' έβενους,
και ηδονικά μυρωδικά κάθε λογής,
όσο μπορείς πιο άφθονα ηδονικά μυρωδικά·

[Hope the voyage is a long one.
May there be many a summer morning when,
with what pleasure, what joy,
you come into harbours seen for the first time;
may you stop at Phoenician trading stations
to buy fine things,
mother of pearl and coral, amber and ebony,
sensual perfume of every kind.]

Constantine Cavafy, *Ithaca*

Contents

Acknowledgments

I am so grateful for the many encounters over years of discussion and research that have helped shape this book, often from many different and curious corners of the globe. First and foremost, I would like to thank Peggy McCracken for her invaluable insights into the questions at stake in this study and her encouragement as it has taken its road to fruition. The University of Michigan's Department of Romance Languages and the Rackham School of Graduate Studies helped make large portions of the original research for this project possible, in particular permitting the manuscript research conducted in the archives of the Bibliothèque Nationale and the Bodleian Library as well as extensive time in minor archives in Greece and France. Domna Stanton and Cathy Sanok both asked key questions about the nature of gender in my project.

I would also like to thank my Byzantinist colleagues for many wonderful hours spent debating cross-cultural contact. In particular, I am grateful to Dimitris Krallis for that first long and delightful conversation about the relationship between Byzantium and the west. I also thank Stavroula Constantinou for her kind invitation to present my work in Cyprus, and for her assistance with the Medieval Greek in this volume, though of course any errors that remain are mine. I am also grateful to Panagiotis Agapitos for his criticism of my work in Cyprus, and for his continued interest in seeing how one western medievalist picks up the threads of Byzantium. Conversations held long ago over pizza with John Fine, Anthony Kaldellis, and Ian Mladjov also proved important to shaping my interests in Mediterranean cross-cultural contact.

I would also like to acknowledge the impact a graduate seminar focusing on the history of the book and manuscript studies taken with

George Greenia has had on my understanding of the process of writing and reading in the Middle Ages. I attribute my interest in manuscripts and their production and consumption – which I maintain deeply affects how we read and understand medieval literature – to that first class. I am also grateful for subsequent conversations with Keith Busby and Douglas Kelly, whose work on medieval French romance manuscripts has grounded this study. I appreciate Raymond Clemens and Paul Saenger for their suggestions when discussing the manuscript methodology of this project with me.

The Newberry Library's Fellows' Seminar provided a much-needed critical testing ground for several of the ideas launched here. In particular, I wish to thank my colleagues Carla Zecher, Jim Grossman, Karen Christianson, Paul Gehl, and Jim Akerman; and fellows Diana Robin, Ellen McClure, Sam Truett, Katie Gucer, Carmen Nocentelli, Laura Edwards, and Natalie Rothman for their suggestions.

I am extremely grateful to the University of Missouri for its substantial support of this project through the Research Council. My colleagues Johanna Kramer, Emma Lipton, and Rabia Gregory were enormously helpful and supportive critics. I also offer warm thanks to Myles Freborg for his meticulousness with research questions. Finally, I wish to thank Toby Oshiro, for reminding me about the joy to be found in writing.

Finally, I would like to thank my family for their continued encouragement and unwavering support as I have trotted off to archives and buried myself with delight in research questions and manuscripts for weeks on end. Throughout much change they still held on to the notion that this book and its ideas were worth pursuing, and I am deeply thankful for that support, especially from Johannes Becker.

EXCHANGES IN EXOTICISM

Cross-Cultural Marriage and the Making of the Mediterranean in Old French Romance

Introduction

Once out of nature I shall never take
My bodily form from any natural thing,
But such a form as Grecian goldsmiths make
Of hammered gold and gold enamelling
To keep a drowsy Emperor awake;
Or set upon a golden bough to sing
To lords and ladies of Byzantium
Of what is past, or passing, or to come.

– Yeats, "Sailing to Byzantium"

At dusk on 13 April 1204 Constantinople lay in a smoking rubble, burnt, pillaged, and assaulted by the western Crusaders who had sworn oaths to leave the world's richest Christian city unscathed. As Byzantines wailed and their city burned, the Frankish and Venetian families at the forefront of its demise began a frenzied race to divvy up the spoils of conquest. They scrambled to claim the city's wondrous relics, textiles, and gold, as well as its women, whom they saw as their main access to legitimization and power. That night soldiers sacked the Hagia Sofia, broke its renowned altar into thousands of pieces, absconded with its gems, and placed a prostitute on the patriarch's throne to sing lewd songs. Byzantine historian Niketas Choniates looked upon his beleaguered city and lamented that

> a certain harlot, a sharer in their guilt, a minister of the furies, a servant of the demons, a worker of incantations and poisonings, insulting Christ, sat in the patriarch's seat, singing an obscene song and dancing frequently.

> [...] In the alleys, in the streets, in the temples, complaints, weeping, lamentations, grief, the groaning of men, the shrieks of women, wounds, rape, captivity, the separation of those most closely united. Nobles wandered about ignominiously, those of venerable age in tears, the rich in poverty. [...] Oh, immortal God, how great the afflictions of the men, how great the distress![1]

Like many of his contemporaries, Choniates expressed inimitable sorrow at the desecration of his beloved city. More importantly for our purposes, however, Choniates, like the crusaders, identifies women as key players in the downfall of an empire. Choniates's outrage reaches its zenith here with the intentional desecration of the patriarch's throne, and he links the colonization of religious space with women's inappropriate actions.

Examples like Choniates's underscore how western crusaders used women's sexuality to support their political and personal goals. While the prostitute offers a powerful single image of how women's sexuality could interface with the goals of political domination, the involvement of women in the construction of empire was more systematic and on a large scale at the level of the nobility. At the very moment the harlot was belting out her bawdy tunes, for example, the crusaders flooding into the newly captured city were seeking out her exact opposite – the most highly born Constantinopolitan maidens – to legitimize their power through cross-cultural partnerships. From the prostitute whom they placed upon the Byzantine throne to the marriage patterns of medieval colonial Greece, it is clear that women were integral to the processes of exchange at the heart of Mediterranean empire building.

The sacking of Constantinople reveals how essential women – all sorts of women – were to the processes of negotiating culture and empire. As the soldiers pillaged the Hagia Sofia, the three main western contenders for rightful rule of the new crusader empire sought access to the best palaces in Constantinople, and with them, access to the best Byzantine brides. The shrewdest of western men saw the capture of Byzantine women as a means to instantiate familial and dynastic claims to power through strategic cross-cultural marriage.[2] Both Old French and Medieval Greek sources about the fall of Constantinople suggest that the essential work of plundering involves not only managing the flow of riches and the desecration of cultural icons, but also managing how women are allocated and exchanged, determining what kinds of new relationships they forge and what kinds of empire they transmit in cross-cultural marriage.

Six hundred years later, and despite its destruction and decline, Byzantium's treasures still exerted a draw on the minds of elite artists who sought to spin a tale of relations between east and west. Both William Butler Yeats and Constantine Cavafy were fascinated by the pull of the golden empire, and its reinterpretation and use in the modern sphere. In his 1928 poem "Sailing to Byzantium," William Butler Yeats compares returning to Byzantium with a return to a place where old ideas (and old bodies and artistic masterpieces) are all highly regarded, away from the hustle and bustle of British modernism and its unsympathetic youth, a place he deems "no country for old men." For Yeats, Byzantium becomes a refuge from the ceaseless interest in the future, a place promising artistic multi-temporality, where bards (even old bards, ones without much of a future) can sing of what is "past, or passing, or to come." Byzantium's treasures – its "hammered gold and gold enamelling" – transcend era or epoch, and those who are able to inhabit them, to *narrate* through them, become endowed with a unique timelessness, too. In short, Yeats conflates Byzantium and its fantastic riches, artistic narration, and eternal fame as the underpinnings of the story of western glory, in this case his own as a poet. Though unconcerned with the smoking rubble of Constantinople in 1204, like Choniates, Yeats focuses readers' attention on how the articulation of the self across chasms of geography, language, and time remained deeply tied to the wonders of Byzantium.

Yeats's contemporary Greek-speaking counterpart, Constantine P. Cavafy, wrote one of his masterpieces, "Ithaca," in 1911. Though "Ithaca" harkens well beyond the ken of Byzantium, and is written by a Greek-speaking Alexandrian, it springs from the pen of a Greek master poet who had a deep and abiding interest in articulating the self in relation to a Greek past.[3] "Ithaca" narrates Odysseus's return, and it focuses on the pleasures of the voyage, of the movement and development of the self over time and through travel. The most memorable lines remind the reader to enjoy the voyage, to take pleasure in the wonders seen while under way throughout the long years sailing the fair winds of the Mediterranean, a voyage not only of discovery of the foreign, but of refashioning the self through encounter with the other. Cavafy's voyage of self-discovery, like that of crusaders years before him and of Yeats shortly after him, is defined by his relation to narratives of Greekness, to a Mediterranean that stretches out not only around shorelines, but also along boundaries of empire and time; it is a Greekness articulated through exchange, exotic goods, and, above all, the journey of encounter with the other.

Though wholly unrelated, these three authors from three different places – Choniates, Yeats, and Cavafy – all imagine Byzantium as a way of negotiating the relations between the self and the other, as a meeting ground and melting pot of goods, peoples, ideas, and history. They also imagine Byzantium as a way of lending authority to their writing of the self. Like these writers, in *Exchanges in Exoticism* I explore how literature imagines interactions with Byzantium – from its exotic goods to its cultural products – to permit the articulation of noble identities. This study focuses especially on Old French literature about cross-cultural marriages with Byzantium. As it turns out, cross-cultural marriage is a perfect place to examine the kinds of identities Cavafy imagined the Mediterranean voyage to articulate in the mythical "Ithaca." It is a space in which, as Choniates's lamentations suggest, women had unique – but relatively unexplored – access to refashioning empire.

Defining identity has always been more complicated than situating the self in any single ethnic, linguistic, gendered, geographic, or political construct. People have shifting and multiple determinants for self-identification; medieval people were no different in this regard, nor does the evidence left to us about them make them any easier to triangulate than ourselves. They were framed by their various loyalties to family, to loosely defined governmental structures, religious beliefs, and local practices of gender and inheritance. The terminology we use to address identity must accommodate its many layers. The same kinds of complicated discourses that are woven around the problematic of "French" plague the ways we struggle to define a coherent nation or culture in the Middle Ages, when shifting allegiances and familial holdings continually reshaped the geopolitical landscapes in which literature was being patronized and composed. Therefore, this book explores Mediterranean – and, in particular, Byzantine – cross-cultural exchange as expressed in Old French and Medieval Greek romance as a way of examining multiple layers of identity.

Whereas nineteenth-century nationalist discourses suggested we should conceptualize medieval France as a static site for the founding myth of French identity, recent scholarship suggests that we may be better served by framing questions of cross-cultural exchange and Mediterranean identity in the more fluid realm of shared linguistic practices. In this study, Patrick Geary's recent work on nation building, interrogating Horden and Purcell's rereading of Braudel, helps to formulate a reading of Old French literary representations of nobility in a wider Mediterranean context, one constructed without a deep attachment to the notion of an internally cohesive medieval France.[4] The centre of this study can be defined in *linguistic* rather than nationalist terms, then, where Old French romances, no matter where written, explore and describe identities created in cross-cultural marriage around the medieval Mediterranean. Moreover, studying romance from the point of view of linguistic unity highlights the stretch of Old French around the Mediterranean, as crusaders colonized, settled, and wrote stories in many places not typically considered "French."

By focusing on exchange in these ways this study in some sense creates its own geography of the Mediterranean. It argues that the Mediterranean provides a geo-cultural space in which identity is not relegated to fictitious feudal borders, but rather created through patterns of patronage and exchange, through trade and warfare. The sea itself is not the unifying factor of medieval existence, but it provides a constantly ebbing landscape on which change and exchange are inevitable facets of existence. The ever-shifting sands of the shoreline reflect the extent to which exchange characterizes the sea, negotiating the movement of culture between ports and nations with the ebb and flow of the tide.

The Mediterranean is also, of course, a place, and one that suggests that "medieval France" is a concept better unpacked and situated within a larger framework of trading networks, kin patterns, and political interests that were both highly family-specific and decentralized at best. The invocation of Mediterranean in this study offers a methodological advantage, in that it reaches out beyond the borders of medieval French landholding and recognizes the complexities of being "French"– if one could be that at all – in the time of warfare and exchange that is the Crusades. When extended and powerful portions of originally French families wield control over and physically govern Jerusalem for generations, or when political marriages and familial interests converge in colonial practices in the Greek Peloponnese, it is no longer accurate to think of medieval nobles as being wedded to a singular, and uniquely French, identity. The Mediterranean, then, is a means of tracing and typifying the degree to which the nobility was extended beyond the borders of "France," and it underlines how integral exchange was to the construction of noble power.

The suggestion of unity among a Mediterranean aristocracy is of course problematic. Yet Mediterranean nobles shared a certain unity despite the vast expanse of the sea – most notably they were related to other nobles through blood and marriage, and warfare and trade around its shores structured their lives. Class, for example, meant access to privileges unique to the nobility and from which the majority of people were excluded. This included constructing the noble self through consumption of exotic fabrics, spices, foods, horses, art, literature, and architecture, thus guaranteeing a certain trade in expensive and nearly unattainable goods. It also meant the privileges of education (more for men, less for women); transportation; a variety of possible professions (from knightly to clerical, scholarly to administrative); and, of course, the comforts and entertainments that money could buy. These aspects of being noble were common throughout the Mediterranean, and meant that being a noble in Champagne was most probably more like being a noble in Thessaly than like being a French-speaking serf.

Furthermore, as marital regulations designed to police kinship status spurred nobles to marry further and further abroad, the nobility became even more deeply interconnected, with rulers of Jerusalem, the Palatine, and Byzantium having broad and deep ties to French and Italian (as we would now characterize them) families back in western Europe. The historical realities of this class of people – which in many ways run contrary to the horizons of the average serf, cleric, or servant – make it possible to understand why literature imagines them to travel, marry, and make warfare and trade all across the Mediterranean, often in ways that eschew local political realities and insist on a false sense of cultural unity. Reading, then, from a Mediterranean perspective on nobility permits us to pose the critical question: to what extent does literature imagine medieval Mediterranean noble culture to be interwoven, at least partly created through the exchange of culture, grounded in and permitted by cross-cultural marriage, and wedded to an undercurrent of exoticism diffused around its shores?

Like class, geography, and language, gender, too, is integral to understanding medieval Mediterranean exchange. Gender was as entwined with notions of power and privilege in the Middle Ages as it is today. Moreover, much medieval literature imagines women's choices to affect the construction of men's gender: in every instance that a woman deviates from a prescriptive and stereotypical kind of femininity in the Old French literature in these pages, her partner's masculinity is affected.

The relation between gender and power is perhaps best explored in the interstices of knowledge in the Middle Ages. While scholars have focused on the construction and transmission of men's knowledge – from formal academic exchanges to clerical practices, from exegesis to informal literary production – women's scholarship and knowledge have been more problematic to access and define, but remain equally important for understanding medieval culture.[5] In this vein, Katherine Kong has persuasively argued that women were careful and cogent manipulators of the medieval epistolary tradition in ways that demonstrate their command not only of a genre, but also of a tradition of knowledge and its practices.[6] Likewise, I argue that women were adept at transmitting their knowledge in the interstices of exchange.

Exchanges in Exoticism starts from the premise that women played a fundamental role in the creation and exchange of cultural knowledge as they married and reproduced with foreign men. Considering women's involvement complicates the narrative of Mediterranean nobility, for it offers a unique perspective on how empires were expanded and constructed, not only through politics but also through love. Cross-cultural marriage and the reproductive hybridity it produced created a vessel for the exchange of culture and knowledge as women moved throughout the medieval Mediterranean. While of course in Gayle Rubin's terms, this movement of women might constitute a kind of traffic in their sex, my readings in *Exchanges in Exoticism* seek to reclaim the space of their supposed oppression – cross-cultural marriage – as a space for the celebration of the ways they were imagined to help transmit culture and mores across lines of geography, familial loyalty, and generation.[7]

Medieval intercultural marriages stimulated public and private discourses that interrogated some of the basic categories of identity (like ethnicity, class, and gender) on which exchange depends, and with which this introduction began. These conversations about women's roles in negotiating identity within marriage were expansive in genre and scope, ranging from ecclesiastical tracts and canon law about women's roles to legal enquiries to fantasies of cross-culturalism in medieval romance. Whether traded and exchanged in the crudest of senses between noble households or whether co-travellers on medieval voyages, women provide a unique vantage point for posing essential questions about the culture of exchange around which I claim noble identities were created in the twelfth and thirteenth centuries.

One of the most cogent historical examples of this kind of exchange – propagated by cross-cultural marriage, prompting public commentary, recorded in literature, constructing multiple kinds of identities, and instrumentalized by a woman's performance of her femininity – can be found in a critique of the new dogaressa of Venice, recounted by an ascetic friar, Peter Damian. Damian laments that his doge, Pietro II Orseolo (d. 1009), chose to marry his son Giovanni to Maria Argyropoulina (985–1007), a Byzantine royal woman, in 1005. Maria, it seems, had not only brought her extensive, expensive, and luxurious Byzantine trousseau to influence her new court, but she imposed her Byzantine cultural customs as well. Damian writes: "Such was the luxury of her habits that she scorned even to wash herself in the common water, obliging her servants instead to collect the dew that fell from the heavens for her to bathe in. Nor did she deign to touch her food with her fingers, but would command her eunuchs to cut it up into small pieces, which she would impale on a certain golden instrument with two prongs and thus carry to her mouth."[8] Using fresh rainwater as the basis for a royal bath was no innovation to eleventh-century Venice, but Damian finds excess and sin in the new bride's insistence that the court use forks at her wedding repast.[9] Here, what scholars following Rubin's work might typically qualify as a trafficking in a medieval noble-woman becomes the very vehicle through which a woman finds space to exchange and translate cultural habits herself. Damian's commentary reveals his fear of a woman's power to exchange cultural knowledge in cross-cultural marriage. In particular, her performance of her role as wife transforms not only her environment, but it also affects her husband's own performance of his masculinity. In this case, Damian critiques Maria's inability to be controlled, to become a docile, reformed – and now Venetian – subject of her powerful lord and husband. Damian's very public critique of Maria's performance of "bride" or "wife" is thus also a concomitant critique of the doge's performance of "husband" and "ruler" – and, implicitly, "man" and "lord." The critique itself reveals how deeply gender, power, and exchange coalesce, then, in the space of women's work in cross-cultural marriage. It ties the regulation of her femininity to the performance of his masculinity.

While the overall importance of the fork on western society is certainly debatable, Maria's actions lance a kind of cultural exchange that is both measurable in terms of objects exchanged (the fork), cultural change propagated (the refinement of eating and refashioning of the body's relation to food), and the cultural imperialism it implies (the sway the Byzantine woman held over her husband, and his willingness to adapt his court to her standards, amidst what is ultimately public commentary about his masculinity). More importantly, this passage constructs cross-cultural marriage among Mediterranean nobility as a place for interrogating cultural and gender norms, and, above all, for theorizing cross-cultural exchange as fundamentally entwined with gender. Even when medieval people like Peter Damian stridently object to the kinds of change imposed by Maria Argyropoulina, her influence upon her husband indicates that cross-cultural marriage facilitated the exchange not only of goods, but also of ideas, identities, and cultural habits – all, I argue, mitigated by women.

Through readings like these, this book also seeks to identify how ill-defined categories like nation and gender might be articulated through women's choices in cross-cultural, pan-Mediterranean marriages.[10] Rather than trying to argue for definitive and clear-cut visions of how these categories might operate distinctively, I focus instead on the kinds of questions that reading literature from the intersections of gender, class, and ethnicity staged within cross-cultural marriage might tease out. There are few instances, for example, of women who marry into foreign noble households without facing questions about their gender, ethnicity, or culture raised by their new families, often to the newcomers' detriment. In one prescient medieval story, which I examine in chapter 3, the story of the girl without a hand, a girl who is persecuted by her incestuous father leaves her homeland, her hand, and her eastern identity behind, and so charms a distant western prince that he agrees to marry her, despite the uncertainty of her origins. After they marry, the prince's mother begins to ask questions about the identity of the foreign bride, and, when they cannot be answered, she begins to propagate rumours and seeks to have her daughter-in-law murdered or condemned to death, claiming that she is some sort of foreign monster. That the myth of the nameless, handless girl who marries a western king, retold in stories like *La Belle Hélène de Constantinople*, *Le Roman de la Manekine*, and *Emaré*, carried such force as to be translated, repeated, and widely disseminated in the thirteenth through fifteenth centuries suggests that the major questions it addresses – patrilineal practices of identity, geographic influences upon stories of personal origin, and the relation between gender and empire – are very much ideas at stake in this time period of cross-cultural marriages necessitated by the politics of the Crusades and the stringent prohibitions against intermarriage imposed by the Church.[11]

Culture – and cross-cultural exchange – is necessarily at the heart of this study, but, like gender and empire, it remains elusive to define. Homi Bhabha resists the urge to define culture as an inclusive set of practices, and I follow his lead here to construct medieval noble identities as a shifting set of negotiated practices stemming from disparate experiences of class, ethnicity, gender, and geographic and linguistic origins.[12] By focusing on what Bhabha has termed the "alterity" of a postcolonial sense of culture, this study underlines how Mediterranean noble identity is instantiated through marriage based on the exchange of difference, at the same time that it purports to create a superficially reified sense of "family" and a false sense of similarity. Family, in these terms, becomes a place of hybridity, a mixing ground of identities rather than a place of overdetermined and overly unified cultural, gendered, or political practices.[13]

As the examples of the story of the handless girl and of Maria Argyropoulina suggest, although medieval noble households are for the most part constructed through their collective alterity (through cross-cultural and exogamous marriages between people of dissimilar geographic and familial origins), medieval literature imagines marriage to be a continual site through which the fiction of cultural inclusion and homogeny is propagated. It is precisely at this disjuncture in noble families – between the imagined, idealized literary stagings of cultural inclusion in "successful" marriages that result in patrilinear genealogies and the disorder and disarray caused by the on-the-ground reality of cross-cultural exchange and hybridity – that this study takes its starting point, in the form of examining romances about cross-cultural marriage and reproduction between France and Byzantium.

Byzantium – and the ways it gets taken up in Old French literature – makes a particularly interesting place for thinking about exchange, gender, and Mediterranean identity in the twelfth and thirteenth centuries, not only for the ways that conflict structured these exchanges (as Choniates's critique of the fall of Constantinople suggests), but also for the ways many of the interactions there are imagined as successful moments of cross-cultural exchange.

Many people passed through and travelled to Byzantium in the eleventh through the fourteenth centuries, and yet until recently scholars of western literature have found it easy to overlook its importance (exceptions include in the work of Rima Devereaux and Krijna Nelly Ciggaar). The capital, Constantinople, was a city roughly four times the size of medieval Paris, yet arguably much more important to trade.[14] A cultural and trading capital of the medieval Mediterranean world, Constantinople was overwhelmingly rich, full of artistic, textile, and architectural wealth.[15] When the Franks and Venetians sacked the imperial city in 1204, westerners came in droves to acquire Byzantine riches in the form of material objects, from silks to coins to relics, and in the process many of them stayed on in crusader colonies such as the Morea. As one French-speaking onlooker, Robert de Clari, put it,

> Si comme li avoirs fu la aportés, qui si estoit rikes et tant i avoit de rike vaisselemente d'or et d'argent et de dras a or et tant de rikes joiaus que ch'estoit une fine merveille du grant avoir qui luekes fu aportés, mais puis que chis siecles fu estorés, si grans avoirs, ne si nobles, ne si rikes, ne fu veus, ne conquis, ne au tans Alixandre, ne au tans Charlemaine, ne devant ne aprés; ne je ne quit mie, au mien ensient, que es quarante plus rikes chités du monde eust tant d'avoir comme on trouva u cors de Constantinoble. Et si tesmongnoient li Griu que les deus pars de l'avoir du monde estoient en Coustantinoble et le tierche estoit esparse par le monde.[16]

> [And when the booty was brought there, it was so rich and contained such a wealth of golden and silver dishes and golden cloth, and there were so many rich jewels, that it was marvellous to behold the great riches that had been brought there – never since the world was created was so great wealth, or so noble, or so magnificent, either seen or won. Not in the days of Alexander, or of Charlemagne, or before, or after. Nor do I believe, of my own knowledge, that in the forty richest cities of the world is so much wealth as was found in all of Constantinople. For the Greeks also testified that two-thirds of all the wealth of the world was in Constantinople, and that the other third was dispersed throughout the world.]

Once the loot was distributed, Frankish-Byzantine families sprang up in landed enclaves, and these places became sites of more exchange, as textiles, architecture, art, and stories emerged that reflected a mixed and new tradition, one that women as well as men participated in creating, and one in which new gender structures emerged to deal with the hybridity of these cultural interactions.[17]

Not only was Byzantium a capital of trade in exotic goods,[18] but it was also a place of shifting meaning, a place at once Christian and eastern, a place of well-developed bureaucratic governance structures and a place alive with a culture of literate debate and copious textual production that still remains for the most part unedited and unpublished in manuscript form. While western medievalists have focused more recently on the Mediterranean (and in particular on the Frankish/Muslim interactions staged there) in studies of Old French literature such as Sharon Kinoshita's *Medieval Boundaries* and E. Jane Burns's *Courtly Love Undressed*, this book intervenes to examine Byzantium's role in mediating cross-cultural exchange – whether literary, cultural, or sumptuary – as central to medieval Mediterranean culture.[19] I agree with Rima Devereaux, who in her recent study of Constantinople's influence on western European renewal argues that many Old French texts "are concerned with the achievement of *renovation*, and present contact with Byzantium as a means towards this goal."[20] While Devereaux's study explores Constantinople as a site for imagining western renewal, this study takes cross-cultural marriage with Byzantium as a way of constructing a Mediterranean nobility.

Cross-cultural marriage around the Mediterranean, and with Byzantium in particular, produced one of the founding narratives of noble identity – the genre of romance. The primary methodological advantage of my focus on the west's manipulation of Byzantium to stage its own noble Mediterranean origins is that it reveals how cross-cultural marriage develops in tandem with the genre of romance itself. I argue that the romance story arises concomitantly with its thematic treatment of love across the border, a love often staged to reflect the exotic and authorizing Hellenic origins of western nobility through romance's incessant interest in noble genealogies. The methodology of *Exchanges in Exoticism*, then, offers generic as well as thematic implications for the understanding of Old French romance.

Some of the first stories to emerge as romance do so precisely because they narrate the difficulties of pairing disparate lovers, of bridging a cultural gap, so to speak, and these stories point to the rise of romance as coterminous with the work of women in mitigating difference in cross-cultural marriage. *Cligès*, one of the earliest twelfth-century Old French romances, and *Digenis Akritas*, an eleventh-century Byzantine border tale of mixed genre, are two literary explorations of how cross-cultural exchange constructs new – and different – kinds of identities and gender structures. Both of these tales, which I examine in detail in chapter 1, pore anxiously over the sexuality and fecundity associated with out-of-the-ordinary cross-cultural couplings. *Cligès* details the reproductive felicity of two generations of Franco-Byzantine lovers, and *Digenis* examines how two generations of Syrian and Byzantine families intersect in the identity of the protagonist, Digenis, the "double-blooded border lord." Though separated by language, geography, and time, the texts' explorations of how cultural melding warps fixed norms of gendered and politicized identities imply they share more than a common plot. Reading the French and Greek narratives together reveals anxieties about gender structures – and the power of women to effect change in cross-cultural marriage – to be inimitably caught up in struggles over cross-cultural identity, and to be one of the founding problematics of romance.

Despite their many differences, Byzantine and Old French literatures share many commonalities, not the least of which is the way they imagine women to be crucial in the making of empire. Not only are they both interested in the ways that medieval nobles exchanged culture through cross-cultural marriage, they are also deeply tied to their status as emerging forms of vernacular literary composition. Unlike Latin, the academic *lingua franca* since the mid-third century, vernaculars like Medieval Greek and Old French came to offer a glimpse into how noble – but perhaps not extensively educated – people enjoyed and experienced their worlds. This is particularly important when considering marriage as a site for vernacular (rather than clerical) exchange and textual creation. Women, in particular, had less access to education than men, and yet cross-cultural marriage affords them a space in which their knowledge and their "texts" – though not those of clerical reasoning and erudition – are exchanged and in which they find influence, often to the point of pushing the boundaries of gender in their new households.[21] While of course this kind of knowledge is vastly different from the intellectualism of the medieval universities or even the devotion to scripture and canon law in monastic settings, it is still a space in which women's knowledge of and interest in literary culture could be cultivated and circulated; as such, it offers a more relaxed space for considering what qualifies as "cultural knowledge" and what kinds of ideas literature imagines women to patronize, manipulate, and exchange.

Another interwoven, but distinctly separate, question also arises: how does cross-cultural marriage create new gender/power frameworks in which exchange can flourish? Maria Argyropoulina's story provides a compelling touchstone to which to return when thinking about gender. Her marriage, apparently a forceful place for the movement of culture and its artefacts, is also simultaneously a highly typical paradox of incomplete transmission, of powerlessness, and of persecution. Peter Damian, for example, elaborates that not only does she use the pitchfork of the devil to eat her food, but "[h]er rooms, too, were so heavy with incense and various perfumes that it is nauseating for me to speak of them, nor would my readers readily believe it. But this woman's vanity was hateful to Almighty God; and so, unmistakably, did He take his revenge."[22] Damian's critique (that God punished Maria for her excesses with an early death) points to anxieties about foreign women marrying into positions of rule, anxieties that continued to circulate well into the eighteenth century.[23] Foreign women represent danger on a number of levels, not the least of which is their ability to reproduce and influence the new royal progeny with their foreign culture, religion, and ideas. Such critiques predate but also predict the rise of Salic law.

The anxieties expressed here also reveal the degree to which medieval foreign brides operated from within a unique kind of vantage point, similar to what feminist theorists like Patricia Hill Collins have dubbed "the outsider within."[24] Never completely assimilated and never completely exiled, never quite as good as indigenous royal brides, these women and their marriages provided a unique perspective from which to explore the dominant culture of the region and family into which they married. Like Cynthia Enloe's "cultural ambassadors" in her study of women in postcolonial diplomatic circles, medieval noblewomen who married into new families had the unique opportunity to bring their culture with them, and to implement that culture in unique ways.[25] In Maria's case, Damian's critique of her Byzantine fork provides insight into anxieties about the corruption of Venetian cultural practices and mores.

Although I am primarily interested in the ways that women's work helped to transmit and instantiate noble identities, I want to stress that cross-cultural marriage offers a unique platform for examining the ways that gender itself is a very fluid construct, one which permits the kinds of exchange and transformation this book seeks to examine. That is, while women and their reproductive bodies may do much of the physical work of moving knowledge in cross-cultural marriage and reproduction, the very fact that they are able to wield such a degree of influence reveals men's identities – and masculinity itself – to be much less solidly fixed around an immovable, immutable structure of primogeniture and paterfamilias and grounded squarely in exchange, cultural hybridity, and the performance of femininity.

Perhaps nowhere is this more evident than in the medieval French romance *Floire et Blancheflor*, which I examine in chapter 2. In this romance, the protagonist lovers are a pagan boy and a French Christian girl, who are raised together, fall in love, and become virtually indistinguishable when caught sleeping together nude in the same bed. Cultural, religious, and geographic difference is effaced by the likeness of these lovers' bodies. I argue that it is in this space of likeness – rather than difference – that the romance stages the majority of the work of cross-cultural marriage, revealing it to be a place in which both gender and national difference can be brought into question.

While the blossoming of twelfth-century romance in tandem with the thematic development of cross-cultural marriage opens a space for women to bring new ideas with them as they move across lines of family and empire, thirteenth-century romances depict these relationships in full bloom. However, thirteenth-century narratives of exchange are increasingly at odds with the celebratory Byzantium first figured in earlier romances like *Floire et Blancheflor* and reiterated centuries later in the romanticism of Yeats. My readings of thirteenth-century romance in chapters 3 and 4 suggest that literary – and perhaps, according to manuscript evidence, also patrons' – attitudes towards Byzantium had shifted after the sacking of Constantinople in 1204 and the establishment of not-so-successful crusader states.

The cross-cultural romances *Le Roman de la Manekine, La Belle Hélène de Constantinople,* and *Floriant et Florete,* which I examine in the second half of the book, stem from mid-thirteenth-century imaginings of new ways that women's choices in where and how to love could have an impact not only on the construction of noble genealogies, but also on the shape of empire. Whereas the twelfth century saw romance reaching out to Byzantium (and, I argue, Hellenism) to establish its claims to glory, after the fall of Constantinople to the west, romances like *La Manekine* and *Floriant et Florete* slowly begin to reimagine what it means to be a western noble outside of genealogical and cultural claims to Greek glory. I argue that the historical backdrop of crusader disappointments in their colonies underlies the shifting visions of identity that are staged by women's choices within these texts. In the first case, the story of the handless girl becomes a narrative about how women's choices frame the glory of western masculinity – the triumph, so to speak, of west over east in the bedroom. In the second case, *Floriant et Florete* stages a new kind of Arthurian geography, one in which Arthur's crusade to conquer Sicily ends up defeating not only Byzantine men but their women as well. In short, my readings suggest that as the thirteenth century advances, the Old French romance as a genre seeks to put greater distance between itself and Byzantium, building new narrative models for establishing the glory of western aristocrats through women's choices in literature.

The geography of the Mediterranean has meant that for millennia people have been trading and exchanging goods and ideas on its shores.[26] Historians have sketched out macro- and micro-portraits of the kinds of interactions and identities that the sea itself has created,[27] and this study furthers these efforts by arguing for regional networks of literary patronage based on Mediterranean trading routes and familial landholding patterns, rather than rigid nationalized borders. I use the terms "nation" and "empire" throughout this study, then, to resist fixed constructs or borders through which people easily differentiated from one another, and to refer rather to a set of practices (cultural, linguistic, even genealogical) through which families sought to expand their influence around the Mediterranean, particularly through cross-cultural exchange in the form of strategic marriage practices and carefully chosen involvement with war and trade during the Crusades. Empire, then, is more about familial dreams of expansion and influence in the colonial context than about highly organized, state-sponsored practices of domination.

Scholars have recently begun to explore the fluidity of places like medieval Sicily and Spain as a means to access a more complicated discourse of identity (coded as "textuality") in these places of frequent and heavy cross-cultural encounter.[28] Suzanne Fleischman has dismissed nineteenth-century medievalists' calls for a unified linguistic form of literary composition (say, something like "French literature") as the "myth of monoglossia,"[29] and Karla Mallette builds on this work to identify the ways in which literary polyglossia might unify and define – rather than fragment – the complicated history of Sicily, from its conquest by Muslims to its rule by Normans and then Hohenstaufens.[30]

In my conclusion, I follow out recent work on Mediterranean multilingualism to explore how exchanges in exoticism might really have looked, by examining literary, linguistic, and dynastic hybridity in the Frankish-occupied region of the Greek Morea. *The Chronicle of Morea*, a pseudo-historical chronicle composed by second-generation inhabitants of a Frankish crusader state in Greece, was probably written first in Medieval Greek and then immediately translated into Old French. In its narration of cultural encounter and its attempt to historicize this new hybrid colony, the text calls into question, I argue, recent theoretical assumptions that "cultural integrity ... underl[ies] such linguistic complexity."[31] The degree to which *The Chronicle of Morea* depends on cross-cultural exchange, marriage, and encounter suggests that rather than focusing on integrity, we should instead focus on the gaps through which alterity constitutes culture, through which typical peripheries (like odd marital partnerships, gender/power configurations, and ethnic encounters) become *constitutive* of the core of Mediterranean noble society and are mitigated as much by women as by men as the thirteenth century unfolds.

The medieval identities I imagine Old French romance examining, then, are ones legible by their patterns of exchange and by the networks of obligations through which they prosper. The identities I explore in these pages are deeply linked to their position around a sea of trade, warfare, commerce, and exchange, and they radiate like spokes from this centre, this Mediterranean that both effaces nationalized differences and functions as a buffer zone. It is a Mediterranean that literature imagines women to shape, both through their practices in exchanging knowledge and in creating empire in cross-cultural marriage around its shores. Byzantium – and the ways women mitigate its exchange and meaning through cross-cultural marriage – does indeed form part of the narration of that mythic voyage towards Cavafy-esque identity, and provides a kind of literary timelessness that lends gravity to texts and bodies both old and new.

1 Women and the Making of Mediterranean Identities in *Cligès* and *Digenis Akritas*

"Einc mielz nel firent nules dames" ["Never did women do better"].[1] With these five words, Chrétien de Troyes interrupts *Cligès* to judge a women's rebellion, lauding more than two thousand Byzantine women who storm the imperial palace to save their German-born empress from being tortured to death by Salernian doctors. His interjection is unusual for its endorsement of many things romance as a genre usually resists: female agency, political rebellion, and plebeian success. In the space of five words an interpretive gesture is born, one that imagines a place within romance for the agency of women, a space in which the plot depends as much upon feminine rebellion as it does on cross-cultural political intrigue. With these five words, Chrétien invites us to consider how romance depends on women to negotiate the exchange facilitated by cross-cultural encounters.

As Chrétien's remark intimates, romances like *Cligès* imagine exchange and contact as the very heart of the story of medieval nobility. *Cligès*, a tale of cross-cultural love between a Byzantine imperial heir and a German princess, reimagines the western love affair of romance in an exoticised eastern setting. At first glance, this might be a move designed to generate plot and stimulate an already saturated market of romance narratives mostly centred on the Arthurian court. Yet I would argue that *Cligès*, like the other romances examined in this book, incorporates eastern references to explore how the medieval French-speaking nobility is deeply dependent on its relation to multifaceted and ahistorical easts. Essentially, romances like *Cligès* invoke eastern courtly settings to explore how the western noble self is dependent on exchange with its Mediterranean neighbours, past and present.

The literature I examine throughout this book imagines cross-cultural marriage as a site for the exchange and translation of culture. In particular, it imagines exchange as deeply dependent on women. As we shall see in *Cligès*, this manifests itself both in the group rebellion of the Byzantine women, whose push to save their empress sparks Chrétien's dubious endorsement of their mob justice, and in the personal empire-building effected by Fénice, the female protagonist. In a contemporary Medieval Greek romance that I examine in this chapter, *Digenis Akritas*, women are imagined to have central roles in the movement of culture. As we shall see in the pages to come, the borderland love affairs in *Digenis* imagine women as both warriors and victims of rapt, positing them as crucial to the negotiation of cross-cultural contact along the frontiers of empire. These romances, then, imagine cross-cultural love affairs as a site for staging women's agency in personal and political terms.

Perhaps most importantly, cross-cultural encounters permit women – and not just men – to articulate and critique alternate gender positions, in particular alternate masculinities. From the confrontation between the enraged Byzantine women and the Salernian doctors, to the cross-cultural love affair between Cligès and Fénice, cross-cultural marriage is a space in which women critique masculinities that are aligned with the East. In this chapter, I claim that *Cligès* imagines women to participate in the forging of Mediterranean culture, not only through cross-cultural exchange and dynastic hybridity, but also through their critique of non-hegemonic masculinities. Chrétien's striking commendation that "never did women do better" in condemning the erroneous Salernian doctors, then, becomes a way of marking both women's participation in the melding of Mediterranean nobility, and a prelude to the ways their participation should be read as a complex critique of gender.

The Romance of Byzantium: Hybridity and the Story of Cross-Cultural Encounter

The rage-fuelled rebellion of the Byzantine women who liberate Fénice in *Cligès*, like Peter Damian's scornful rejection of Maria Argyropoulina and her Byzantine forks, which we saw in the introduction, complicates our understanding of the ways in which medieval identities were created and represented, for it points to cross-cultural exchange – of stories, goods, and even people – as the norm, rather than the exception, among the medieval French-speaking nobility. In fact, in the romances explored throughout this book, exchange is the basis for noble identity. Through myriad markets, wagers, and transactions, people and goods move all around the Mediterranean; it is movement, exchange, and cultural transformation that generate narratives of nobleness.

The widespread practice of political marriages, which I explored in the introduction, and which Rima Devereaux explores in her recent study *Constantinople and the West in Medieval French Literature*, meant that French-speaking noble families' interests and genealogies, once so limited by local clan warfare, swiftly stretched all around the Mediterranean during the Crusades.[2] For most noble French-speaking families – the very families who patronized and enjoyed the romances discussed throughout this study – cross-cultural marriage was the norm, and hybridity the staple of their dynastic endeavours.[3] In this study, I use hybridity to refer to both the cultural and the genealogical mixing through which the nobility cemented its political ambitions. Though I suggest that Mediterranean noble hybridity was the *norm*, I use the term "cross-cultural" to draw attention to partnerships between people of *different* linguistic, geographic, religious, ethnic, or economic backgrounds, in a move designed to highlight how these encounters permitted cultural exchange, transformation, and fusion.

While the term "hybridity" can address racial difference, in the Middle Ages it is best understood in terms of cultural melding, something that has long caught the attention of medievalists seeking to understand the primary geocultural encounter of the European Middle Ages, the Crusades. Gaston Paris and Joseph Bédiers's nineteenth-century readings of *La Chanson de Roland* as a nationalist epic spurred medievalists to become interested in the relations between east and west, inciting a set of textual analyses founded on cultural comparison and exchange in the service of modern-day French nationalism.[4] Though in the past studies contrasted Muslim East with Christian West, current work from a postcolonial perspective invites us to consider in-between spaces that may help us nuance our understanding of medieval identity.[5] If, as Homi Bhabha has suggested, reading from peripheries can help us better understand how centres are constructed, then reading from what western literature posits as the margins of Christendom can help us better understand how noble identities were forged and negotiated through literary encounters.[6]

One of the most important and overlooked "margins" between what we now think of as myriad easts and wests is Byzantium, a place neither here nor there, neither, as Bhabha would have it, centre nor periphery. When *Cligès* was written in 1176, Byzantium was a place of shifting meaning for western nobles, at once providing safe overland passage, food, and supplies to crusaders; trading in silks, spices, oils, and other valuable goods with Muslims, Christians, and Jews; and offering political and military assistance in increasingly complicated and questionable ways.[7] Yet Byzantium, for all its might, was in turn conquered and invaded by its Christian neighbours, colonized and suppressed by its one-time partner in crusade, with French and Italian families controlling most of the Peloponnese after 1204. In medieval western literature of the late twelfth and early thirteenth centuries, Byzantium is at once Christian and yet eastern, at once on the fringes of Europe and replete with oriental wonder; it is always both other and self through its unique position as both empire and colony. Byzantium makes informed, negotiated representations possible, at once standing for access and encounter, and fantasy and projection, through its status as a Christian but eastern neighbour to the western literary traditions.

Byzantium figures in a number of Old French texts, so many that some medievalists identify "Byzantine romances" as a subgenre of Old French texts defined by their connection to ancient Greek stories and events. In these Old French narratives, exoticized, orientalized peoples and goods figure strongly in ways that hark back to Ancient Greek literary motifs. They include some of the romances explored in this book (e.g., *Cligès* and *La Belle Hélène de Constantinople*) as well as the *romans antiques* (*Le Roman de Thèbes, Le Roman de Troie, Le Roman d'Alexandre*) and texts with geographical connections to Greece, like *Athis et Prophilias*. Yet grouping these texts together merely because they invoke and rework Ancient Greek narratives or because they reference Greece is an oversight. While all "about Greekness" to some extent, these texts have more in common than thematic elements, the usage of ancient Greek narratives, or an interest in representing Greekness throughout the ages. These texts all invoke, repeat, and negotiate relations with Byzantium (and, I would argue, so do many other romances).

In the texts known as Byzantine romances, identity hangs upon hybridity, upon the intersection where the exchange of blood (in the form of mixed lineage) meets the exchange of culture (in the form of ideas, goods, religions, languages, even textual practices), usually at the locus of cross-cultural marriage. This is borne out most clearly in the prologue to *Cligès*, where lineage is articulated as the narrative framework. According to Chrétien, the story of lineage begins with genealogy: "D'un vaslet qui an Grece fu / Del lignage le roi Artu. / Mes ainz que de lui rien vos die, / Orroiz de son pere la vie, / Don il fu et de quell lignage" [10–13] [a new tale about a Greek youth of the line of King Arthur. But before I tell you about him, you will hear of his father's life, of his family and where he was from].[8] The traditional articulation of the protagonist's "lignage" in the familiar court and genealogy of Arthur inserts the story squarely into the tradition of Arthurian lore. Yet, unlike many tales, the name of the protagonist himself is eschewed in favour of naming his king, "Artu," which most pointedly rimes not with Brittany, the locus we might expect for his court and genealogy, but with "Grece fu," Greece, a surprising locale for an Arthurian tale.[9] The prologue ties the exotic locus of the story – Byzantium – to the more familiar Arthurian genealogy, thereby conflating the concerns of genealogy with geography. As such, it offers a first glimpse at *Cligès*'s larger concern with the movement of ideas and genealogies around the Mediterranean.

Chrétien's tale opens out from its familial locus, its focus on paternity and bloodlines, to stretch along the coasts of the Mediterranean, with action reaching from the shores of Constantinople to the westernmost part of France itself.[10] It is a story about two generations of cross-cultural love affairs between Byzantines and Westerners, first from Arthur's court and then from the German empire. The first-generation love story occurs when the Byzantine emperor, Alexander, departs his lands in search of renown at Arthur's court and falls in love with, and eventually marries, Soredamors, the niece of one of Arthur's liegemen. They have a son, the hero of the romance, Cligès, and return as a family from England to rule Byzantium, only to find that Alexander's younger brother, Alis, has stolen the throne. The brothers resolve their conflict with an oath of allegiance through which Alis swears never to take a wife or have children, so that Alexander's son Cligès may rightfully inherit the throne. Shortly after Alexander dies, Alis breaks his oath and marries a German princess, Fénice, who is secretly in love with Cligès. Fénice, unhappy with Alis's betrayal of his oath, refuses to consummate the marriage for fear that reproduction would endanger her lover's claims to the throne. She and her nurse concoct a potion to deceive Alis into believing he takes pleasure in his wife every night, and, after many trials and tribulations, including the torture and subsequent rescue of Fénice, Alis is finally removed from the throne, Cligès reinstated, and Fénice given to him as his wife.

Several of the longest fundamental manuscripts of *Cligès* show that reading Greekness has codicological – and not just thematic – resonance. If, as Keith Busby suggests, a manuscript should be read within a larger codex with its own story, then reading *around Cligès* becomes an interpretive act as well, and one in which I argue Byzantium becomes a central interpretive tool.[11] Two of the most renowned manuscripts in which *Cligès* is found are the thirteenth-century megalith codices BnF Fr. 375 and 1450, which I argue stage thematic interests in Franco-Byzantine connections.[12] Manuscript 375 is traditionally cited as one of the primary sources for Arthuriana in Old French, for it also contains *Erec et Enide, Le Chevalier de la charrette,* and *Le Chevalier au lion.* Yet nestled amongst these literary heavyweights are a host of other stories, ones that detail the wonders of Greece, from antiquity to the medieval present. Containing not only *Cligès,* but also the stories of Thebes, Troy, Alexander the Great, *Athis et Prophilias,* and *Floire et Blancheflor,* MS BnF Fr. 375 can also be read as working through the legacy of Hellenism in the medieval world. In fact, almost half of the codex is dedicated to Greek material, with eight of the eighteen secular stories stemming from Greek sources or treating contact with medieval Byzantium. The same is true for BnF Fr. 1450, which contains the more obviously Greek-inspired *Roman de Troie, Eneas, Brut, Cligès,* and *Dolopathos;* and *Le Chevalier au lion, Le Chevalier de la charrette, Erec, and Perceval.* While the latter romances, including *Perceval* and *Le Chevalier de la charrette,* are not overtly about contact with Byzantium or any other East, as Jane Burns has shown, the textiles through which the nobility's worth is articulated have decidedly Eastern referents.[13] Similarly, even BnF Fr. 1450, in which *Cligès* is bound with one remaining page of the *Roman de Troie,* suggests that Byzantium must be understood as a key player in the medieval French imagination of exchanges in exoticism.

These graecophile manuscript codices were all assembled in the thirteenth century, long after the composition of Cligès in 1176, and long after historical events like the sacking of Constantinople in 1204 had permanently changed Franco-Byzantine relations. The fact that they are bound together suggests that people were interested in reading programmatically about the crossing, the exchange, of all kinds of Greek motifs. These stories depict the movement of peoples and goods across the cultural and linguistic frontier between two great Christian forces. Furthermore, and as I will show throughout these pages, they imagine women as essential to this movement, in ways that extend beyond the pages of literary representation. Reading this literature from its codicological context helps us to understand the importance of Greek traditions within Old French romance; in particular, it invites us to pay attention to the ways cross-cultural marriages, featured in almost every tale bound together with *Cligès*, facilitated the transmission and interpretation of eastern cultures for western audiences.

Reading these codices within their historical context further invites us to consider how Byzantium figured into the making of the Mediterranean in Old French romance. The late twelfth century, during which *Cligès* and its manuscripts were composed, was a time of increasing contact between Byzantium and the west. Crusaders strayed into Byzantine lands and made pacts permitting travel and trade as they voyaged to the Holy Lands, and sometimes they were too poor or weak to return home, so they stayed and started families.[14] The Byzantine capital Constantinople was, at its height, five times more populous than medieval Paris, and its fairs and markets were filled with luxury goods traded under a highly bureaucratized and literate Byzantine administration.[15] Just twenty-eight years after *Cligès* was composed, frustrated at deteriorating relations with the Byzantines and unable to make it all the way to Jerusalem, the leaders of the Fourth Crusade would divert their troops to sack and burn Constantinople itself to set up some of the first French colonies, in what is today the Greek Peloponnese.

The codicological and historical contexts suggest that Byzantium was an important referent in shaping medieval noble identities staged in Old French romance. Though Byzantium might be just one of many "peripheries" of Old French texts, in many ways the theme of cross-cultural marriage permits us to theorize it as a centre underwriting the narrative of exchange in Old French romance. The narrative thrust of *Cligès*, which moves from Chrétien's concerns about speech, genealogy, and empire in the prologue, to the complicated space of cross-cultural negotiation in Fénice's marriage to Alis, to her subsequent rebuke in the epilogue, also imagines Byzantium to be a site for interrogating the literal and literary fecundity of Mediterranean empire.

In this larger codicological and historical context, the hybridity staged in *Cligès* is not only about the exchange of lineage, it is also about the movement of culture. Hybridity is not only genealogical, but also cultural. It is about the movement of blood in tandem with the movement of a certain set of beliefs, ideas, daily practices, or linguistic preferences. In *Cligès*, hybridity begins within Chrétien's prologue itself when Chrétien marries the concerns of lineage and geography to the concerns of intellectual reproduction under the general rubric of *translatio*. Chrétien pairs lineage with language, and in so doing he entwines the concepts of writing and reproduction within a larger story about cross-cultural nobility.

The first words of the romance are penned in service of propagating ideas, in connecting stories to their dissemination; in short, they are publicity that allows self-promotion to function simultaneously as literary reproduction, much in the vein of *translatio studii*:

Cil qui fist d'Erec et d'Enide,
Et les comandemanz Ovide
Et l'art d'amors an romanz mist
Et le mors de l'espaule fist,
Del roi Marc et d'Iseut la blonde,
Et de la hupe et de l'aronde
Et del rossignol la muance,
Un novel conte recomance
D'un vaslet qui en Grece fu.[...]
Ceste estoire trovons escrite,
Que vonter vos vuel et retreire,
An un des livres de l'aumeire
Mon seignor saint Pere a Biauvez. [1–9; 18–21]

[The man who wrote of Erec and Enide, translated Ovid's *Commandments* and his *Art of Love*, composed *The Shoulder Bite*, and wrote of King Mark and the blonde Iseult, and about the metamorphoses of the hoopoe, the swallow, and the nightingale, takes up a new tale about a Greek youth of the line of King Arthur. [...] we find [it] written down in one of the books in the library of Saint Peter's Cathedral in Beauvais.]

In the very first lines of the romance, the singular use of "cil" contrasts starkly with the anaphoric repetition of "et," putting emphasis on the divide between the one wonderful author and his many literary progeny. The "cil" not only reinforces the grandeur of the author, but also posits him as the father of his narrative offspring; the "cil" becomes, then, a genealogical claim to a male literary authority, a kind of authorial paternity. The first word of the romance – about the author and his own prodigious talent – foreshadows a connection between text and genealogy even before Chrétien himself cements it in the next lines, when he introduces the familial background of his titular protagonist Cligès and his father, Alexander. His final authorial interjections in the prologue serve to further entwine literature and genealogy as he literally reproduces *Cligès* (here, "retreire") from an exemplar found in the library of St Peter of Beauvais.

Chrétien's prologue situates him as an intellectual forefather, one who seeks to delineate the past from the present, the source from its new interpretation, and he writes of his innovation in geographic terms, calling attention to Greece and Rome:

Ce nos ont nostre livre apris
Que Grece ot de chevalerie
Le premier los et de clergie,
Puis vint chevalerie a Rome
Et de la clergie la somme,
Qui or est en France venue.
Dex doint qu'ele i soit retenue
Tant que li leus li embelisse
Si que ja mais de France n'isse
L'ennors qui s'i est arestee.
Dex l'avoit as altres prestee,
Que des Grezois ne des Romains
Ne dit en mais ne plus ne mains,
D'esu est la parole remese
Et esteinte la vive brese. (30–44)

[These books of ours have taught us that Greece once stood preeminent in both chivalry and learning. Then chivalry proceeded to Rome in company with the highest learning. Now they have come into France. God grant that they be sustained here and their stay be so pleasing that the honour that has stopped here in France never depart. God had lent them to the others, for no one ever speaks now of the Greeks or the Romans. Talk of them is over; their burning coals are spent.]

Chrétien claims his project as one of intellectual and cultural supremacy, one in which "talk of [others] is over" and in which French mastery of lyrical love poetry reveals itself. The prologue is steeped in the medieval tradition of *translatio studii*, in which old texts are reinterpreted for a new linguistic, geographic, and cultural climate – one pointedly Mediterranean.[16] It connects the intellectual project of *translatio* with a kind of cultural imperialism, in which all things French should supplant all things Greek and Roman.[17] Chrétien's *translatio* serves, then, as a kind of framework for reading the valuation of East-West relations staged in the body of the romance through the love affairs of Alexander and Soredamors and Cligès and Fénice. By marrying lineage and literature to geography, Chrétien's text creates a reading program deeply interested in cross-cultural exchange with Byzantium.

The cultural context of twelfth-century crusading, the codicological context of Byzantine romances, and the thematic interest in the geography of narrative genealogies combine to suggest, then, that the movement of culture is one of the primary themes of Old French romance. The prologue to *Cligès* joins a long tradition of writings that theorize Mediterranean exchange – in particular the exchange of narrative and culture between Greece and Rome – as the domain of men. Women's work in cross-cultural exchange, though often eschewed in favour of men's narratives and men's deeds, is in fact essential to the movement of ideas and the construction of nobility around the Mediterranean. As we shall see, in *Cligès* the "sorplus" of Byzantium permits the literary fantasy of women's agency, the projection of a space for female empowerment in the service and critique of empire.

Women's Interventions in Empire

Chrétien's prologue posits men as the primary makers and transmitters of culture (after all, Chrétien names himself and Arthur as the cornerstones of this story). Yet the body of the romance depends increasingly on women and their work in cross-cultural love. The women's rebellion, in which "einc mielz ... firent nules dames," is the perfect starting point from which to explore the intersection of cross-cultural exchange and women's agency. Though I do not wish to read the Byzantine-inflection as what David Shirt has critiqued as "a romance à clef, in which fact is thinly disguised as fiction,"[18] as Krijna Ciggaar has pointed out, there are certainly historical parallels between the women's rebellion in *Cligès* and the women's rebellion that saved the Byzantine consort Zoë Porphyrogenita.[19]

Whatever the historical roots of women's participation in Mediterranean cultural exchange, it is clear that romance struggles to articulate how women's interventions into Mediterranean society – normally couched as "the personal" and aligned with their reproductive functions – are transformed into actions with political consequences. That is, moving beyond conceptualizing women for their reproductive functions, medieval sources imagine women who married into foreign courts as transmitters of their own culture. This depiction of women's roles in cross-cultural encounters resonates with how Cynthia Enloe theorizes the work of diplomatic wives, which, while certainly obscured by their husbands' more obvious political negotiations, often serve a fundamental and complementary role in exchanging values in cross-cultural environments.[20]

Whereas diplomatic wives work to transmit their own cultural values *in tandem with* their husband's political goals in cross-cultural interactions, most obviously in texts like *Cligès*, the female protagonists married in foreign courts work *in opposition to* their new husband and his culture. The women's rebellion is only the beginning of how *Cligès* stages women's personal interventions as having political consequences for the transmission of empire. The most cogent example of women's interventions comes when Fénice herself censures her new husband's morality. The success of cross-cultural encounter at the heart of romance is brought sharply into question, its fecundity as a model harshly interrogated when Fénice censures her husband's disloyalty to his brother, policing his feudal obligations.

When Fénice realizes that Alis has broken his feudal oath of loyalty to his brother she quickly takes action to preserve Cligès's rightful claim to the throne. She commands her nurse, Thessala, to brew her a potion so that her husband can never consummate their marriage, and in so doing, bring about the disinheritance of his nephew. She says:

> Mais se voz tant saviez d'art
> Que ja cil n'eüst en moi part
> Cui je suis donee et plevie
> Molt m'avriez en gré servie.
> Maistre, car i mettez entente
> Que cil sa fiance ne mente
> Qui au pere Cligès plevi,
> Si com il meïsme eschevi,
> Que ja n'avroit fame espousee …
> Ja de moi ne puisse enfes nestre
> Par coi il [Cligès] soit deseritez.
> Mestre, or vos en entremetez. (3131–48)

[But if you could use your skill to prevent the man to whom I am promised and given from having any part of me, you would do me a great service. Nurse, devote all your efforts that this man not break his promise. Under oath he swore to Cligès's father never to take a wife. Since he will soon marry me, his oath will be violated. May I never be able to bear a child and so bring about his disinheritance. Nurse, see to now that I am in your debt forever.]

Fénice constructs a man's honour using a lexicon of feudal obligation steeped in speech (plevi, servie, fiance). She is ready to police her husband's actions – his preference for personal gain over feudal oaths of loyalty – as if she were still living under the standards of a western court, like that of Arthur or of her father. In describing both of their actions using "plevie" and "plevi" – the Old French word for pledging – she clearly contrasts her own duty of loyalty to her spouse to the duty her husband has undertaken to be loyal to his lord. The doubling of "plevie" highlights her choice to privilege the duty of feudal loyalty over spousal duty, and shows that she is ready to wager not only her marital felicity, but also her bodily integrity, that her own western feudal values will, in the long run, prove to be more tenable than her husband's Byzantine disloyalty. In short, she bets that, against all odds, she can impose her western world view of the oath onto an eastern court organized around the gift. Fénice's cross-cultural relationships permit her to assert the primacy of her own western political structures in ways that preserve her personal bodily integrity for her would-be lover. Her personal loyalties become the politics she imposes on her body, her marriage, and her new court.

Fénice's solution to her problem is both ingenious and dangerous. Whereas western courtly protocol for punishing Alis for breaking with their social mores would require that *men* hold a trial by judicial ordeal or deliberate whether to launch a war, neither Cligès nor Arthur is able to diminish Alis's grasp on the throne by force. Instead, inverting gender roles, a western noblewoman and her Byzantine nurse – two rogue *women* – act in collusion, both identifying the Byzantine man as disloyal and punishing him for his disloyalty. Not only do women's actions in negotiating culture name Byzantines as deviant, they construct women as political agents.

When Cligès returns to the court, they hatch a plan involving yet another potion and a faked death, through which Fénice's almost-dead body would, in a provisory wink towards *Romeo and Juliet*, allow them to escape and live together happily ever after.[21] Like in Shakespeare's play, the lovers' idea fails miserably, but here it does not end with their deaths. Luckily, like her namesake the phoenix, Fénice has the ability to be reborn again and again. The potion does not fool everyone, for three Salernian doctors ask to "interview" a half-dead Fénice alone, leading to her eventual torture and subsequent rescue by the Byzantine ladies' rebellion.

Fénice and Thessala's plan to prevent reproduction and impose Fénice's western values onto the Byzantine court in *Cligès* constructs women as fundamental to the negotiation of empire. Indeed, the spaces where women seem the most repressed – those spaces where they are traded as political pawns in men's larger plots of dynastic empire – come to be niches in which they carve out their own kinds of transmission, sometimes at odds with the men who have shuffled them from one household to another.

Women's work in *Cligès* also constructs cross-cultural marriage as a locus for the negotiation of empire, and not just through genealogical hybridity. In fact, the problematic sterility at the heart of *Cligès* – Fénice's wilful sterility – constructs women's work in cross-cultural marriage pointedly outside of the work of reproduction. *Cligès* theorizes women's participation in cross-cultural encounters as that of negotiation, transmission, and imposition.

Yet for all the women's courage in the romance, for all the cultural changes they enforce, and for all the rescuing they do, the epilogue of the romance averts any celebratory readings of female empowerment when Chrétien comments:

> Unques ne fu tenue anclose
> Si com ont puis esté tenues
> Celes qu'après li sont venues,
> Qu'ainc puis n'i ot empereor
> N'eüst de sa fame peor
> Qu'ele nel deüst decevoir,
> Se il oï ramantevoir
> Comant Fenice Alis deçut
> Primes par la poison qu'il but
> Et puis par l'autre traïson.
> Por ce einsi com an prison
> Est gardee an Constantinoble. (6680–91)

[Since then there has been no emperor who did not fear being deceived by his wife after hearing the story of Fénice deceiving Alis, first with the potion he drank, and then with the other treachery. For this reason every empress, no matter who she was, no matter how high-born or noble, was guarded in Constantinople as though imprisoned.]

Many have focused on the misogyny of these comments, yet inherent within this misogyny is a stringent critique of women's work in empire.[22] Perhaps it is not so much for her affair with Cligès that the narrator at the end of the epilogue condemns Fénice as "treasonous." Rather, I would argue that Fénice is condemned for her continual hard work – the "other treachery" – that undermines her new husband's court. It is work that supplants his avaricious bid for the throne with her foreign ideals of loyalty. In the end, the epilogue marks Fénice's agency as dangerous to the men who are trying to use her body and marriage to extend their empires. She is reprimanded for conflating empire with female agency, for appropriating and policing the mechanism of cultural transmission outside of men's control.

While women have agency, and while this agency is one that is transformative, bringing cultural change to the Byzantine court, their agency is of course over their own bodies, not directly over the empire. Women's agency is motivated by love, described as politics, accomplished by trickery and magic – but nonetheless it is an effective agency that has political consequences. The critique of Fénice's actions suggests that while literature may imagine women as active participants in cultural imperialism, it does not necessarily approve of that participation. Indeed, the critique of Fénice suggests that any reading of women's participation in transmitting culture and empire through cross-cultural marriage must be strictly nuanced to admit the transience of women's agency and control.

When we juxtapose the project announced by the prologue, in which the romance is all about the movement of knowledge, about *translatio* and all its cultural imperialism, with the moralizing of the epilogue, in which women's power to effect cultural change is simultaneously announced and castigated, we begin to see that the story of cross-cultural marriage cannot be told without women. Read in this light, the prologue's interest in the movement of knowledge – and its directionality *away* from all things Greek (of whom "talk is over, their burning embers spent") and *towards* all things western – can be thought of not only in relation to Chrétien's prowess as a writer, but also for the ways it reveals the creation and critique of empire to be deeply dependent on women's choices. Though condemned in the epilogue for her double treachery mixing love and politics, Fénice's insistence on policing her husband's feudal obligations shows how romance imagines noblewomen to play a crucial role in the transmission of culture and in the creation and policing of empire in the contested space of cross-cultural marriages around the Mediterranean.

The Making of Byzantine Empire in *Digenis Akritas*

It is possible to read the in-between spaces of Old French romances to understand Byzantium's significance in staging the intersection of women's work and empire, but in order to fully understand how these themes may represent concerns that resonate on both sides of cross-cultural interaction, we must also read from within a Byzantine romance about exchange in cross-cultural marriage.[23] Perhaps no Medieval Greek text offers a better comparison than *Digenis Akritas*, which has striking parallels to *Cligès* in both narrative content and structure. *Digenis* is a Medieval Greek story of two cross-cultural love affairs stretching over two generations and played out along the Byzantine frontier.[24] Though the original song was probably composed in the tenth century (the Grottaferrata manuscript), scholars argue that the earliest extant demotic Greek manuscript copy stems from twelfth-century versions of the tale.[25]

In ways that prefigure *Cligès*, and with material that in many ways resonates with the concerns of the later Old French romance, *Digenis* is the story of two generations of Byzantine nobles living on the borderlands with Syria. In the first part of the story, an Arab emir invades the borderlands of the Byzantine empire, Cappadocia, and abducts the daughter of the local Byzantine lord, converts to Christianity out of love for her, and fathers their son, Digenis Akritas, or "double-blooded border lord." The second part of the song details Digenis's skills as a warrior, and then turns to his prowess as, like his father, he abducts a Byzantine bride and then marries her. Though ostensibly an epic song focusing on the martial prowess of a hero of the Byzantine borderlands, the text is also a romance about the difficulties of frontier life in cross-cultural marriage. For all its obvious differences from *Cligès* – from its language, to its geographic separation, narrative tradition, and compositional timing – *Digenis* nonetheless reveals a parallel concern with the articulation of noble hybridity within cross-cultural marriage, this time between Byzantium and the Syrian frontier it seeks to colonize.

Reading *Digenis Akritas* and *Cligès* together does not imply that one influenced the other, nor does it mean that Byzantine or Old French literary motifs circulated in one direction or another.[26] Rather, putting Byzantine and Old French texts into dialogue during a moment of historical encounter and exchange reveals how the literature of both cultures imagined hybridity to be a position of power, a centre from which to enunciate a critique of borderland identities, be it in Byzantium (in the case of *Cligès*) or in modern-day Syria, on the Byzantine frontier (in the case of *Digenis*). By marrying the concerns of lineage with the concerns of empire, texts like *Digenis* and *Cligès* create a space in which the felicity of hybridity can be explored.

Of course, it is unlikely that there are any direct influences between the Byzantine epic song and the Old French romance. Yet it is still possible to compare their concerns and work to see what two ostensibly different cultures are grappling with as they face the problems of a nascent medieval Mediterranean hybridity. The larger non-literary wars of the Mediterranean, the need for more extensive geopolitical alliances, and the ecclesiastical pressures to marry exogamously meant that nobles exchanged not only goods, tropes, and myths, but also their own flesh and blood in ways that broke down the borders between east and west.[27]

Digenis offers a natural platform for reading about noble identities in the borderlands, and it fleshes out exactly what it might mean to be a noble participating in the colonial project, one whose home base is far from the centre of imperial life in Constantinople, one whose life and family are created and lived out on the in-between space of the frontier. The tale of love between a Syrian Muslim and a Byzantine Orthodox woman addresses not only religious difference (as when the emir's mother accuses him of converting to the faith of the "pig eaters" [πάντα μασυιδίον] for love of a Byzantine woman (E270) but also cultural praxis (as when men change clothing to pass between Syrian and Byzantine households).[28] Though there is ample description of difference, as Elizabeth Jeffreys points out, there is little likelihood that *Digenis* explores direct colonial encounters in a way that is any more historically informed than the fictitious portrayal of Germano-Byzantine interactions in a text like *Cligès*.[29] What is imagined in *Digenis* is the force of cross-cultural love on constructing life along the border; what is at stake are the ways that Byzantine glory are affirmed and transmitted through cross-cultural marriage. Like *Cligès*, then, *Digenis* imagines marriage as an essential locus of cultural exchange.

Digenis's story begins with the cross-cultural love of his parents, which is initially predicated upon the rapt of his mother. The rapt foreshadows the systematic disenfranchisement of women in the romance and abnegates their subjectivity in the borderlands. In Byzantium, women who unlawfully left their father's households were considered stolen property, and, in keeping with that understanding, the girl's brothers lament her abduction as a loss of property from their family:[30]

> ʽΟ πατήρ μας έξόριστος διὰ τὴν τιμωρίαν ...
> Οὐδεὶς ἀφ᾽ ἡμῶν ἔτυχεν είς τὴν ἐπέλευσίν σου,
> καὶ γὰρ ἡμεῖς ὑπήρχομεν στρατηγοὶ εἰς τὰς ἄκρας·
> εί γὰρ έκεῖ έτύχομεν, ούκ ἂν τοῦτο συνέβη,
> ούκ ἂν είς οἶκον μάς ποτε εἴχετε πορευθῆναι·
> άφ᾽ οὖ δὲ ούκ έτύχομεν, καλῶς νὰ τὸ καυχᾶσαι. (I:270, 272–6)
>
> [Our father is in exile as a punishment …
> None of us were present at your attack,
> for we were serving as generals on the frontier.
> If we had been there, this would not have occurred,
> you would never have invaded our house.
> Since we were not there, you can well boast of it.]

Here, the brothers lament the loss of their sister on two fronts: both as a loss of familial property, and as a loss of their own masculinity. Their lament ties men's bravery to two locales, to shaping the frontier and to protecting their homesteads. Tying men's duties to protecting kingdom and homestead suggests that *Digenis* imagines masculinity as essentially tied to the control of property.

Cross-cultural love is a locale that permits the exchange of household belongings. When rapt is redeemed by marriage, it is also simultaneously assuaged by the exchange of copious goods, tying the family's worth to the gifts exchanged. In the Grottaferrata version, book 4 is almost entirely dedicated to enumerating the copious gifts, goods, and people exchanged by men as dowry and counter-dowry in celebration of the cross-cultural marriage. For the bride's father gift giving serves a double purpose, both to reveal his daughter's worth and, more innovatively, to test a man's worth. He elaborates that for his daughter's wedding, he will offer both his consent and part of his household:

> Κεντηνάρια εἴκοσι, νομίσματα παλαῖα, ...
> βιστιάριον χρῇζον τε πεντακοσίας λίτρας,
> κτήματα πολλὰ άκίνητα τριανταὲξ είσόδων,
> καὶ μετὰ τούτων πάντων <τε> εὑρισκόμενα ζῷα,
> πρωτεῖα τετρακόσια, στράτορας όγδοήντα,
> μαγείρους δεκατέσσαρας καὶ μάγκιπας ὡσαύτως ...

ὡσαύτως καὶ ἐξαίσια κόσμια τῆς μητρός της ...
Ποιήσω καὶ τοὺς γάμους σου ἀκουστοὺς εἰς τὸν κόσμον
τοῦ μὴ κράζειν σε πώποτε κλεψίγαμον οἱ νέοι,
καὶ ὅτι κόρην ἥρπασας πραγμάτων ἀμοιροῦσαν,
ὅπερ αἰσχύνη πέφυκε πᾶσι τοῖς εὖ φρονοῦσιν.

[Twenty *centenaria* in old *nomismata* ...
a wardrobe worth five hundred *litrai*,
much landed property providing thirty-six revenues,
and with all the livestock they contain,
four hundred beasts of the first quality, eighty grooms,
fourteen cooks and as many bakers ...
likewise exceptional jewellery from her mother ...
And I shall make your wedding renowned throughout the world,
so that young men can never call you a match stealer,
saying that you abducted a girl who lacked possessions,
which is a reproach to all men of good sense.]

(IV:706, 709–18, 713, 724–7)

Here, ravishment is directly mitigated by gifts, marking exotic goods as a way to alleviate the injury to father and suitor caused by the actions that would be a "reproach to all men of good sense." Both fathers (as givers) and sons-in-laws (as receivers) are honoured through the reciprocal bonds created by the exchange of marriage gifts.

Cross-cultural marriage in *Digenis* is predicated on violence against both men (as they lose property) and women (as they are abducted), and it imagines women as property in ways that seem to eschew their agency. Women are to be exchanged across borders and between families in ways that bridge the gulf established by rapt, turning the personal abduction of daughters into a political tool for expanding empire on the border. As Kathryn Gravdal has pointed out, the violence of rape is one of the foundational narratives of western romance; whether or not her analysis typifies Greek romance, the violence of life on the frontier in *Digenis Akritas* is certainly as much structured by the threat of rape as it is by the threats posed within combats between men.[31] As such, the formulation of women's agency on the frontier is complicated at best.[32] Essentially, we must ask the question: if women are continually the subject of men's domination in the romance, whether through ravishment redeemed by marriage, or through the continual threat of rape that is living life on a warring frontier, then in what ways is it possible to posit their subjectivity?

The reading of rapt from a women's perspective offers insights into how love, hybridity, and empire coalesce, even within a disempowered subjectivity. If the brothers' lament constructs rapt as an injury to their masculinity, the women of the romance – both the mothers and their abducted daughters – interpret it differently. For women, ravishment offers the possibility of choosing cross-cultural love and bridging the borders of empire, but at the precarious price of wagering one's life and familial honour against the happy outcome of marriage. While the mothers are active letter writers who spur their sons to action, begging them on different occasions to save their sister, avenge their father, protect their children, and preserve the family's honour, the daughters who are abducted tell a pointedly different tale.

In the daughters' formulations, rapt has a complex relationship to agency, one that turns around the articulation of women's desire, their illicit and personal desire for foreign men of whom their fathers do not approve. The second generation of rapt, for example, begins with a love story of Digenis and his Doukas bride that transcends language, religion, and even political borders. Importantly, the kidnapping is consensual, and the girl acknowledges that with illicit cross-cultural love comes the threat of disrupting her own family's status:

᾿Αφ᾿ ἧς γὰρ ὥρας πρόσωπον τὸ σὸν εἶδον, ὦ νέε,
ὡς πῦρ κατέφλεξεν εὐθὺς τὴν σώφρονα ψυχήν μου,
μετήλλαξε τὸν λογισμὸν ὁμοίως καὶ τὴν γνώμην,
τὸ φρόνημα ἐδούλωσεν, ἀναίσχυντόν μ᾿ ἐποίησε.
Εἰς σὲ καὶ μόνον, ποθητέ, καὶ πρὸς τὴν σὴν ἀγάπην
πείθομαι νῦν καὶ βούλομαι μετὰ σοῦ πορευθῆναι,
δι᾿ οὗ ἀρνοῦμαι συγγενεῖς, γονέας ὑστεροῦμαι,
ἀλλοτριοῦμαι ἀδελφῶν καὶ τοῦ ἀπείρου πλούτου
καὶ μετὰ σοῦ πορεύομαι ὅπου δ᾿ ἂν καὶ κελεύῃς.

[From the moment I saw your face, young man,
a kind of fire immediately enflamed my chaste soul,
it transformed my reasoning and likewise my nature,
it enslaved my mind and made me shameless.
To you alone beloved, and to my love for you
I am now obedient, and I want to journey with you,
for whom I renounce my kinsmen, I deprive myself of parents,
I make myself a stranger to my brothers and our boundless wealth
and with you I journey wherever you command.] (IV:506–14)

The formulation of rapt – which in many ways resonates with the staging of Cligès's escape from the German emperor's household with Fénice – permits a space for imagining *women*'s personal desires (their cross-cultural love) to have political consequences for both their families and their empires. While women are constantly the subject of rape and physical violence throughout *Digenis*, and while they lack all the obvious markers of empowerment and agency, women's choices to love across the frontier and beyond the ken of their father's households create unique spaces in which love on the borderlands becomes a site for negotiating cross-cultural exchange. As in *Cligès*, *Digenis* imagines women's desires as one of the cornerstones of cross-cultural exchange and the negotiation of hybrid identities. Even while women remain nameless in *Digenis*, their personal desires are articulated as borderland politics, forging avenues of exchange in which gifts, family dynasties, and borderland are exchanged. Women's work in cross-cultural love assures that marriage becomes a bridge across which women – and not only their fathers or husbands – exchange ideas.

If cross-cultural marriage permits us to imagine women as bearers of cultural knowledge, it also allows us to interrogate the location of the borderland, the "other." In *Digenis*, the borderland is Syria and the centre is Byzantium; in *Cligès*, the borderland is Byzantium and the centre is the Arthurian court. Though these borders are decidedly different, both romances capitalize on the idea of centre and periphery to typify the self and the other, to try to locate and name the differences that women and their desires are meant to bridge. Cross-cultural marriage is not only a space where women's personal desires have public consequences; it is also a space in which the border is revealed to be fragile, impermanent, and illusory.

In particular, the comparison between *Cligès* and *Digenis* makes it clear that east and west become, as I see them, terms used to denote *relative* geographic directions, rather than a set of cultural values fixed to hard geographic or religious determinants. Even the stereotypes that typify Byzantines in many of the romances contemporary to *Cligès* are, in fact, reversible when read from another point of view. As Byzantine imperial princess and historiographer Anna Komnene relates in her *Alexiad*, the Byzantines themselves depicted the Latins (as they referred to westerners) as fickle oath-breakers, as people motivated only by their greed for gold and their willingness to lie and deceive.[33] Reading *Cligès* in tandem with *Digenis* reveals the necessity of revising fixed ideas about centre and periphery as east and west are blurred and relativized. No longer marginalized at the frontier of Old French literature,

Byzantium becomes a larger methodological avenue of enquiry for reading for a spectrum of identities produced by cross-cultural matches across the Mediterranean and negotiated by women.

Most importantly, and as we shall see, marriage becomes the space in which women's personal feelings become a public critique of their men's worth, formulating and advertising their masculinity. As staged in *Digenis*, and as the brothers' lamentations predict, cross-cultural love permits romance to articulate women as makers and keepers of masculinities.

A Man Is as Good as His Word: Masculinity, Empire, and Oaths

It may not be surprising that romance as a genre constructs western victories over eastern others – be they Byzantines, Syrians, or other "others." Reading Byzantine and Old French texts together suggests that medieval cross-cultural marriage is a site for women to exchange culture and critique empire, most often in favour of the imagined literary centre. *Cligès* and *Digenis Akritas*, for example, suggest that cross-cultural encounters permit the articulation of women's love as political agency. Women's work in cross-cultural marriage on the *frontier* helps make the *centre*, helps pull values that may be liminal to their new courts and homes back to the centre of discourse and storytelling, back to the centre of courtly culture.

But women's work in cross-cultural marriage extends beyond the reproduction of their native cultural structures in a foreign man's court, or even, in the best cases, beyond their ability to translate them for a new courtly setting. Their critiques not only reify their own cultural structures, they also provide a link between women's empire-building and the kinds of gender structures it produces. In essence, women's critiques of empire as articulated in texts of cultural encounter like *Cligès* and *Digenis* construct cross-cultural marriage as a site that proffers the possibility of alternate genders.

One of the most important and savvy critiques couched in women's rebellions in cross-cultural romance is the critique of masculinity, positing cross-cultural love as the locus for alternate formulations of gender as well as empire. In *Cligès*, as in *Digenis*, the critique of masculinity is articulated as a critique of men's relations to language. In twelfth-century French courts like that of Marie de Champagne, in which Chrétien wrote and where *Cligès* would have been performed, speech was one of the currencies of a man's worth, and nobles swore oaths of fealty to their king, who in turn confirmed their hereditary right to titles, lands, and rents.[34] The special relationship of mutual defence and loyalty that bound the king and his nobles was enacted through speech, and, to a great extent, speech guaranteed a man's worth.[35] Whether made between king and vassal or between husband and wife, the oath became an act that ensured succeeding generations' claims to money and power, cementing dynastic – rather than individual – rights to land and titles over several generations.[36] While of course speech was not the only way of aligning or of maintaining the noble-king relationship, speech acts such as oaths were the primary way of doing so.[37]

In French-speaking courts, the widespread use of vassalic oaths suggests that speech played a substantial role in instantiating and maintaining hegemonic masculinities, and that masculinity was essentially bound to the truth that speech could enact. Without speech, a man was hardly a man in medieval romance, for without speech to report and promise renown, without speech to *enact* renown, a man's reputation faded quickly away. One need only to think of the heroes who lose their identity in western romances like *Le Chevalier au lion* or *Le Chevalier de la charrette* to see that dominant masculinities are constructed through speech – through storytelling about men's exploits and through speech acts forging bonds between knights and kings. The quest for personal identity is structured as a quest for encounters with other men and is enacted through speech about that encounter. Narratives of personal glory in romances like *Yvain, Erec et Enide,* and *Lancelot* depend on language to perform and transmit renown.

Byzantium, unlike the west, was highly literate and bureaucratic; moreover, the court had a different relation to speech. In Byzantium, it was the gift of money, rather than the oath of honour, that organized and structured court life and loyalty, at least until the late twelfth century.[38] The emperor personally doled out yearly salaries (*roga*) in the form of bags of gold given to his vassals in an elaborate ceremony involving the whole court and written down by court historiographers.[39] Byzantine loyalty vacillated wildly. As Byzantine historians Michael Psellos and Niketas Choniates point out, power struggles wracked the imperial court; over eleven Byzantine rulers were violently deposed from 1150 to 1390, often blinded or worse by their own relatives who sought control of the imperial coffers. While of course medieval French romances are *not* based on Byzantine cultural praxis, both fictional and historical representations of the Byzantine court point to a system of allegiance in which the oath held a very different function than in the west.

Byzantium seems to be a place in which goods, rather than speech, created masculine worth. Western medieval literature recognizes Byzantium as a site for figuring masculinity through gold and goods, through the strategic use of the gift. In *Le Roman de Thèbes*, for example, another contemporary text of *Cligès* and bound with it in several manuscript codices, when eastern emperor Atys dies, he is remembered for his gift giving, not his oath-making:

> Car tu donoies les contreis,
> Donoez muls et palefreis,
> Armes, festreials et couvertors,
> Et beals levriers et genz ostors;
> Tu donoes les chevals gras,
> Or et argent et riches dras.
> Ti chevalier errant joyos,
> Onc ne furent jor soffraitos:
> Tu donoes les granz aveirs,
> Tu faiseies touz lour voleirs;
> Tu amoiez les chevaliers,
> Tu les teneies forment chiers;
> Qui te servit n'en reprentit,
> Onc sofraite oue tei ne sentit.
> Onc ne fut homme de ta proece,
> Ne qui eust si grant largece. (6899–914)[40]

> [you gave away lands, you gave mules and palfreys, arms, decorative ribbons, horse blankets, beautiful dogs for hunting rabbits, and falcons. You gave great horses, gold and silver and rich cloths. Your knights were joyful, they never were suffering: you gave them great things, you did all that they wished; you loved the knights, you held them very dear to you; he who served you did not regret it, they never felt suffering with you. There was never a man of your prowess, nor one who is so generous.][41]

Atys's masculinity is caught up in the process of gift giving: his prowess ("proece") is directly linked to his generosity ("largece") in the end rhyme of the Old French passage. His vassals remember him explicitly and exaggeratedly not only in terms of the battles he has won, but also in terms of the wondrous gifts he has given, and his masculinity is established through the copious goods he gives away. The *Roman de*

Thèbes, then, imagines eastern rulers' prowess as directly linked to their gift giving.

Several other medieval French texts bound with *Cligès* also explore the tension between the two ways of describing masculinity and maintaining loyalty at court. The *Roman d'Alexandre*, for example, describes Alexander the Great (who in this romance is born to Greek, rather than Turkish, parents) in terms of his hardiness ("hardiesse") and his generosity ("largesse").[42] On his deathbed at the young age of twenty-six, the emperor calls each of his twelve pairs over to his bedside in order to present them with fantastic gifts of lands and rents. Each stanza invokes a formulaic notion of giving, and the repetition of the verb "doner" (to give) highlights that it is Alexander's ability to give – rather than his ability to speak or fight – which is to be remembered as the core of his identity, cemented through reiteration. This is just one of several examples in which eastern rulers are imagined as gift givers, their masculinity commensurate to their wealth, rather than to their martial abilities or verbal trustworthiness.

In many romances, it is the gift giving and the wondrous, exotic goods that mark the power of the Byzantine court, not its adherence to western vassalic practices rooted in speech. The Byzantine court was represented in Old French literature as a place where gifts could not necessarily guarantee loyalty, and speech most certainly did not guarantee anything. Of course, this is not to say that speech acts did not occur at the Byzantine court, or that they did not represent or enact anything; rather, it points to the ways literature conflated gift giving and eastern masculinity, and it contextualizes this reading of the structural differences between the courts of pseudo-Byzantine emperor Alis and King Arthur in *Cligès*.[43]

Arthur, for example, is preoccupied with speech throughout the romance. He understands a man's worth to be instantiated through speech, through the ways that his deeds reflect his words. In essence, he is interested in the ways oaths function as speech acts, how they *instantiate* and *promise* masculinity through loyal service. Arthur understands a man's speech to perform his masculinity, to instantiate his trustworthiness as a vassal. When Alis breaks his vow of loyalty, then, he breaks with western structures of masculinity. For Arthur, there is no question that broken oaths merit swift military retribution, as when he readies an army to defend Alexander's right to the throne (2380–8).

In contrast to Arthur, the Byzantine emperor Alexander is typified as a gift giver. In his encounter with the Arthurian court, for example, the young Byzantine creates his renown not through speech but through gifts of exotic things:

> largement done et despent
> Si come a sa richece apent
> Et si com ses cuers li conseille,
> Et toute la corz s'en merveille
> Ou ce que il despent est pris,
> Qu'il done a touz chevaux de pris
> Que de sa terre ot amenez.
> Tant s'est Alixandres penez
> Et tant fet par son bel servise
> Que molt l'aime li rois et prise
> Et li baron et la reïne. (410–21)

> [giving and spending generously, according to the promptings of his heart and befitting his wealth. The entire court wondered where he had acquired what he had spent, for to all he presented valuable horses, which he had brought from his own land. Alexander's fine services won him the love and high esteem of the king, the queen, and the barons.]

Though the association between Byzantines and gifts is at first positive, as the romance progresses it devolves, becoming markedly pejorative. Already in this passage there is something sinister in the rumours of his wealth that are articulated through the sibilance of "si," "sa richece," "si," "ses," "cuers," "conseille," and "corz s'en merveille," audibly associating the sinister with a masculinity predicated upon goods.

By the time Fénice and Thessala brew the potion, that "something sinister" is revealed in the complex relation between gifts, oaths, gender, and speech. In Byzantium, language does not reflect truth; gifts, rather than oaths, are what structure courtly loyalty. The "something sinister" begins with the disjuncture between language and loyalty at the Byzantine court, and it seeps into the construction of masculinity in empire. And women's actions in cross-cultural marriage provide both the link and the critique.

Women's actions throughout *Cligès* permit the articulation and critique of alternate systems of masculinity. From the women's rebellion against the Salernian doctor's inability to "read" Fénice's body correctly, to the rebellious potion brewed by Fénice and Thessala, women take actions that directly comment upon and critique the relationship between speech and masculinity as performed in Byzantium. In the former case, women gathered because they recognized foreign men as unable to read their empress's body correctly; they rebel not only against her torture, but also against the men's inability to understand the truth her body is supposed to represent. As such, the rebellion is not only a moment in which women uphold another *woman*, it is also a moment in which women cite and condemn *men's* inability to perceive reality as told to them through a woman's body. They articulate and denounce, essentially, men's inability to perceive truth in the language of the female body, aligning foreign men with an inability to see truth in language. In *Cligès*, hordes of eastern ladies not only famously defenestrate foreign doctors, they also make apparent one of the central problematics of eastern masculinity as writ in western romance: its inherent disjuncture from language.

Women's work in *Cligès* is not only about censuring particular men, it is also about constructing a critique of eastern masculinity. When Thessala and Fénice concoct their plan to disenfranchise Alis, they are concocting a plan that names Byzantine masculinity as different from western masculinity, and they simultaneously articulate that alternation as deviant and dangerous. As we have already seen, their personal politics have public ramifications in the exchange of culture and the formation of empire. Another consequence of Fénice's speech is to create Alis's masculinity as separate from that of Cligès and to name it as inferior. Her speech enacts and condemns an alternate masculinity predicated on gift giving. It constructs western masculinities, deeply tied to speech and oath-taking, as preferable and worth sacrifice. Fénice recognizes two kinds of men, one for whom speech (language, oaths) reports reality (loyalty), and the other for whom speech is essentially opaque and independent of its relation to truth.[44]

Women's actions in cross-cultural encounters in *Cligès* not only help make empire and impose western values onto the Byzantine court; they also help tie the language of empire to gender. That is, empire is articulated not only through court politics, but also through gender politics. In this case, Alis and the Salernian doctors are both condemned for their deviancy – not for their deviant desires or their deviant sexuality, but for their deviancy in relating to language. Whereas western masculinities are predicated on the ways valour is constructed through truthful language, through speech either instantiating positions (like speech acts such as "I dub you Sir Lancelot") or reporting renown (such as stories of the knightly encounter with other men), the women in *Cligès* interpret eastern masculinities as essentially predicated on the lie, on the disjuncture between language and reality. Though it is not unexpected that eastern masculinity be labelled as deviant, moments like Fénice's speech and the women's rebellion reveal how deeply dependent the articulation of masculinity is on women and their understanding of how men should relate to language.

Though the overt work of men in *Digenis* is to make war and exchange gifts, that process is also deeply dependent on women and also offers a pointed critique of masculinity. Women are letter writers in *Digenis*, and their words are what create action. They castigate and cajole their men into warfare, or they curse their sons for their failings (I:70–81). But their words do more than prescribe men's martial, marital, or filial duties, they also help forge frontier masculinities, in ways that suggest that the Byzantine romance, too, imagines cross-cultural marriage to be a space for women to articulate and critique alternate gender positions. Their words *enact* men's worth.

Not only does letter writing in *Digenis* imagine a relation between language, women, and femininity in cross-cultural encounters, it also explicitly stages cross-cultural marriage as a locus for the critique of masculinity. After the emir marries Digenis's mother, his own mother castigates cross-cultural love as a detriment to her son's masculinity. In a scathing letter to her newly married son, she bemoans his failures as a man:

> Πῶς γὰρ ούκ έμνημόνευσας τὰς πράξεις τοῦ πατρός σου,
> ὅσους Ῥωμαίους ἔσφαξε, πόσους ἔφερε δούλους; ...
> Ἀλλ' έκεῖνος προστάγματα φυλάττων τοῦ Προφήτου
> δόξης μὲν κατεφρόνησε, πλοῦτον δὲ ού προσέσχε·
> καὶ μεληδόν τον ἔκοψαν καὶ άπῆραν τὸ σπαθίν του.
> Σὺ δὲ άνάγκην μὴ είδὼς πάντα ὁμοῦ παρεῖδες,
> τὴν πίστιν μέν, τοὺς συγγενεῖς κάμὲ τὴν σὴν μητέρα ...
> ὅταν ἤθελες δοξασθῆν παρ' ὅλην τὴν Συρίαν,
> τὰ πάντα προσαπώλεσας δι' άγάπην χανζυρίσσης.
>
> [How could you not remember your father's deeds,
> how many Romans[45] he slew, how many he carried off as slaves? ...
> But he kept the Prophet's commandments,
> spurned renown and paid no attention to wealth,
> and they hewed him limb from limb and took away his sword.

> But you, not even under compulsion, have abandoned everything at once,
> your faith, your kinsmen and me, your mother ...
> When you were about to be honoured by all Syria,
> you destroyed everything for the love of a pig-eater.]
>
> (II:60–1, 70–4, 81–2)

Here, a mother's words construct masculinity on the frontier in terms of fighting other men and renouncing conversion – that is, fighting to the death to extol one's beliefs and expand one's territories. Creating empire creates masculinities predicated on encounter, but not upon exchange. These are identities predicated upon domination and extermination, not upon negotiation, mitigation, and exchange.

In the mother's speech, the danger of the cross-cultural love affair lies in the renunciation of this identity of empire, the identity of propagation and extermination, rather than exchange and hybridity. The women from across the border, the "pig eater(s)," represent not only a threat to religious and political order, they also represent a threat to the systems of monocultural identity. Cross-cultural marriage becomes a point of contact, a beginning of a conversation in which ideas are shared, practices melded, families blended; it threatens to disrupt the empire-building upon which she understands masculinity to be based, as demonstrated by her vitriolic outburst against cultural hybridity. Hybridity and cultural exchange are clearly condemned when the encounter is typified by words like "plunder," "slew," and "renounce," only a fraction of the condemnation coursing throughout the longer letter from which this excerpt stems. Cross-cultural love produces not only cultural hybridity, according to this mother's speech, it also threatens the basis of a man's identity, his masculinity. In the end, her critique equates cross-cultural love with the loss of masculinity.

Digenis's father is deeply wounded by his mother's censure; like his wife's brothers, who were spurred to action by their mother's pen, Digenis's father must in turn negotiate a new identity in relation to his mother. He does so by convincing his whole Syrian household, of which she is a part, to convert to Christianity and come live with him as Byzantines. Thus in *Digenis*, cross-cultural marriage becomes a place for conversion, for the change of religious and cultural practices and for the articulation of new, hybrid kinds of masculinities. In particular, shortly after having converted his whole household to Christianity (III:230–31), Digenis must negotiate his borderland masculinity, his crossing over to Roman territory, through clothing (III:257–62).

The text constructs cross-cultural love as the vehicle for cultural exchange, and it is Eros who controls it:

Ὄντως θαῦμα παράδοξον ἔργον ὀρθῆς ἀγάπης.
τίς τοῦτο μὴ καταπλαγῇ ...
καὶ καταμάθῃ ἀκριβῶς ἔρωτος τὰς δυνάμεις,
πῶς ἀλλοφύλους ἥνωσεν, εἰς μίαν φέρων πίστιν; (III:319–22)

[The results of sanctioned love are truly a strange wonder.
Who would not be astounded ...
to learn precisely the power of Eros,
how he united those of different race, bringing them into one faith?]
(Jeffreys 63)

Though the translation ascribes the exchange of culture to the "power" of Eros, the Medieval Greek term "δυνάμεις" also connotes the "workings," the "dynamics" of love. That is, the text is as much interested in the *process*, the dynamic, of identities forged through cross-cultural love, as it is with the outcome of conversion and cultural hybridity. The Byzantine text constructs love as a mechanism for a celebratory, hybrid masculinity. In *Digenis*, masculinity is based upon the exchange made possible through borderland love affairs, rather than through the destruction and annihilation of empirical warfare. In the end, cross-cultural marriage permits the articulation of an alternate, non-warring masculinity, within the confines of the love affair; it is this masculinity that bridges cultures torn apart by rapt.

When combined with other episodes in which love is predicated upon women's beauty and, later, women's desire to love illicitly across the border, *Digenis* can be read as a romance that constructs women at the heart of negotiating masculinities on the frontier. Whether through mothers who castigate their sons and spur them to action – to fight for their familial monoculture – or through daughters who love across the borders of religion and "race," the Byzantine romance imagines, like *Cligès*, cross-cultural marriage as a space for women to manipulate the exchange of culture and shape their men's masculinities.

Historical context, codicological evidence, and literary themes spanning Medieval Greek and Old French literature come together to suggest, then, that Byzantium was a complicated but essential signifier for the west, a place neither here nor there, neither completely Christian nor certainly Muslim, a place neither friend nor foe, a place of glamorous exotic gifts and treacherous military traps. Literature depicting the complicated and evolving relationship between Byzantium and France in the late twelfth century suggests that Byzantium became a site for articulating alternate gender positions to both construct and critique empire. Women had an important role to play in negotiating how and what got exchanged and transmitted, amplified, or silenced, in the pan-Mediterranean relations forged through cross-cultural marriage. Whether, like Fénice, in a move that prefigures the later historical conquest of Constantinople by the Franks and Venetians, they refused assimilation and blazed ahead to impose western mores onto an eastern court, or whether they opted to assimilate, women's work in negotiating empire seems to have extended well beyond their reproductive capacities and into the imaginative realm of literary imperialism, a place which we have, until now, reserved squarely for the work of men, as authors, characters, and crusaders.

2 Exchanging Exoticism: Narrating Mediterranean Nobility in *Floire et Blancheflor*[1]

The twelfth-century Old French romance *Floire et Blancheflor* depicts how a pagan boy's love for a Christian maiden leads him to convert his kingdom to Christianity out of love for her. It has long been read as a story of cross-religious love and conversion. Most obviously at stake in this text are a Christian military victory over Islam and a romantic victory over a foreign other in the context of cross-cultural love. It would be easy to read the story as another iteration of the basic storyline of *Cligès*, in which marriages spanning the Mediterranean become spaces through which women's work in cross-cultural marriage permits the expansion of western empires. Yet, this reading relies on a number of assumptions about who these "others" are, and what they represent.

Recent critical work on *Floire et Blancheflor* has focused on exchange between medieval France and its eastern neighbours, and in particular scholars are asking questions about how exotic goods are showcased in their reading of a story about Muslims and religious conversion.[2] Several recent studies focus on the teleological ends of religious encounter, that is, on Christian France and its Muslim others, leaving a whole middle Mediterranean geography unexplored, though they acknowledge its presence.[3] Jane Burns and Sharon Kinoshita, for example, have each examined how *Floire et Blancheflor* depicts Mediterranean trade in medieval French literature.[4] Yet I would go further to argue that this romance invites differentiation between what Burns calls a "courtly west" and an ambiguous "mercantile east," for within its leaves lies a whole host of intertexts, going well beyond the borders of Islam. [5]

Nestled in the crevices of much of the solid scholarship about *Floire et Blancheflor* lies an assumption that the pagans peopling its pages are to be understood as *Muslims*, and that the courts, objects, and genders that are described in the text are uniquely Muslim.[6] An alternate reading of *Floire et Blancheflor* invites us to broaden our ken to focus on cross-cultural trade beyond the souks of the Arab-speaking world, the markets of Venice and other Italian coastal cities, and the well-known *foires* of medieval France, to which we have contented ourselves until now.[7]

While of course this text *is* overtly about Arab Muslims living in Spain, there is an important subtext in which many different kinds of peoples invoked by the term "pagan" play a role, and which changes our reading of how nobility is constructed through the trade and consumption of exotic goods within the romance. The trade in and display of unattainable foreign goods – goods that no plebeian people would ever own and most nobles could not obtain – was not only a marker of one's own power and value, but it also created an economy of what I am calling "exoticism," of wonder at the power of mythicized foreign goods and ideas in the marketplace.[8] This economy has deep roots in Byzantium and thrives in part through connections to Hellenism, as well as through the more obvious contemporary intertexts interpellated by *Floire et Blancheflor*: Mozarabic Spain and Muslim Cairo. I suggest that we must consider a multiplicity of easts when considering the figuring of pagan exoticism within *Floire et Blancheflor*.

When Edward Said's landmark study *Orientalism* appeared, it was one of the first scholarly attempts to grapple with the convergence of exoticism, gender, and the power struggles of the colonial encounter.[9] While scholars have contested his framing of the colonial encounter as exclusively post-medieval, in medieval studies there has been less attention paid to the gendering of the exotic encounter – that is, the narrative as told from the point of view of the masculinized western observer of the feminized native (man). Though Said's work aligned the exotic with the feminine in the colonial encounter, some medieval texts imagine a narrative space for figuring masculinity precisely *through* exoticism. *Floire et Blancheflor*, for example, imagines exoticism as empowering, and the so-called "other" as integral to fashioning the noble self. This romance, which exists in several manuscripts and is widely translated,[10] is a text I claim is predicated on the desirability of exoticism, the currency that the exotic holds in transactions of gift giving, book commissioning, and outright mercantilism across boundaries of religion.

Though the term "exotic" is certainly not a medieval one, and though I clearly mean to engage with Said's discussion of the politics of exoticism, I also use the term "exotic" to refer to the sense of wonder expressed by medievals when faced with beautiful foreign *objects* – from architecture to relics, from technologies of war to magical machines, from beautiful fine cloths to wondrous spices and gems – that were not produced in their own area.[11] Whereas "exoticism," then, refers to a set of cultural practices surrounding the encounter with the foreign, I claim that exotic goods help create an economy of conspicuous consumption through which the nobility – and in particular, noble masculinity – is fashioned in relation to the other.

The economy of the exotic is a real-life economic structure of supply and demand – the paucity of wondrous, exotic goods from far away redoubled the noble desire to fashion the self through the consumption and giving of these goods. My reading of the codicological contexts of *Floire et Blancheflor* (especially its two main manuscripts, BnF Fr. 375 and 1447) suggests that this economy included the production of expensive manuscripts in which narratives about exoticism figured prominently. *Floire et Blancheflor* is both a narrative about the sway of exotic goods and itself an exotic good, a manuscript and a story, commissioned, traded, and compiled within a particular noble context, creating an economy of exoticism that I will explore further in the coming pages.

In this chapter, then, I argue that *Floire et Blancheflor* creates an economy of the exotic in which exotic goods and stories are imagined as fundamental to the construction of the Mediterranean noble self. Such a reading most obviously changes the stakes for the eponymous protagonists Floire and Blancheflor, in that it reshapes them into Mediterranean – rather than particularly Christian or Muslim – characters. Yet the reading, as we shall see, also has implications for the relationship between exoticism, nobility, and gender in the medieval Mediterranean.

The Pagan Paradigm: Remapping Religious Others

Floire et Blancheflor begins with the story of religious strife between pagans and Christians somewhere in Spain, where Blancheflor's pregnant mother and her retinue are brutally attacked while on pilgrimage by pagan marauders. Floire's father's ruthlessness is aligned with his religion: "Fenix ot non si fu paiens / Passé ot mer sus crestïens / Pour u païs la praie prendre" [Fénix was his name and he was also a Pagan; he had gone by sea to the land of the Christians to take their land from them] (61–3).[12] As I have remarked elsewhere, the paratactic repetition of the plosive "p" tying together the words "paiens," "paies," and "prendre" creates a tight association between inter-religious violence and pagans.[13] Yet what do we really know about these pagans? And just how culturally specific are their practices to Mozarabic Spain?

The "pagan" court in *Floire et Blancheflor* is a space of transformation and flux. In fact, there are several places where descriptions of this exotic, purportedly Muslim, other resembles as much people and goods from French-speaking courts or Byzantium as they do any part of Muslim Spain. Blancheflor's mother – captive, Christian, and French – integrates into her new courtly environment easily, and her changes allow her to forge alliances with her captors. Her integration permits her to participate in the queen's retinue and is so complete that she even gives birth to Blancheflor on the same day that her new protectress gives birth to her son, Floire. She goes on to help raise the children, assisting in their upbringing and care. As such, the friendship of the two women – one a pagan, the other a Christian – and, subsequently, between their two children renders the narrative conflict of the frame story formulaic at best and bridges the gulf that supposedly delineates pagans as bad and Christians as good. The narrative frame of inter-religious strife that purportedly sets the reading program for the romance is thus called into question by the first moments of cross-cultural amity in the romance.[14]

The etymology of "paiien" ("pagan"), the only term used to identify the religion of both Floire's parents and the Egyptian emir in the earliest extant Old French manuscript, BnF Fr. 375, derives from the Latin word *paganus*, a term denoting rustic peoples.[15] In keeping with these roots, its medieval usage did not point exclusively to Muslims, and while it most frequently described Muslims, it often connoted other non-Western peoples, specifically in its association with rustic religious practices, including the worshipping of icons as practised by Byzantines. Such a reading of "pagan" suggests a much wider set of religious and cultural referents for the courtly milieu of *Floire et Blancheflor*, expanding well beyond the borders of Islam and into other non-Catholic traditions, such as Byzantine Orthodox Christianity. While in the Orthodox Church, for example, iconoclasm had not totally routed the deeply engrained popular rituals of image worshipping, the veneration of images in medieval Islamic practice was totally forbidden. It is therefore possible to read beyond the borders of Islam if one reads "pagan" as a label that invokes not only non-Roman Christians, but in particular, *image-worshipping* non-Roman Christians – that is, Byzantines – within conversion texts like *Floire et Blancheflor*.

The careful use of the term "pagan" to describe Floire and his parents in MS 375 invites a reconsideration of how this text stages commerce, exchange, gift giving, and gender politics between fictive Spanish and eastern courts. Focusing not on these extreme boundaries of the crusader world, but instead on the complex grey space of interaction and conversion staged in a world neither specifically eastern nor exclusively Muslim, opens up a broader space for considering just what is being exchanged within the world of *Floire et Blancheflor* and what this exchange might allow the romance to do. Passages that critics have read as black-and-white descriptions of Muslims in *Floire et Blancheflor* are actually much more nuanced, creating a grey space layering subtle influences from Christian – if geographically separate – neighbours to the courtly west on top of descriptions of the Islamic east. In particular, this grey space should be extended beyond the boundaries of the Muslim world to include eastern Christian neighbours like Byzantium, whose trading networks and patterns of exchange are fruitfully resonant with narrative elements of *Floire et Blancheflor* as well as other territories mentioned in the romance, such as Bulgaria and Hungary.[16]

The Mediterraneanism of the romance – that is, its usage of many Mediterranean cultures and religions to figure multiculturalism within the medieval nobility – is best exemplified in the ways it equates noble identity with exoticism, and, in particular, with exotic goods. After Floire and Blancheflor are raised and educated together in this pagan world, they fall in love. However, Floire's parents are so opposed to the match that they concoct a plan to sell her off for the price of a costly golden goblet in order to get her away from Floire without having to kill her. Jane Burns has recently read this goblet as one "neither Christian nor Muslim: an extraordinarily costly goblet from ancient Troy."[17] It is precisely the very hybrid nature of this goblet – and of the court in which it appears within the romance – that offers the first glimpse of how noble identity is caught up in a Mediterranean taste for the exotic. The cup is meant to directly figure the value of the noble Christian maiden in terms of an exotic and rare mercantile good, and is:

Une ciere coupe d'or
Qui fu emblee du tresor
Au rice empereour de Rome;
Ainc a plus ciere ne but home,
A grant mervelle fu bien faite
Et molt fu soutiument portraite

Par menue neeleüre;
Vulcans le fist, s'i mist sa cure. (441–50)

[A costly golden goblet which was stolen from the treasury of the rich emperor of Rome; from something more costly no man has ever drunk, and it was made in a very marvellous fashion and much was subtly painted upon it in miniature hand-drawn portraits; Vulcan made it, and with it went his care.]

This wonderfully adorned golden chalice is itself a treasure, crafted and traded in ways that have been examined in the context of connections to a Spanish court. Scholars have recently argued that it is a cup wrought of *Spanish* gold, carved and emblazoned with intricate figures like golden birds, studded with jewels and gems, and adorned in miniatures by an expert goldsmith.[18] Yet the narrative history of the cup itself (here, "forged by Vulcan," a Roman God, and then stolen from the Romans), points instead towards its firm rooting in the *Mediterranean* lineage of the transfer of both objects and stories westwards, best exemplified in the process of *translatio*. As the text itself points out, the cup narrates the *Greek* story of Troy through an object made by Vulcan, a *Roman* god ("Vulcans le fist ... Une ciere coupe d'or / Qui fu emblee du tresor / Au rice empereour de Rome"); there is nothing in the story itself to limit its origins to a Spanish court. Squarely within the tradition of *translatio studii* and *imperii*, all roads lead away from the Spanish court and back in time, first to Rome and then to ancient Greece and Troy itself, in a search for the signification of an expensive exotic object and the worth of the noblewoman it replaces.

Indeed, upon the cup itself, and highlighted most prominently in the passage quoted above, is a story that in many ways itself supplants the cup's testament to the glory of the Spanish goldmeisters, exchanging their own artistry for the most powerful narrative of ancient Greece. The cup assumes a Mediterranean significance when its Romano-Spanish history is supplanted by an elaborate illustration program detailing the story of Troy:

El hanap ot paint environ
Troies et le rice doignon,
Et com li Griu dehors l'assaillent,
Com au mur par grant aïr maillent,
Et com cil dedens se deffendent,

Quariaus et pex agus lor rendent.
En l'eur après fu paint Helaine,
comment Paris ses drus l'en maine.
D'un blanc esmail ot fait l'image,
Assise en l'or par artimage.
Aprés i est com ses maris
Le suit par mer, d'ire maris,
Et l'os des Grius com il nagoit
Et Agamennon quil menoit. (451–64)

[On the chalice was Troy and its surroundings and its rich tower, and how the Greeks assailed them from without, how they beat at the walls with great effort and how those within defended themselves, throwing back sharp spears and stones at them. In the next scene Helen was painted, how Paris took her as his wife. The image was made with white ceramics, put down into gold by artisanship. Afterwards it shows how the husband followed by sea, enraged by anger, and the daring of the Greeks as he swam and how he led Agamemnon.]

The story of Troy, of the abduction of Helen, was well known throughout the Middle Ages from Latin sources and was gaining increasing attention in mid-twelfth-century France, when manuscript history suggests that *Floire et Blancheflor*, with all its attention to exotic craftsmanship, became so popular.[19] Even though medieval French authors would only have known the Troy story through the distant lens of translation, the story is nevertheless one of the founding narratives of Mediterranean noble identity.[20] By invoking Troy, the romance enters into a dialogue and a medieval manuscript tradition focused squarely on reanimating ancient Greek and Roman stories, often through the lens of Latin authors like Virgil, and often in ways that posit western noble familial authority through genealogical claims to Troy.[21]

The Spanish artisanship is clearly impressive, but in my reading, its purpose is to showcase narratives about the transmission of ancient Greek glory to contemporary medieval Mediterranean nobles. The move to reanimate the Hellenic past was often concomitant to an interest in documenting epic genealogies for medieval French noble families, and the move to cite the Greeks becomes in this context a move to instantiate Blancheflor's own grandeur.[22] While the cup itself might function as a testament to Spanish craftsmanship, the depictions over which so many lines are carefully spent recalling the wonderful narrative elements of the romance between Helen and Paris is a testament to the forging of a uniquely Mediterranean object, with both value and meaning: the Greek story and the exotic Spanish object, eventually exchanged in an Egyptian market. This blending is further cemented by the manuscript context of the larger story of *Floire et Blancheflor*, in which two different codices, BnF Fr. 375 and BnF Fr. 1447, offer different and competing understandings of how nobility is connected to Mediterranean exoticism.

Narrating Exoticism: The Codicological Context

Manuscript evidence is integral to understanding the staging of nobility in terms of Mediterranean exoticism in *Floire et Blancheflor*.[23] MS BnF Fr. 375, which contains one of the two earliest and most complete examples of *Floire et Blancheflor*, provides a key to understanding *why* Byzantium might be figured as a crucial subtext of the romance, and as integral to understanding this as a *Mediterranean* vision of nobility, rather than as a *Muslim* one. MS 375 is a late thirteenth-century codex containing, among other texts, *Athis et Prophilias, Cligès, Le Roman d'Alexandre, Floire et Blancheflor, Ille et Galeron, Blancandin, Le Roman de Thèbes, Le Roman d'Enéas*, and *Le Roman de Troie*.[24] It is a well-known anthology of famous medieval texts; as I argued in chapter 1, it figures the foreign other in medieval French literature at a time of intense scrutiny of relations between France and its eastern neighbours. In particular, many of the romances bound around and near *Floire et Blancheflor* depend on the adaptation and rewriting of Hellenic material.

In MS 375, *Floire et Blancheflor* is part of a codex in which difference – religious, cultural, geographic, linguistic – is thoroughly explored. As Keith Busby et al. have pointed out, the scribal evidence and the assembly of the quires nearly guarantee that the manuscript was copied programmatically as a whole in or around Arras between 1288 and 1289, about 130 years after its narrative composition.[25] The several *romans antiques* as well as the *contes du Graal* from Chrétien de Troyes were copied together, and though they remained unbound for quite some time, part 2 of the manuscript (which contains all of these Mediterranean literary texts) seems to have come into being together as a package in which references to Greece figure prominently.[26] Though the thirteenth-century bindings that now unite these texts can offer no unimpeachable reading program to document twelfth-century authorial intentions, they do point to a grossly enlarged conception of "pagan" for at least one binder.

When read in the context of this heavily Greek-influenced codex, *Floire et Blancheflor*'s use of the term "pagan" to figure the foreign other should, as I stated earlier, be understood in a broader sense to refer not only to Muslims but to non-Catholic Christians, such as Orthodox Byzantines, as well. Indeed, within the context of codex 375, that golden chalice circulating ever westwards may be as much in commerce with ideas stemming from neighbours like Byzantium as from courts in Moorish Spain or Cairo. Like the chalice with its Greek stories of ancient Troy, the manuscript itself points to a way of figuring the relation between exoticism and nobility in which it was the Greek context – rather than the Spanish one – that interested at least some medieval readers, and in particular, one medieval scribe and binder.

MS 375 is often called the "aristocratic" version of *Floire et Blancheflor* because it is typically read for its attention to detailing life at the aristocratic court. It is the oldest of the extant manuscripts, and is the one I read in the first part of this chapter to explore its interest in figuring noble identity and difference through figuring "pagans." In the later version of the manuscript, MS BnF Fr. 1447, the so-called popular version, the pagans do explicitly become Muslims, but the majority of the narrative is virtually identical to MS 375. This shift to Islam coincides with a shift in the codicological framing of the material.[27] As I will explore in the later part of this chapter, MS 1447 figures the noble self through genealogy, focusing on how Islam and religious conversion served as the backdrop for narrating the ascension of Charlemagne's Christian lineage. Although these two codicological contexts focalize our readings in different directions, ultimately, both manuscript versions narrate Mediterranean exoticism as the primary way of forging the story of the noble self.

In a sense, both the manuscript context of *Floire et Blancheflor* and its meta-story of the rapt of Helen detailed upon the chalice combine to create several levels through which the text creates a nobility dependent upon the exchange of exotic eastern goods. First, the *narrative* itself traces a literary voyage westwards. *Floire et Blancheflor* details the westward movement of eastern narratives, in a literal translation of the Troy story (engraved upon the gilded chalice, which belonged at one point to the "rich emperor of Rome" and seems to have been taken there from Troy by Aeneas as a gift to his Lavinia). Second, in several intertextual references to the rapt of Helen in other stories found within codex 375, notably *Le Roman de Troie* and *Cligès*, the *codex* in which the manuscript is bound becomes a physical indication of how thirteenth-century audiences might have appreciated this story within a larger context of tales about the exotic east, in general, and about Greeks, in particular.[28] Finally, within *Floire et Blancheflor*, *objects* such as the chalice, luxurious silk fabrics, and magical architecture are all moving westwards to be digested and appreciated by a medieval French audience, constructing them as noble through their consumption of exotic goods.

Read in the context of MS 375, the Hellenic stories on the chalice forge the fundamental story of Mediterranean nobility (that of Troy and of Aeneas) as instantiated through a trade in wondrous materials of eastern origins – certainly of Spanish origins, but also, I would argue, with strong resonance to depictions of Byzantine luxury goods. The cup is adorned, for example, with a magical gem:

Li coupiers ert ciers et vaillans,
D'un escarboucle reluisans;
n'est soussiel si orges celiers,
s'il i estoit, li boutilliers
ne peüst sans autre clarete
cler vin connoistre d'ysopé.
D'or avoit deseure un oisel
Trifoire, qui molt par ert bel,
Qui en son pié tenoit la geme,
plus bel ne vit ne hom ne feme:
c'ert vis celui qui l'esgardoit
que vis estoit si voletoit. (491–502)

[The chalice was expensive and a treasure, and sparkling with a ruby; in no cellar was there such a renowned wine keeper that if he were there, he would not be able to see without any opacity the clear wine of Hyssop. There was a trefoil-gilded bird perched atop the chalice, which was very beautiful and held a gem in his beak – no woman or man had ever seen more beautiful. It showed him who looked into it the thing that he most wanted.]

In this passage, the process of narrating nobility becomes entwined with the process of obtaining exotically crafted materials. That is, exotic goods begin to beget exotic stories, showing their owners "the thing [they] most want," stories about the status of the nobility. Here, the thing that is most desired is a narrative about nobility, the founding narrative of the story of European noble lineage, and it is one crafted – even literally reflected – through an exotic object, the gem studded onto the Troy chalice. The story of the Mediterranean nobility is woven through exchanges in exotic goods, both literary (in the Troy story of the origins of the nobility) and literal (in things like chalices, gems, and other wondrous goods) within the rubric of cross-cultural love.

Stories of the East: Automata, Byzantium, and the Story of Exoticism

After Blancheflor is sold for the chalice, Floire's parents try to trick him into believing his beloved is dead, and they construct an elaborate and well-decorated tomb for her. Floire's grief renders him inconsolable, and on several occasions he tries to kill himself. Finally, we find him weeping beside the tomb, where he is astonished to see talking and breathing statues of himself and Blancheflor, as well as seemingly magically enchanted statues of birds that sing songs in the wind. The long description of the tomb culminates in a depiction of the two children as automata, mechanical figures that kiss when the wind blows through them:

> Quant li vens les enfans toucoit,
> L'un baisoit l'autre et acoloit,
> Si disoient par ingremance
> Trestout lor bon et lor enfance.
> Ce dist Flores a Blanceflor:
> "Basiés moi, bele, par amor."
> Blaceflor respont en baisant:
> "Je vos aim plus que riens vivant." (597–604)

> [When the wind struck the children, the one kissed and hugged the other, and magically recounted all of their deeds and childhood together. This is what Floire says to Blancheflor: "Kiss me, beauty, for love of me." Blancheflor responds in kissing him, "I love you more than any other living thing."]

Although the tomb where Floire spends so much time grieving is inscribed with gold Arabic lettering, much of its adornment points again to an object better read in its larger Mediterranean context.

In particular, the use of automata, carefully constructed moving statues, suggests that it should not merely be read for its Moorish artistry, but more likely for its relationship to Byzantine craftsmanship. In the passage above, the creation of narrative is explicitly entwined with exoticism and cross-cultural love. Cross-cultural romance is imagined as the space of narrative transmission, where the children "si disoient par ingremance / trestout lor bon et lor enfance." The space for the creation of narrative is one figured through exoticism, in the reconstruction of the narrating children as wondrous machines.

From as early as the tenth century, literary and fictional narratives in both Medieval Greek and Old French all point towards Greece as the source of the fantastic magically animated automata.[29] The first literary depiction of an automaton occurs in Homer's *Iliad*, when Thetis visits Hephaestus, and though by the medieval period Latin and Arab literature had reworked the Greek legends and also imagined automata in connection with wondrous places, the origins of the trope are decidedly Hellenic.[30] Ambassadors' accounts of the emperor's palace in Constantinople, for example, recount that emissaries were often startled by the roaring lion automata that surrounded the Byzantine throne of Solomon.[31] Liutprand of Cremona reports in the tenth century that he was escorted to the Byzantine imperial palace and humbled before an elaborate mechanical throne on which the emperor himself sat when receiving official guests.[32] Several were even more surprised when he and his throne disappeared into the floor while they prostrated themselves before him.

Literary references like the kissing children in *Floire et Blancheflor* show that French authors knew about automata by as early as the twelfth century; intertexts suggest they associated them with Byzantium. One of the earliest references to automata occurs in a passage in *Le Pèlerinage de Charlemagne*, an early twelfth-century French fictional account of Charlemagne's voyages to Jerusalem and Constantinople. In this text, Charlemagne is entranced by whistling figures present in the Byzantine emperor's palace in Constantinople, a sumptuous residence full of magical automata that interact with each other just like the statuary versions of Floire and Blancheflor on Blancheflor's fake tomb:

Li paleis fu listez de azur e avenant [...]
De quivre e de metal tregeté douz enfanz;
Cascun tient en sa buche un corn d'ivorie blanc.
Si galerne is de mer, bise ne alter vent,
Ki ferent al paleis devers occident,

Il le funt turner e menut e suvent,
Cumme roe de char qui a tere decent;
Cil corn sunent e buglent e tunent ensement
Cumme tabors u toneires u grant cloches qui pent.
Li uns esgardet le alter ensement cum en riant,
Que ço vus fust viarie que tut fussent vivant. (344–61)[33]

[The palace was decorated with blue edgings, and pleasing to behold … and there was a moulded figure of two children in copper and metal, each carrying in its mouth a horn of white ivory. If any winds, blowing in from the sea, strike the palace on the west side, they make it revolve quickly and repeatedly, like a chariot's wheel rolling downhill. Their horns blare and bellow and thunder, just like a drum, a clap of thunder or a huge, hanging bell. One looks at the other as if they were smiling, so that you would have sworn they were actually alive.][34]

While the description must be grossly exaggerated, there were historical precedents for imagining such wondrous technology using nearly identical language ("as if they were actually alive") as contemporary fictional texts invoking Byzantium. A later pseudo-historical account of Constantinople written by French crusade chronicler Robert de Clari specifies that the Byzantine emperor, Manuel I Komnenos, had a stadium for jousting and games full of just such animated statues:

Du lonc de chele plache, si avoit une masiere qui bien avoit quinze piés de haut et dis de lé; deseure chele maisiere, si avoit il ymages d'ommes et de femmes et de chevaus et de bués et de cameus et de ors et de lions, et de molt de manieres de bestes getees de coivre, qui si estoient bien faites et si natureument formees qu'il n'a si boin maistre en paienism ne en chrestienté qui seust miex pourtraire ne si bien former ymages comme chil ymage estoient formé; et soloient cha en arriere giuer par encantement, mais ne juoient mais nient.[35]

[Along this wall, there was a wall that was fifteen feet tall and ten feet wide; there were images of men and women and horses and oxen and camels and bears and lions and all manners of beasts cast in copper, who were so well made and so naturally shaped that there is no better master in all heathendom nor in Christendom who would know how to better portray or form images as these images were formed; and these images used to play by enchantment, but now they no longer do.]

Though the text acknowledges a sort of automata diaspora ("n'a si boin maistre en paienism ne en chrestienté"), Byzantium is the centre of this world of wondrous statues. Robert de Clari's historical assertion of Byzantium's mastery of the technology is echoed throughout contemporary Old French literature, and Clari's descriptions validate Byzantine historiographers' comments on the use of automata at court to impress and frighten foreigners.

Like the Old French texts, Medieval Greek sources forge a tight association between Byzantium and exotic courtly architecture, especially automata, furthering our reading of the Hellenism coursing throughout the pagan court in *Floire et Blancheflor*. Medieval Greek romances like *Velthandros and Chrysandza*, for example, in which a young prince leaves home on a quest for adventure and instead discovers a marvellous stream in the centre of which flows liquid fire bubbling forth from a wondrous castle, employ the same features of wonderful gems, exotic architectural features, and speaking statues as do the medieval French texts *Le Pèlerinage de Charlemagne* and *Floire et Blancheflor*. Velthandros, the princely protagonist, is surprised by magical automated figures atop the Castle of Love:

> Καὶ δέκα περιεπάτησεν ἡμέρας ὁλοκλήρους
> καὶ τότε κάστρον ηὕρηκε μέγα, πολὺν τὴν θέαν,
> ἐκ σαρδωνύχου / λαξευτοῦ κτισμένον μετὰ τέχνης
> ἐπάνω δὲ τοῦ κτίσματος τοῦ λαμπροτὰτου ἐκείνου
> ἀντι πυργοβολήματα ἦσαν συντεθειμένα
> λέων, δρακόντων κεφαλαὶ ἀπὸ χρυσῶν ποικίλων.
> Τεχνήτης τὸ ἐσκεύασεν ἀπὸ πολλῆς σοφίας,
> ἐκ δὲ τὸ στόμα των αὐτῶν, ἄν ἔλεψες [sic], νὰ εἶδες
> πῶς συριγμὸς ἐξήρχετο φρικτώδης, ἀγριώδης
> νά εἶπες ὅτι κίνησιν ἔχουσιν ὥσπερ ζῶντα
> καὶ νὰ λαλοῦν ἀμφότερα καὶ νὰ φωνολογοῦσιν.[36]

[For ten whole days [Velthandros] travelled and finally came to a mighty castle, vast in appearance, wonderfully constructed from chiselled sardonyx. On top of the shining edifice, placed together instead of battlements, were a lion and the heads of dragons made with variegated gold. An artist had constructed them with much skill, and if you looked you could see from their mouths there came a wild and terrible whistling. You would have said that they were possessed of movement like living things and they were talking and shouting together.][37]

Here, the "terrible whistling" in the Medieval Greek text resonates with the descriptions of both the automata on Blancheflor's tomb and, later, of wondrous statues in the emir's garden. The whistling also resonates with other Old French descriptions of automata found in the Byzantine emperor's palace, like in *Le Pelèrinage de Charlemagne*. The romance explicitly situates this courtly milieu to the east of Byzantium (positing Byzantium as the centre, rather than an eastern referent, as it often figures in Old French texts). Like in *Floire et Blancheflor*, the exotic automata offer narrative; they are literally "talking and shouting together." In both Byzantine and Old French texts, wondrous exotic architectural features seem to narrate the story of exoticism as one concomitant to the figuring of noble prowess.

Of course the subject matter and physical descriptions – all in Medieval Greek, written far from the place of composition of *Floire and Blancheflor*, and most likely much later – make it unlikely that there is any direct connection between the authoring of these texts.[38] Certainly the extant manuscripts we have of them are much later than those we have of *Floire et Blancheflor*. The point, however, is not to claim a particular primacy of either the French or Greek sources, but to instead point to the ways that images of Byzantine exotic architecture, statues, and goods were circulating throughout the medieval world during the Crusades, certainly within medieval French crusader texts, and probably also within medieval French romances. It seems that some of the wonders of Byzantium – wonders like automata, architectural innovations, and amazing fabrics seen by merchants, crusaders, and pilgrims since the eleventh century, and reported ever since the *Iliad* in stories – figure strongly in the medieval imagination of Mediterranean exoticism.[39] Read with the depiction of the story of Paris's rapt of Helen on the golden chalice, the invocation of automata and magical gems in *Floire et Blancheflor* offers a subtext that ties western nobility to a genealogy of Hellenic glory, and points to Byzantium as a contemporary marker of wonder in the western medieval noble imagination.

The later Medieval Greek version of *Floire et Blancheflor*, *Florios kai Platziaflora*, also stages a world of cross-cultural love (in fact, it is explicitly inter-religious love in this text, between a Christian and a Muslim) in a trading romance filled with exotic goods and places.[40] This version, which appears in the sixteenth century, is nonetheless interesting for its staging of the exotic in Greek terms. If automata are exotic to the westerners writing *Floire et Blancheflor*, perhaps they are less so to the Byzantines, and indeed, in *Florios kai Platziaflora*, the trope of exoticism is the joust (lines 630–70), an added scene in which Florios takes up arms in order to battle for his beloved.

Medieval Greek courts were unfamiliar with the joust until Manuel I Komnenos brought it as a wonder from one of his encounters with westerners.[41] Manuel I is remembered, among other things, as a lover of all things western.[42] The Medieval Greek rendition of the tale highlights the two key elements of the story – exchange and exoticism – and shows a transposition of both elements as the courtly milieu and tropes of exoticism shift, but the essential nature of the trading romance remains clear. That is, the medieval Greek version suggests that tropes of exoticism circulate between cultures, and that what is recognizable at the base of the narrative is not the figuring of any particular cultural referent, but the figuring of nobility through its relation to obtaining, trading, and showing off exotic goods and narratives, creating what I call an economy of exoticism.

Byzantium, then, becomes an important cultural referent, an undercurrent informing much of the exoticism coursing throughout *Floire et Blancheflor* and other medieval French texts figuring the east. But more importantly, reading the multivalent significations of Byzantium and other eastern others together shows that it is exoticism – and not one particular cultural referent – that is meant to figure nobility in the medieval Mediterranean imagination. Medieval Mediterranean fiction suggests that the taste for exoticism – to consume and produce narratives about it, to stage the self through it – unifies the Mediterranean nobility in a time when religion, geography, language, and politics suggest much sharper divisions among even the most empowered echelon of society.

Exchanges in Exoticism: Narrating Masculinity

The body is often theorized as a site for writing the narratives of men's glory in Old French romance, but in *Floire et Blancheflor*, it is also a place for disrupting the relation between gender and exoticism. The process of bartering for narrative makes explicit one of the underlying tenets of romance itself, namely, that romance is constructed through the movement of narrative in exchange for sacrifice: most obviously, the sacrifice of men's bodies as they are wounded in combat. While other contemporary texts bound with *Floire et Blancheflor* such as Chrétien's Arthurian romances stage a masculinity defined by domination and broadcast through contests of physical strength and martial prowess,

Floire et Blancheflor narrates a world of Mediterranean encounter structured around the gift and mercantilism, in which war-mongering, physical combat, and physiological signs of gender difference are all but effaced. In *Floire et Blancheflor*, gifts – and not men's bodies – are sacrificed, exchanged for the greater necessity of narrative.[43]

In *Floire et Blancheflor*, the traditional gender roles of romance are eschewed to the point that the young lovers are indistinguishable from each other in several passages. They are both, for example, educated in Latin reading and writing by the same tutor. They read the same romances together, and Floire argues consistently and persuasively that everything he does should be in the company of his childhood friend, much to the growing chagrin of his parents. The character doubling and, as others have argued, gender play is predicted from the outset, where the children do everything, and become everything, together.[44]

Ensemble vent, ensenble vienent
Et la joie d'amours maintienent.
Chaucuns d'els deus tant aprenoit
Pour l'ature que merveille estoit;
Li dui enfant mout s'entramoient
Et de biauté s'entresembloient. (213–17)

[Together they go, together they come back and maintain the joy of love. Each one of them learned so much for the other that it was marvellous; the two children loved each other a lot and resembled each other a lot in beauty.]

Their names, too, offer a reflection of the day they were born, that "Pakes florie" that inspired Blancheflor's Christian mother to name her after the lily of Easter and to repeat the story of Christ's rebirth to her pagan captors. As many scholars have remarked, the children are virtually indistinguishable.[45] One of the women who lodges Floire while he trades his way towards rescuing Blancheflor, for example, says that she thinks Blancheflor is his twin sister, because they not only look alike, they also have similar bodies:

Ce m'est avis, quant je le voi,
Que ce soit Blancheflor la bele ;
Je cuit qu'ele est sa suer jumele.
Tel vis, tel cors et tel semblant

Conme ele a voi en cest enfant.
Bien voi qu'il sont prochain parent
Au vis et au contenement. (1542–8)

[This is my opinion, when I see him, that he must be Blancheflor the beautiful; I believe that she is his twin sister. The same face, the same body and the same demeanour as she has, I see in this child. I see well in their face and comportment that they are of close parentage.]

Here we are reminded of the doubling of characters in romances like *Ami et Amile* or *Erec et Enide* – the documented physical mirroring of the heroes, the strange, almost incestuous terminology used to describe their corporeal closeness. In fact, probably referring to their common upbringing, Floire responds to the woman's enquiries, "Damë, en penser ere, / Ele est ma suer, je sui son frere" ["Lady, truth be told, / she is my sister, and I am her brother"] (1557–8). Passages like these, dispersed in snippets throughout the conversations Floire has with innkeepers while engaging in the mercantile questing of the romance, suggest that there is a certain amount of substitutability in the characters, who are continually mistaken for one another, and who suffer for one another, throughout the romance.[46]

Whereas we might expect that Floire's masculinity would be continually described in pejorative terms (he is, after all that pagan other who must be converted and recuperated by Christianity at the end of the text), here the depiction of doubling blurs the lines between masculine and feminine, between pagan and Christian, creating if anything confusion rather than condemnation. The character doubling of our protagonists and their mutable bodies is consistent with the mirroring of protagonists in other texts, and indeed is even to be expected with a title like *Floire et Blancheflor*. Yet it is surprising that the markers of masculinity that usually make the errant male's quest for his lady remarkable – even *narratable*, through stories of chivalric glory sent to far-away courts – are eschewed in favour of mercantile savvy, shrewd gift giving, and physical gender ambiguity, without any pretence to physical combat or knightly bravery.

The markers of masculinity that normally facilitate the episodic narration and storytelling so prominent in Old French romances – a man's physical ability to fight and defeat other men, a fight repeated and retold in countless iterations that become the storyline itself – are nowhere present. Instead, the kind of contest staged within the narration and at which women are at the centre is a *mercantile* one dependent not on the power of men's muscles, but on the flexing of gift giving from a man's bottomless purse. Unlike other romances, which imagine heroic masculinity in terms of knightly combat, *Floire et Blancheflor* insists on Floire's heroicism as a gift giver, far from the realm of combat.

Floire et Blancheflor focuses insistently on gift giving as a way of constructing Floire's success as a man. For example, when Floire's mother finally relents and admits that his beloved has been sold off and is captive in the east, Floire equips himself for the quest for his lady in ways that are markedly different from the usual preparations undertaken by other noblemen in contemporary romance narratives.[47] Rather than arming himself for combat, as most errant men in romance do, he arms himself for trade, beginning a new narrative association between the construction of medieval noble masculinity through narratives of exoticism, rather than warfare. Floire spends long days stockpiling the right items to trade for information – for narratives – about his beloved, and sets off not nobly clad as a knight but rather disguised beneath his own class as a simple merchant.

Floire's quest is pointedly one for narrative, not combat, and as such defines the text as one in which masculinity is predicated on the ability to exchange exotic goods not for lands or titles, but for information. In many ways, Floire's mercantile quest for Blancheflor, in which the quest equates exotic goods with narration, recalls the very depiction of the golden chalice on which the story of nobility was forged and advertised through exotic goods. More inclined to gift giving than lucrative trading, Floire essentially barters his way to knowledge of his beloved, and he does so with exotic and expensive gifts. Each common innkeeper who hosts him becomes a source for information about the movement of his beloved, and each episode is predicated on the exchange of costly goods for narrative:

> Ensement au mangier pensoit
> Et un sien ami regretoit,
> Flore, cui amie ele estoit;
> Por lui tolir on le vendoit.
> Ele fut çaiens .xv. jors [...]
> Ele fu a cest port vendue.
> Cil qui l'acaterent disoient
> K'en Babiloine l'en menroient,

De l'amiral tant en aroient
Qu'il au double i gaigneroient.' [...]
Flores un coupe d'or fin
A fait emplir de molt bon vin,
Tous lies a la dame le tent:
"Iceste, fait il, vos present
por çoi que m'avés dit novele
de Blanceflor la damoisele." (1301–30)

[She was deep in thought at dinner and missed her friend, Floire, whose girlfriend she was; for stealing him [his heart] they sold her off. She had been captive already for fifteen days [...] she was sold at this port. Those who bought her said that they would take her to Babylon, where they would get double her price from the admiral. [...] Floire had a cup of fine gold filled with very good wine, and, completely relieved held it out to the lady: "This," he said, "I am giving to you because you have given me news of the lady Blancheflor."]

Floire's discussion with the innkeeper's wife over dinner on the first night on his trip presages the collapse of the difference between the nobility's ability to buy exotic goods (like the "coupe d'or fin," here another reference to the chalice) and to buy narratives and information ("novele / de Blanceflor la damoisele"). Floire's quest will instantiate his prowess as dependent on his ability to exchange exotic goods most innkeepers and commoners could neither find nor afford, in what seems an incommensurate trade for narratives they gladly offer.

Whereas other medieval French love stories explore men's prowess in terms of their physical ability in combat, constructing masculinity in tandem with physical strength, *Floire et Blancheflor*'s insistence on Floire's acumen as a merchant suggests that another model for masculinity is possible. If, as I have suggested, *Floire et Blancheflor* is indeed a story of the Mediterranean nobility, it is also simultaneously a story of Mediterranean masculinity, of the ways that noble masculinity is instantiated and promised by the act of exchanging exotic goods for narrative. In *Floire et Blancheflor*, exotic goods are exchanged for narratives about a lady, and the romance systematically builds the story of noble Mediterranean masculinity not upon the common tropes of physical fighting and martial ability, but upon markers of class: the ability to enact one's personal status by narrating the story of one's wealth. In effect, in *Floire et Blancheflor*, unlike in traditional French romances in which masculinity is deeply rooted in physical combat, masculinity is enacted through exchanges of exoticism.

While one way of reading this masculinity would align the nobility with the merchant class – an unlikely association – another way of approaching it would be to read how exchanges in exoticism relate to gift giving. As we have already seen, *Cligès* and *Digenis Akritas* suggest that gifts were essential to Mediterranean culture, even more so in Byzantium than in western courts. Both *Cligès* and *Digenis* imagine Byzantium as the centre of a world for better or worse predicated on the power of the gift, where the emperor himself aligned noble status with sums of gold, doling out yearly salaries in exchange for the work of noblemen.[48] Medieval gift theory about Byzantium suggests, too, that at its very base the gift enacted a kind of reciprocity, one that had both symbolic and economic value.[49] If, as these fictional texts, contemporary historiography about the Byzantine court, and medieval gift theory suggest, gifts created an essential reciprocity, staged in *Floire et Blancheflor* as between exotic goods and the narrative of nobility.

The Mediterranean practice of gift giving – in *Cligès* aligned with the Byzantine court, and here with the "pagan" court of Floire – becomes another (non-martial) way of marking masculine prowess. The prominence of men's gift giving suggests that some Old French narratives recognize a space for a parallel construction of masculinity, one that functions outside of the space of the homosocial knightly encounter, and instead depends on the exchange of exotic goods. One might surmise that this must be a pejorative kind of masculinity, especially following the colonial narrative about the feminization of the native (read here as "pagan"). However, as we shall see, *Floire et Blancheflor* resists this negativity, at worst casting Floire's masculinity as ambiguous. While in the earliest versions Floire does not fight, his masculinity is not negatively affected. Rather, Floire's masculinity is simply ambiguous, a kind of masculinity that rests uncomfortably next to the dominant narratives of the time, in which knightly masculinity is determined by bodies in physical combat, rather than purse strings.[50]

If masculinity is linked to trade in exotic goods in the first night of Floire's stay, that narrative is only amplified and reiterated throughout the rest of Floire's journey towards Blancheflor in Babylon.[51] His next stay is with the rich bourgeois merchant (1418) who had bought Blancheflor; again, he expects to have "novele" of the "pucele" (1428a/b). When Floire enquires about Blancheflor, he once again exchanges an expensive gift for narrative: "'Quant de ci tornerent, / en Babiloine s'en alerent.' / Flores li done un boin mantel / Et un hanap d'argent molt bel" (1471–4) ["When they left from here, they were headed to Babylon." Floire gave him a nice coat and a very beautiful chalice made of silver]. Jane Burns has explored these passages of exchange for their connections to a mercantile trade in sumptuary goods, and in particular she focuses on how *Floire et Blancheflor* figures romance through the movement of exotic textiles.[52] In passages like these, however, which narrate the movement of goods in exchange for narratives, another reading suggests that nobility is also created through narratives of exchanges in the exotic, creating not only a *sericultural*, but also a *narrative* economy of exoticism.

Floire et Blancheflor posits masculinity in terms of a quest – but not for physical renown, rather for narrative, for the story of noble glory. When Floire stays with his last host before he makes the move to Babylon, for example, he explains the relation between exchange, exoticism, and narrative quite bluntly:

> "Sire, fait il, por Diu, merci!
> Fius de roi sui, je vos afi,
> Et Blanceflor si est m'amie. [...]
> Rices home sui d'or et d'argent,
> Si vos en donrai largement
> Se de cest plait me consilliés." (1751–9)

> ["Sir," he says, "in God's name have mercy! I am the son of a king, I swear it to you, and Blancheflor is my lady. [...] I am a rich man with plenty of gold and silver, and will give you lots of it if you will give me counsel."]

As Floire wanders in search of his beloved, passage after passage reveals the nobility to be dependent on Mediterranean goods to display and instantiate its power. More importantly, however, the exchange of goods for narrative (here, "counsel") simultaneously constructs a nobility deeply interested in and dependent upon the creation of narrative. Put simply, the exchange of exotic goods is both a cause for narration and a result of it; as shown throughout these passages and made explicit by Floire here ("si vos en donrai largement / se de cest plait me consilliés"), in *Floire et Blancheflor*, the exchange of exotic goods and narrative work together to propagate the renown of medieval Mediterranean nobility.

The Gift of Narrative: Women, Exoticism, and Medieval Book Economies

In the story of masculinity, trade, and narrative woven through *Floire et Blancheflor*, we might conceptualize gift giving as the foundational story of medieval Mediterranean encounter, serving as the fundamental capital in an economy of the exotic. This economy of the exotic represents the system of exchange and reciprocity that gift giving produces at a time when all things exotic (medical, architectural, agricultural, or sericultural) actually helped cement the authority of the Mediterranean nobility, as they visually enacted the power they and their families wielded.

In this light, exchanges in exoticism are not only about literary motifs; they become an economic structure underlying medieval book production, propagating medieval noble power. As we have seen, literary representations of gift giving in exchange for narrative course throughout MS 375, and in the last chapter we explored how *Cligès* typified gift giving as one of the central ways of organizing Byzantine courtly life. *Cligès* is not the only story to bear witness to the power of Greek gifts – in fact, many Old French texts coupled Byzantine gift giving with what Caroline Walker Bynum has elsewhere characterized as "wonderful" and exotic things, as well as with more negative accusations of perfidy and verbal fickleness.[53] Like literary texts, medieval Greek court historiography and Old French crusader chronicles imagine gift giving as a way of instantiating power, in ways that recall Marcel Mauss's formulations of the power structures involved in recipients' duties towards reciprocity.[54] Given in noble courts in France or England, Byzantine gifts became a mnemonic for the far-off splendours of Constantinople's wealth and power; Byzantium's treasures became portable reminders of the greater treasure to be found in its capital and, more importantly, within the purse strings of its emperor.

The exchange of fantastic exotic goods within fictional texts also propagates extra-textual exchange. The economy of the exotic becomes a living, breathing medieval economic structure, in which authors and patrons, scribes and bookbinders, and bards and audiences engage with the exotic as a hot topic of medieval storytelling. The proliferation of stories about foreign markets in MS 375 indicates that the nobility actively pursued stories about the exotic. The objects in the story are not only traded because they *are* exotic, but rather help support a trade *in* the exotic, in which the exotic becomes a kind of capital circulating between medieval authors, scribes, patrons, and audiences.

Indeed, the manuscript history of *Floire et Blancheflor* and its over forty subsequent translations reveals it to be one of the most popular secular medieval texts that has been passed down to us today.[55] Whereas scholars have considered the popularity of many types of medieval literature, the economy of book consumption around the exotic story has not yet been systematically explored, despite several codices that point to a thriving network of stories that link the power of the nobility to the exchange of exotic goods, women, and lands. Codicological evidence alone would suggest that there was an audience for these stories, and that they, like the objects they detailed within their margins, were traded in and had inherent economic – as well as symbolic or political – value within a culture of medieval book production and consumption.

Manuscript evidence indicates that not only were texts about the exotic being commissioned and consumed, but that this trade was influenced by women. Some of the exchange of stories about exotic places took place precisely in the locale of cross-cultural marriage and was dependent on the work of noblewomen. Richard and Mary Rouse have explored women's participation in the manuscript trade in detail, and they show that women not only appreciated stories in which exoticism figured, but they likely also commissioned them and brought them in their trousseau when they married. Manuscript evidence for Adenet le Roi's *Cleomadès*, for example, suggests that Blanche de Castille brought the story with her from North Africa when she returned to Paris from Spain around 1276.[56] The miniatures depicting scenes of patronage in the two most authoritative surviving manuscripts of *Cleomadès*, BnF Fr. 24404 and Arsenal 3142, foreground Blanche de Castille as she narrates the story to Marie de Brabant, who commissioned the manuscript, with Adenet le Roi sitting in the background recording the story.[57]

Historical documents combine with literary and artistic depictions to indicate, then, that not only were exotic *goods* such as forks exchanged in cross-cultural marriage, as in the case of Maria Argyropoulina that we explored in the introduction, but, as one would expect, exotic *stories* were exchanged in cross-cultural marriage, too. Literary, codicological, and historical sources all imply that women are essential both in the movement of empire in marriage (as we have already seen in *Cligès* and *Digenis Akritas*), and also to the movement of stories of exoticism (as in *Floire et Blancheflor* or *Cleomadès*).

Not only was there an ideological interest in commissioning texts about the east during the twelfth and thirteenth centuries, but for bookmakers in medieval Paris, texts about the east were also an important source of income. As the Rouses put it, "the *libraries* who were demonstrably in business on the rue Neuve by the date of the taille rolls of the 1290s were present at that location, and in large numbers, for a reason. There was money to be made."[58] Manuscripts like MS 375 suggest that the economy of the exotic staged within medieval French fictional accounts of trade in fantastic eastern goods resonated with a real-life economic paradigm, in which authors, scribes, and bookbinders themselves gained money and reputation from the exotic.

Exchanges in exoticism, then, stem from both the desire for exotic Mediterranean goods and a desire to represent the self in relation to those goods – through displaying fantastic architecture or automata, through wearing wondrous silks, and through commissioning exotic stories. The desire for narrative, staged metatextually within the opening scenes of *Floire et Blancheflor* as a desire to tell stories about exotic goods, is concomitantly a historical economic structure, a manuscript trade. Exoticism is the fundamental *narrative* of the medieval Mediterranean, one that interweaves different Mediterranean cultural referents (literary and manuscript, sumptuary and statuary, Byzantine, Arab, and Spanish) and relies on the movement of wealth to construct noble power. The narrative of exoticism, so essential to the story of the Mediterranean nobility, is one that, in the other predominant manuscript of *Floire et Blancheflor*, is deeply entwined with the twelfth-century nobility's desire for a narrative of familial identity through genealogy.

The Exoticism of Genealogy: Reading the Narrative of Lineage in BnF Fr. 1447

We have already seen how the central concerns of *Floire et Blancheflor* – trade, exoticism, and gender – have begun to overlap narrative in BnF Fr. 375. Yet another manuscript, BnF Fr. 1447, offers a different codicological context for reading *Floire et Blancheflor*, one in which I would argue the narrative of nobility – that is, genealogy – is at stake. The so-called popular version, BnF Fr. 1447 is the first of two texts, including *Berte as Grans Piès*, that document the emergence of Charlemagne from the mixed and Mediterranean ancestry of Floire and Blancheflor. In particular, Floire's conversion to Christianity permits the couple to produce Charlemagne's grandmother, Bertha Broadfoot. Though in this manuscript *Floire et Blancheflor* is still about exchange and cross-cultural love, its location at the outset of a codex detailing the lineage of Charlemagne spurs us to focus on the links between genealogy and narratives of exoticism. Reading from this alternate codicological perspective offers another interpretation of the same story, allowing us to see facets of the story that reading from within the context of MS BnF Fr. 375 does not. Though different in focus, in both manuscripts the exchanges of exoticism depend on women's contributions and result in alternate constructions of medieval masculinities.

The codicological context of BnF Fr. 375, which situates *Floire et Blancheflor* among several other texts about the exotic other, constructs masculinity in relation to the trade of exoticism; the codicological context of BnF Fr. 1447 implies that *Floire et Blancheflor* can also be read as a commentary on how medieval women help construct the narrative of Mediterranean nobility. If BnF Fr. 375 tends towards the construction of a noble mercantile masculinity valorized by exchanges in exoticism, then BnF Fr. 1447, with its interest in genealogy and narrating the reproductive body (ultimately, recounting in detail the maternal lineage of Charlemagne), suggests that *Floire et Blancheflor* must also be read as a commentary on how exchanges in exoticism are linked to practices of femininity, particularly by linking lineage and maternity. It is only by reading these two texts in their codicologically inspired contexts that one can fully appreciate their overall themes of narrative, exoticism, and exchange as concomitant to the construction of the gendered noble self. Since the two texts offer basically the same storyline, their codicological framing becomes a medieval gloss that underlines what should be read as important in each of them.

While, as I argued in chapter 1, medieval noblewomen participated in the exchange of ideas around the Mediterranean, of course one of the most direct and frequent ways they participated was through their bodies, in the form of cross-cultural reproduction. Though in chapter 1 I argued for the ways women's cultural work contributed to the practices of empire, to some extent this corporeal model is *the* work of the kinds of exchanges facilitated by cross-cultural marriage. New, hybridized stories of nobility are forged through the generation of children and therefore new narratives of renown. If one thinks of reproduction as not only creating new heirs to a family dynasty, but also as creating the possibility for the expansion and reworking of narratives about family renown, the processes of narration, reproduction, and lineage become intextricably entwined.

This anxiety about and interest in documenting reproduction in Old French texts corresponds to a time when patrilinear primogeniture was the primary method of transmitting familial power in western Mediterranean courts; manuscripts like MS 1447 reveal this preoccupation through their codicological intent to document a lineage for Charlemagne.[59] Indeed, the first lines of the codex (and therefore of *Floire et Blancheflor*) are dedicated to naming the lineage in which the story of exchange and conversion must be read:

C'est du roy Floire l'enfant
Et de Blancheflor la vaillante
De cui Berte aus granz piez fu nee
Puis fu en france coronne
Fame fu au gentil baron.
Pepin le roy pere charlon
Berte fu mere charlemaine
Qui puis tint et france et le maine
Floire son pere que vous di
Uns rois paiens l'engenoi
Et Blancheflour que tant ama
Uns quens crestiens l'engendra
Floires fu touz nes de paiens
Et Blancheflour de crestiens. (9–20)[60]

[This [story] is about the child King Floire and Blancheflor the valiant, from whom Bertha Broadfoot was born, and then was married into [the house of] France. King Pepin was the father of Charles. Bertha was the mother of Charlemagne, who afterwards held France and all of Germany. Floire her friend of whom I speak, a pagan king engendered him, and Blancheflor whom he so loved, a Christian count engendered her. Floire was born completely of pagans and Blancheflor of Christians. Floire had himself baptized during his life for his friend Blancheflor.]

In this passage, the syntax belies the content: though ostensibly about Floire and Christianity, the Old French attributes all of Charlemagne's lineage to the work of women, namely Blancheflor and Bertha Broadfoot.

It is argueable, then, that the prologue of codex 1447 frames the entire story in terms of lineage, announcing its importance and relevance to a courtly audience for the ways it outlines Charlemagne's genealogy. It conceptualizes cross-cultural marriage as a place for empire-building dependent upon the bipartite elements of reproduction (rhyming "nee" and "mariee," for example, and "ama" and "engenra") and conversion (in this case, religious conversion, highlighted through the rhyme of "paiiens" and "crestiiens"), and the syntax associates those actions with women. While the prologue insists that primogeniture is defined through a father's line – "uns rois paiiens" and "uns cuens crestiiens," after all, did the work of engendering the two protagonists – it situates the work of negotiating and channelling identity squarely in the court of the mothers in the story of Charlemagne's lineage. Charlemagne's great-grandmother (Blancheflor's mother), for example, is an exemplary Christian captive who gives birth on Easter Sunday ("Pakes florie") and serves as both companion to the pagan queen, and educator to the two newborn children. Her service to the pagan court ensures that her daughter, born in captivity, still maintains her culture, language, and faith. While MS 1447 offers virtually the same plot as MS 375, its codicological framing suggests a separate concern with articulating the genealogy of nobility in ways that implicate women.

In this text we have a rare glimpse of how cross-cultural motherly nourishing – and not just birthing – might look.[61] *Floire et Blancheflor* suggests that cross-cultural nourishing provided a space for the transmission of culture. Blancheflor's mother takes such good care of the children that she "ne savoit / le quel des .ii. plus cier avoit" [she didn't know which of the two of them she cherished more dearly] (187–8). However, this care is carefully divided when it comes to mixing bodily fluids across boundaries of culture and religion, as when Blancheflor's mother is expressly forbidden to breastfeed Floire. According to the text, "Une paiienne l'alaitoit / car lor lois l'autre refusoit" [a pagan woman nursed him / because their laws prohibited the other woman from doing so] (184–5). Bodily fluids can be considered dangerous and polluting; here, it is clear that mother's milk and the act of breastfeeding would cross too many cultural boundaries and risk infecting the child with an outsider's values.[62] All of the Old French versions of *Floire et Blancheflor* imagine mother's milk as a fluidic marker of a biologically based religious difference between the two children; breast milk becomes a signal for the ways that women could literally transmit foreign culture and religion to children through their bodies' fluids, and it marks women's bodies as powerful sites for the transmission of culture. Yet MS 1447, with its codicological insistence on framing the novel as a genealogy of Charlemagne's Christian ancestry, invites readers to focus on women's involvement in producing narrative and shaping masculinity.

The problem with exploring women's participation in narrative is that women are purposefully excluded from narrating in many Old French texts. In *Erec et Enide*, for example, one of Enide's cousins comes along to narrate her struggles, but her tale is muted by Chrétien, who intervenes to say that we do not want to hear the same material twice.[63] Other texts, too, imagine women's narratives as inferior to those of men: at the end of *Cligès*, for example, we are told that nobody ever heard from Byzantine empresses after Fénice (and her dangerous interventions) was suppressed in a tower. Likewise, when Floire and Blancheflor stand accused of treasonous infidelity, having been caught *in flagrante delicto*, Floire does all the defending at the trial, purposefully obscuring Blancheflor's narrative of her harrowing near-rape and sale into captivity with his own account of glorious, mercantile questing. The exotic goods bartered by Floire in exchange for narratives about Blancheflor metonymize the message coursing through the whole love affair: the story of nobility, its genealogical claim to power, is told through the movement of women and exotic goods around the Mediterranean.

Women's relation to narrative – and their roles in inspiring, constructing, and exchanging it – is as much at the heart of *Floire et Blancheflor* as the exotic goods described throughout its pages. Even as the voyage of cross-cultural encounters serves to construct and recount Floire's masculinity (here, concomitant to the exchange of exotic goods), both men and women participate in exchanging stories about the exotic that serve to construct noble identity.

When examined in their codicological context, the two oldest original manuscripts of *Floire et Blancheflor* offer two different glimpses into the ways the various concerns of the romance – personal love, reproduction across cultural boundaries, cross-confessional marriage, and Mediterranean trade – coalesce differently for different medieval readers. The genealogical narrative of the MS 1447 version imagines Charlemagne's heritage as one stemming from courts steeped in Byzantine exoticism and marked by their increasing success as they turn ever westwards for women and religious beliefs (typified across the codex as the voyage made by Floire and Blancheflor as they move from pagan Spain to Egypt to settle in Hungary; their daughter Bertha of Hungary married further west to Pepin of France); the MS 375 version cements the power of the story through its narration of the recuperation of all things eastern – from goods to religions – for a new western courtly context. Taken together, these manuscripts suggest that the in-between spaces of the Mediterranean become the founding *centre* for building lineage, dynasty, and empire through the movement of narratives in cross-cultural marriage.

While the two versions of *Floire et Blancheflor* cast emphasis on different themes coursing throughout the text, these concerns need not be read as mutually exclusive. On the contrary, when read together, these codicological signs – in which MS 375 can be read as a codex with interest in the east and MS 1447 as a genealogical record of Charlemagne's Christian lineage – make it possible to see how important and intertwined the two central concerns of the romance – exoticism and genealogy in the context of cross-confessional marriage – ultimately are. When read together, these two manuscripts suggest that, at least for some medieval manuscript readers, the success of cross-confessional marriages was predicated as much upon religious conversion as upon how gender affected the transmission of ideologies *and* lineages in bicultural settings. Ultimately, *Floire et Blancheflor* paints a picture of exoticism in which the wonders of Byzantium and its past – from automata to fantastic gems and textiles – construct a medieval Mediterranean masculinity predicated on exchange within cross-cultural romance.

Nestled within the lines of cross-confessional exchange in *Floire et Blancheflor* is the fundamental similarity of its protagonists; in fact, they are often mistaken for siblings. As we shall see in the next chapter, the intimacy of incest, only hinted at in the indistinguishability of the protagonists in the twelfth-century *Floire et Blancheflor*, becomes a full-blown problematic in later cross-cultural texts such as *Le Roman de la Manekine* and *La Belle Hélène de Constantinople*, one that also grapples with the struggle of Mediterranean identities.

3 Masculinities and the Geographies of Empire in Thirteenth-Century Incest Romances

While twelfth-century romances such as *Cligès*, *Digenis*, and *Floire et Blancheflor* were written before the fall of Constantinople in 1204 and figured marriage with various "easts" as a fertile site for both ideological and mercantile exchange, as the Crusades wore on and victories by French-speaking households diminished, literature commissioned in these courts began to imagine the near east in more negative terms.[1] Yet even as Byzantium's exoticism – from its fantastic exotic goods to its rapidly depleted golden coffers to its architectural, sericultural, and artistic influence – began to wane, thirteenth-century Old French literature imagined women to be as active in making and breaking ties between eastern and western households as ever. Texts such as *Le Roman de la Manekine* and *La Belle Hélène de Constantinople* imagined women shaping their own destinies, not only falling in love with men from far-off lands, but renouncing their own familial origins in order to fulfil their desires, changing empires and political ties in the process.

During the thirteenth century, when *Le Roman de la Manekine* was written, political relations between Byzantium and the west deteriorated, yet Old French literary sources nevertheless imagine cross-cultural love affairs as a fertile and productive site for figuring exchange.[2] Women's work in underwriting the story of Mediterranean nobility flourished at the very moment that contemporary sources would have us imagine that, as Chrétien put it nearly half a century earlier, "que des Grezois ne des Romains / ne dit en mais ne plus ne mains … et esteiente la vive brese" [talk of the [Greeks] is over … their burning embers spent].[3] Nowhere is the supposed turn away from the Greeks more evident than in the popular and widely translated story of the handless girl, first recounted in *Le Roman de la Manekine* and then later redacted in *La Belle Hélène de Constantinople*, a story of love and exchange framed by questions of empire and gender.

Le Roman de la Manekine, a mid-twelfth-century Old French story written by Philippe de Remi, is arguably the first incarnation of this story; *La Belle Hélène de Constantinople* is an anonymous early fourteenth-century retelling.[4] In these two tales the king of an eastern country marries a beautiful woman who dies giving birth to their first and only child, a young girl named Joïe (in *La Manekine*) or Hélène (in *La Belle Hélène*). The infant is raised by her father, who falls in love with her when she reaches puberty; he informs her that he will marry her. She refuses, cutting off one of her hands in order to preclude the marriage, on the grounds that a king cannot legally marry an imperfect woman. After her father condemns her to death, the young girl flees the eastern court by boat and eventually ends up in northwestern Europe (Scotland in *La Manekine*, England in *La Belle Hélène*). Once she arrives on shore, the king of that land falls in love with her, marries her, and they have either a son or twin sons together. The handless girl's mother-in-law, jealous and hateful, conspires to make her son, who is away on campaign at the time of the birth, believe that his wife has given birth to (a) monster(s). Once again persecuted by her family members, the young mother flees a death sentence with her infant(s). She is separated from her son(s) and wanders for several years, fleeing her husband and her father, who both desire to seize her for their own. Eventually, the mother-in-law is killed or imprisoned, wife and husband peacefully reconciled, children reunited with parents, and the father-daughter incest scene is forgiven.

Though manuscript and literary evidence suggest that the handless girl story was popular,[5] representations of incest form a relatively small part of the corpus of Old French literature.[6] Incest stories represent only a small subset of tales that are arguably as concerned with exchange and exogamy as they are horrified by the problematics of endogamy.[7] Some scholars have read them as proponents for the newly minted and church-controlled practice of confession and penitence, as in many of them incest is considered both a legal problem and a sin.[8] What most scholars can agree upon is that nearly all of the incest texts stage incest as a metaphor for a social problematic, ranging from corrupted kinship patterns to church control of marriage to the implosion of the Arthurian court.[9]

The few medieval literary texts in which incest is pointedly about deviant sexuality have been, until now, either disregarded or analysed in tandem with the ecclesiastical regulation of interfamilial reproduction.[10] Yet as Kathryn Gravdal, Thelma Fenster, and Elizabeth Archibald have all separately pointed out, there is a subset of texts in which incest – or, more often, the threat of incest – is the central concern of the narrative.[11] In these romances, interfamilial sexual violence predicates the narrative and propels children to flee their families and their identities.

While scholars have analysed literary stagings of sexual violence against children from a feminist perspective, until now the historical and cultural specificity of the incestuous milieu in Old French literature has been largely unexplored.[12] Yet, as we have repeatedly seen in other medieval texts staging confrontation, contact, and even exchange between courts around the medieval Mediterranean, this kind of specificity offers new insights into understanding how cross-culturalism is imagined as the base of medieval nobility. The scant medical and legal records from the Middle Ages do not suggest that incest – that is, interfamilial sexual violence – was any more or less common in the medieval period than it is today.[13] One is tempted to enquire, then, why the handless girl story had enough traction in the medieval imagination that it was translated into many languages.[14] In its later iterations, the handless girl story was even incorporated into texts by the Brothers Grimm, and is now called "one of the most widely-spread of the European folk tales."[15]

While others have sought to understand the ecclesiastical resonances of the handless girl story, in this chapter I instead place the Old French versions and their eastern courts into the cultural context they themselves invoke: the Mediterranean. As with *Cligès*, *Floire et Blancheflor*, and *Digenis Akritas*, understanding the dynamics of the later medieval story of the handless girl requires a careful exploration of its cultural context. In keeping with the other stories explored throughout these pages, *Le Roman de la Manekine* and *La Belle Hélène de Constantinople* weave a narrative tapestry using the threads of culture, gender, and empire to consider cross-cultural Mediterranean relationships. When *Le Roman de la Manekine* and *La Belle Hélène de Constantinople* imagine fathers lusting after their daughters, they are taking part in a larger literary tradition that stresses the importance of exogamy and cultural exchange as the heart of medieval Mediterranean noble identity. As we shall see, the incest motif reveals gender to be tantamount to the construction of empire, and it posits women as fundamental to constructing both.

The Story of Incest, the Narration of Deviancy

Though both the *Manekine* and the *Belle Hélène* are ostensibly narratives about their protagonists – that is, narratives about the travails of *women* and their lifetime voyages westwards – both open with lengthy descriptions of the eastern *men* whose incestuous embraces they flee. In fact, the audience is held captive by a description of men and their desires for the first fourth of the romance, suggesting that *men's* desire is as much the core story of this text as women's ability to mitigate and shape those desires to suit their own needs. And this male desire is one that is repeatedly cast as deviant.[16]

In *Le Roman de la Manekine*, the earliest of the handless girl stories, incestuous desire is inaugurated by the king's barons, who decide that the only acceptable match for King Henry is his daughter.[17] From the outset it is clear that the decision to marry father and daughter will be problematic, both spiritually and politically:

"Signeur, li rois ja mais n'avra
Femme, n'on ne le trouvera
Tele comme il le veut avoir,
S'on ne fait tant, au dire voir,
Que il puist sa fille espouser :
Ou monde n'a forst li son per. […]"
De tex i a qui s'i acordent,
Et de tex qui mout s'en descordent.
Longuement entr'eus desputerent.
En la fin li clerc s'acorderent
Que il le roy en prieroient
Et sur aus le pecié penroient. (319–38)

["the king will never have a wife, nor will anyone find one such as he wants to have, unless, truth to tell, it is arranged that he can marry his daughter; except for her, her mother's peer is not in the world. […]" There are those who agree and those who disagree strongly. For a long time they argued amongst themselves. At last the clerics agreed that they would entreat the king to do it and would take the responsibility on themselves.][18]

Here, the barons resolve their problem of female inheritance and governance by suggesting that King Henry should marry his daughter; it is a suggestion that meets with resistance on many fronts. The rhyme scheme functions as a literary echo of the cultural crime, highlighting the deviancy of this unorthodox marriage by employing a stunning audible double-entendre between "espouser" ["marriage"] and both "père" ["father"] and "per" ["equal"], for example. It also clearly highlights the clerics' objections – namely that they will commit a sin in order to secure a male heir to the throne (in the end, they, too, will petition the king to commit incest ["prieroient"], but they construe their petition as a sin for which they will take the punishment ["pecié penroient"]). In their agreement to be held accountable, the barons' use of the conditional Old French form of *pendre* (to take upon themselves, from *prendre*), "penroient," resonates clearly with the other acoustic meaning of the verb "to be hung," from *pendre*. Not only will the sin weigh heavily on their conscience, it could possibly be a fatal error on their part.

While the clerics interrogate the spiritual implications for authorizing incest, the king's response brings into question the social situation of the body by interrogating what it means to be a man. The king's initial response suggests that he, too, understands incest not only to be a *sin* (a "pecié," according to the barons) but also a *transgression* against normative masculine desire. He refuses to acquiesce to his barons' desires, citing the abjection it would cause him: "sacciés, pour riens ne le feroie. / Trop durement me mefferoie" ["know that I should not do this for anything. It would frighten me too greatly"] (360–3).[19] In Henry's terms, incest is a sin that will contaminate the fabric of the Hungarian courtly society, both by threatening the king with abjection and by polluting the princess.

Indeed, so great a transgression is this act of incest that the king agonizes alone in his chamber for an entire night. His *veille* and inner turmoil recall the sleepless nights of legitimate lovesickness in other romances and foreshadow his eventual acquiescence. King Henry's restlessness mixes fierce discussions of rape with sweet sighs of lust, as he begins to burn, ashamedly, for his own daughter. Henry

art de l'estincele
Dont amors seit si les siens batre, [...]
Se laisse en son cemin embatre.
A tant de sa fille se part.
Mais od lui em porte le dart
D'amours, qui grant anui li fait. [...] (431–4)

[burns from the spark with which Love makes his own heart beat, lets himself enter her path. [...] Thereupon he leaves his daughter. But

> he carries away with him the dart of Love, which causes him much distress.

Henry's soliloquy shows him to be enflamed ("art") by his lust, teetering between madness and reason. By aligning his desire with fire (using the term "art"), Henry equates lust with sin, a burning desire that pollutes him.[20] Henry's fright at his own lust situates incest as a transgression of his own identity, against his perception of the way normal men should desire.

The cultural and legal objections to incest raised in *La Manekine* are consistent with those of contemporary medieval writers. Thomas Aquinas (1225–74), for example, held that incest is a sin against proper heterosexual reproduction, against human interest, and one that prevents men from forming good friendships. In his mid-thirteenth-century *Summa Theologica,* Aquinas differentiates between sins of lust, sins against nature, and sins against God.[21] Aquinas creates a moralized hierarchy of sexual sins that range from bestiality, which is the gravest sin because it "corrupt[s] the principle on which all others depend" (i.e., it disrupts human procreative sexuality because the "due use of species is not observed"), to sodomy, which can be equated to male and female homosexuality and to masturbation, which is non-procreative.[22] These sins are grave because they distort "the due use of species" – that is, they represent sins of lust expressed outside the realm of procreative sex. Men accused of bestiality or sodomy are therefore outside the realm of "normative" sexuality, in Aquinas's view, and their non-normative desire is a sin. As such, Aquinas's viewpoint might be considered a theological interpretation of medieval masculinity, in which masculinity is constructed through and inscribed within exogamous male–female sexual desire *with the intent to reproduce.*[23]

Aquinas situates incest as the first sexual sin that represents a possibility of reproduction – the correct "use of species" – but the wrong choice of partner. Aquinas writes that "[a]fter [bestiality and sodomy] comes incest, which ... is contrary to the natural respect we owe persons related to us."[24] Incest is a sin against natural respect, against cultural – as well as procreative – order.[25] Perhaps more importantly in Aquinas's view, incest disrupts society, for its focus on household women bars men from creating external bonds of friendship. Aquinas posits that "a man taking a stranger to wife, all his wife's relations are united to him by a special kind of friendship, as though they were of the same blood as himself."[26]

Aquinas's conceptualization of incest – that is, that it simultaneously instantiates sexual deviancy and removes women from circulation among men – foreshadows its position as a foundational taboo by modern anthropologist Claude Lévi-Strauss. In his now seminal work, *Structural Anthropology*, Lévi-Strauss theorizes the prohibition of incest as the foundation of culture itself, as the necessity for encounter with the other. Lévi-Strauss writes: "Le caractère primitif et irréductible de l'élément de parenté tel que nous l'avons défini résulte en effet, de façon immédiate, de l'existence universelle de la prohibition de l'inceste. [...] dans la société humaine, un homme ne peut obtenir une femme que d'un autre homme, qui la lui cède sous forme de fille ou de sœur"[27] [The primitive and irreducible element of relationship as we have defined it results, in effect, in an immediate way, from the universal existence of the prohibition of incest ... in human society, a man can only obtain a woman from another man, who gives her to him in the form of a daughter or sister]. The organizing force of exogamous marriage is a way of thinking about culture in terms that evoke relationships between different kin groups, defining a family in opposition to outside groups. In Lévi-Strauss's understanding the incest taboo inaugurates the division between "self" and "other," and it does so by encouraging the circulation of women between men.[28] More importantly for our purposes, and as Mary Douglas explains, the incest taboo becomes a sign for the absolute necessity of exchange, for at its base, exogamy is a form of cross-culturalism, a differentiation of the self from the other.[29]

Henry's response in this passage that he will not commit incest because "trop durrement me mefferoie" presages his reading of incest as something that is not only a sin (as in Aquinas's terms), but also something that debases his masculinity. Henry's words align his understanding of masculinity as something constructed through exogamous desire, and they resonate with Aquinas's understanding of incest as the correct "use of species" but a distorted "choice of partner." If masculinity is indeed constructed in romance through the grid of compulsory *exogamous* desire, then any desire a man feels for his family members is automatically problematic, and brings into question the authenticity of his masculinity within the framework of social relations staged by contemporaries like Aquinas.

Henry's terror over committing incest is highlighted by the rhyme that conflates fear and sexual abjection, "mefferoie" and "ferroie." The abjection he expresses showcases how he understands normative masculinity to be predicated on exogamous heterosexual desire. It also eschews the reading (anthropological, literary, or theological) in which women's circulation among men is the primary problem with incest. His response to the situation not only inaugurates this text's understanding of what incest is about (sullying his very essence as a man), it also reveals what normative masculinity looks like (desiring, in essence, exchange). His speech underlines the dangers of transgressing the fundamental social structures of gender and sexuality, for the king would mark himself as an abject deviant, not only in Aquinas's terms a sinner, but in his own mind, an abject subject, a man shuddering without his masculinity.

Rereading Incest: Masculinities at the Borders of Empire

Not only does King Henry's abjection frame incest as a judgment about masculinity, it also interpellates the eastern court specifically as a site for staging deviancy. In *Le Roman de la Manekine*, the incest threat is explored in very clearly delineated geographic environments such as the Hungarian court and the Scottish shores. It is precisely through these opposing milieus that the text entwines and even assigns value to masculinity, geography, and empire. The eastern Hungarian court becomes a site for staging distorted and devalued kinds of masculinity by staging endogamous desire, while the western shores become a fertile ground for exogamous, cross-cultural reproduction and empire-building. Narrating the flight from the east to the west as redemptive (e.g., casting Joïe's Hungarian father as perverted but her Scottish husband as exemplary, or casting Hélène's Byzantine father as abusive but her English husband as liberating) reveals incest to offer not only gendered, but also geopolitical implications. By framing the outcome of incest – that is, deviant masculinity – in geographic terms, *La Manekine* imagines gender politics as inherently related to the geography of contemporary Mediterranean politics. In particular, this reading reveals incest as a trope of empire, in which gender categories become fundamental to the articulation of empire.

While the initial version of the handless girl story, *La Manekine*, is a fascinating study of wayward masculinity, its redaction and retelling across time is even more compelling. By the time *La Belle Hélène de Constantinople* was composed in the early fourteenth century, the courtly milieu shifts from Hungary to Byzantium, and the king becomes obsessed with his daughter without any external interference. In this rewriting, the king's deviant sexuality reinforces *La Manekine*'s initial link between wayward masculinity and (eastern) geographic specificity.

In *La Manekine*, as I have noted, the Hungarian barons provided the authorizing force as well as the deviant suggestion that stoked that first incestuous fire; in *La Belle Hélène*, however, the Byzantine king *himself* is aflame with lust for his daughter from the outset, in ways that are almost iconic:

De plus en plus l'enaime ly fors rois postais,
Et que plus devint grande, plus y a sen cuer mis.
Tant ot a luy d'amour, che nous dist ly escrips,
Que ou non de se fille que tant a cler le vis,
Fist ung paintre mander qui estoit ses subgis,
Et se ly a fait paindre d'or fin et d' aseur vis
Le fourme de se fille en .IX. lieux ou en .X.
Dedens se maistre cambre la ou estoit ses lis.
La furent les ymaignes bien faittes a devis,
En le fourme d'Elaine dont il estoit espris.
Avec li le couchoit et par nuit et par dis,
Douchement lui baisoit et le bouche et le vis. (112–23)

[More and more does the powerful king love her, and the older she gets, the more she commands his heart. He has so much love for her, so goes the story, that in the name of his daughter who has such a bright face he commanded a painter who was his subject to paint her face and form in fine gold in nine or ten places. In his own chambers there where his bed was, were hung up these images of the form of Hélène with whom he was very much taken, and with them he slept by night and by day, and sweetly he kissed her face and lips.]

Unlike the King of Hungary, King Anthony is not conflicted in his desire, and he finds it natural enough to hang and kiss icons of his daughter in his chambers ("douchement lui baisoit et le bouche et le vis"). He also finds incest so natural that he petitions the pope for a papal dispensation to marry his daughter. In the second text there is no connection between abjection and incest; on the contrary, King Anthony's growing lust for his daughter is so righteous that he is willing to threaten the pope with military action if he is not absolved for the illegal marriage with and potential rape of his daughter. The degradation of eastern masculinity within *La Manekine* is further abased by its rewriting in *La Belle Hélène*, in which the deviant Byzantine emperor seeks his own daughter out of own sheer lust.

Where eastern desire is framed as endogamous and perverted, western men offer an exogamous and redemptive partnership for both Joïe and Hélène. In both *La Manekine* and *La Belle Hélène*, western men are described in ways that recall the heroes of western romances; the masculinity associated with them is steeped in chivalric identity and *courtoisie*. Descriptions of western men offer echoes of earlier heroes like Erec, Yvain, Roland, and Lancelot, whose worth was founded upon their chivalric prowess, and whose sighs of lust were directed decidedly outside of their own families.[30] In *La Belle Hélène*, for example, the king of England is well reputed as a man of fighting ability whose courtliness is also renowned:

Tant broche le cheval ly riches rois englois
Qu'il est entrés dedens le castile maginois. [...]
Et quant Elaine vit que Henrys ly adrois
Estoit tant honnerés qu'il estoit clamés rois,
Se dist a soy meïsmes : "Et ! Sainte vraie crois,
Car donnés volenté che princhе demanois
Qu'i me vausist avoir, che seroit biaux explois,
Afyn qu'il me fesist roïne du terrois." (1176–7; 1181–6)

[The rich English King rode his horse so hard that they arrived at his magnificent castle. [...] And when Hélène saw that Henry the upright was so honoured that he was called king, she said to herself, "Ah! True holy cross, because it is your will that I take the prince who must come to me, it would be a wonderful adventure if he made me the Queen of this land."]

In this passage, the king is not only rich and powerful, he is also the object of Hélène's love and desire. Good at both chivalric feats and at captivating the attention of women, he has talents that, in their resonance with other heroes of romance, mark a model for masculinity. Such a passage marks the listener with the sounds of masculinity through the end rhyme of ("rois" / "crois" / "demanois" / "explois" / "terrois"). Adventures ("explois") and lands ("terrois") couple with divine right and faith (the "crois") to make a many worthy to be king ("rois"). The geographic specificity of this chivalric masculinity emerges most clearly when put into opposition with a deviant and lesser masculinity, one rooted in incest, and this is just the work of *La Manekine* and *La Belle Hélène*.[31]

Moreover, and perhaps more importantly, in the passages of encounter with the western rulers, these texts imagine female desire. Whereas the first third of the romances was devoted to detailing the fathers' illicit and incestuous desires, finally we are privy to the enunciation of women's desire. Here we have the point of view of Hélène, whose desires offer insights into the construction of a properly exogamous sexuality. Hélène's desire instils a clear difference between two kinds of men. In both iterations of these texts, the daughter flees the threat of incestuous rape and the court that harbours it. She opts instead to travel westwards in an epic journey that eventually brings her to the shores and arms of a worthy western court. She marries a western king and produces his heirs. The movement here is anything but random, as women and narrative shift ever westwards and find redemption in the west, pausing first at Rome and then journeying on to rest in England or Scotland. The texts trace a narrative journey away from eastern deviancy towards what they imagine to be a redemptive and proscriptive western masculinity. And in both of these texts, women's desires help construct some masculinities/some locales as pejorative and others as desirable.

If, as Jeanette Beer points out, the narrative iterations of *translatio* are always linked to a particular socio-historical context, to a political agenda, then the shift away from the incest proposed by Hungarian nobles towards a later Byzantine man overpowered by his *own* incestuous lust may be telling.[32] Since *La Belle Hélène de Constantinople*, which elaborates Byzantium's incestuous court, is a rewriting of the reproductive dilemma faced by the Hungarians in *La Manekine* precisely at a time when the differences between east and west were programmatically reduced by the hybridizing of eastern crusader colonies, the text may respond to the growing crisis of similarity facing eastern and western men by contrasting their masculinity.[33]

Whether or not the creation of hybridized Frankish crusader colonies after the Fourth Crusade's victory in Constantinople influenced the literary processes of *amplificatio* and *translatio* through which *La Belle Hélène* comes into being as an elaboration of the earlier *Manekine*, it is clear that both texts imagine the Christian near east to be a site for staging masculine competition, for constructing alternate eastern masculinities. The handless girl story, and its subsequent rewritings, do so with ever-increasing force as they imagine first barons and then fathers to implement incest as a viable means for eastern courtly reproduction and endogamous political preservation. Together these texts depict eastern masculinity as not only deviant, but also programmatically compromised and redefined, as we shall see, by women's choices.

Women Making Gender

It may not be surprising that eastern men are constructed as deviant in western romance, nor is it even surprising that women flee the embrace of easterners to find redemption in the arms of a powerful western man. Indeed, we have already had a taste of this in *Cligès*. What is noteworthy, however, is how the construction of masculinity is mediated by women's choices in cross-cultural love affairs. Once the women have mitigated the threat of incest and flown from the threat of their fathers' incestuous embraces, the real work of the romances can begin.

In many ways, the work of women in *La Manekine* and *La Belle Hélène* parallels the work of women in other texts, be it *Gui d'Amaury*, a medieval German story of incest persecution in which women marry eastwards and seek redemption and resolution at the Byzantine court; texts about Frankish-Saracen pairings, like the *Fille du comte de Ponthieu*, where a noblewoman leaves her native court to seek redemption in the arms of exogamy; or even *Cligès*, where Fénice's decision to love abroad helps to reconfigure the structure of loyalty in the east and the inheritance of empire in the west. These texts all imagine women's agency, exogamy, and cross-cultural exchange as cornerstones of Mediterranean identity – from the genealogies of its nobility to the narratives of its glory.

In *La Manekine* and *La Belle Hélène*, women are the protagonists, and thousands of lines are spent detailing their flight from eastern courts, where they excoriate all remnants of their past identities to spite their fathers. Though fairness, youth, and physical beauty often connote desirable femininity in romance, for Joïe and Hélène, self-mutilation becomes a way to reformulate femininity outside of sexuality. Specifically, the girls forfend incestuous rape by cutting off their hands, thereby removing themselves from the economy of marriage by altering their performance of femininity.

The text offers its own logic for the women's actions, explaining that medieval law strictly forbids a king to marry an "incomplete" or damaged woman. "Incomplete" may refer to a woman who is no longer a virgin, of course, but it also refers, at least in these romances, to a woman who has been mutilated in some way, as Joïe explains to her father in *La Manekine*:

"Sire, bien vous ai entendu;
Mais roïne ne doi pas estre,
Car je n'ai point de main senestre,
Et rois ne doit pas penre fame
Qui n'ait tous ses membres, par m'ame !"
Donques a trait hors son moignon,
Loié d'un coevrechief en son. (794–800)

["Sir, I have understood you well; but I may not be a queen, for I do not have a left hand, and a king may not take a wife who does not have all her members, upon my soul!" Then she drew out her stump, bound up with a kerchief at the end.]

As critics have pointed out, the moment of self-mutilation is a moment that equates physical abnormality with social abnormality. The severing of the hand comes to signify the severing of the woman's place in an economy of exchange among men.[34] As the girl severs her hand, she simultaneously severs her father's ability to marry her, effectively disempowering him and forbidding the completion of his incestuous desire. Here, the father is symbolically castrated, unable to fulfil his political and sexual ambition of reproducing his eastern empire with his daughter.[35] The lacking hand reveals the fundamental lack inherent in eastern masculinity, an important critique of eastern desire as power and women shift *wilfully* away from eastern men towards plenitude with men who rule the west.[36]

While the hand effectuates a symbolic castration of the father's wayward lust, on another level, the self-disfigurement functions as betrayal of patriarchal order, as it is the first moment in a long series of steps through which the girls disentangle themselves from their (fathers') eastern identities and from the traditional disempowerment of femininity in patriarchy. Not only does the moment of self-mutilation inaugurate what has been called elsewhere a "symbolic betrayal" of their home culture, but it also is a moment in which the girls take themselves out of an economy of male–male exchange.[37]

In fact, the girls' disfigurement marks a forceful break with two ways that women's desirability is normally constructed in romance. First, their disfigurement renders their bodies incomplete and maimed, distorting their physical perfection. Second, in breaking with the story of their own nobility – their royal genealogies, their royal blood – they remove themselves from the class status through which romance relationships are typically constructed. They effectively rewrite their position – and purpose – in society by seizing control of the story about their sexualized bodies. Their activity – rather than passivity – rewrites the narrative of how women should love, and where, and with them travels a new narrative about what kinds of men are worthy of their love.

Joïe and Hélène literally run with this moment of rebellion, fleeing the east and undertaking an arduous journey westwards and across the Mediterranean. Their movement westwards is a movement away from their families and simultaneously offers a critique of their fathers' masculinities. For over thirty years the girls refuse to disclose their geographic or class origins. When a Scottish provost first meets Joïe, he does not even bother to greet her, but demands to know where she is from, and from what kind of family:

Bele, fait il, de vostre terre
Vous vaudroie gem mout enquerre,
Se il vous venoit a talent,
Dont vous estes et de quel gent.
Dites le moi, et saciés bien,
Ce ne vous grevera ja rien. (1283–90)

["Beautiful one," he says, "I would like to enquire of you about your country, how you came here and what kind of people you are from. Tell me, and know well, that nothing bad will ever happen to you because of it."

The provost's questions show that he understands people by their relationships to other men – to their fathers, to their peers. His questions seek to construct Joïe through her familial background, class status, and geographic origins; this is a common way for people to understand foreigners.[38] Yet Joïe wards off his questions, and, for a while at least, the abjection of narrating incest. By the time she is introduced to the king, she is ready to deflect his questions, too:

Sire, tout cil qui bien me font
I pueent grant aumosne avoir;
Car povre sui, sans nul avoir,
Venue d'estrange contree
Toute seule par mer salee,
Comme une dolente caitive
Et la plus lasse riens qui vive,

Com cele qui ne voldroit estre,
Se il plaisoit au roy celestre.
Ne ja plus nus hom ne m'enquiere.
J'ameroie mix estre en biere
Que je mon anui racontaisse.
Je morroi ains, que le contaisse. (1283–1304)

[Sir, all those who do well by me shall have great recompense for it, because I am poor, without any belongings, and I have come from a foreign land all alone across the sea, as a mournful being and the littlest of nothing that lives, as she who does not want to be alive, if it pleased god, never again would a man enquire about me. I would rather be in a bier than recount my troubles. I will die as soon as I tell them.]

The Manekine's refusal to place herself within the narrative of patrilineal origins is an uncommon move, one that eschews contemporary noble practices of genealogy.[39] Joïe creates her own success story outside of the realms of lineage and without the support of her class status, her nobility. She rewrites the romance love story, anchored in the articulation of nobility, to eschew gender roles by announcing that she would rather "be in a bier" than fulfil her father's dreams of expanding his familial empire through incest.[40] Her speech aligns the process of recognizing people ("reconaisse") with the process of narration ("contaisse"), revealing nobility as something inherently tied to its articulation through iteration, both through lineage and in stories of renown. In Joïe's terms – and in stark contradiction to the traditional narrative of romance – the story of patriarchy is the story of death; she would rather die than narrate her father's glory.[41]

The handless girl's story imagines women's choices to love exogamously to have political and dynastic consequences. The women who seek love outside the bounds of patriarchy, the men they spurn and leave behind in the east, and the western men in whose arms they find solace are all affected by women's desires for exogamy. In this passage, then, women's choices construct masculinity, and the refusal of the story of patriarchy becomes a critique of eastern masculinities.

Women's choices in cross-cultural love construct the cultural norms for femininity, too. When the king of Scotland decides to make Joïe (La Manekine) his queen, it is not his barons who have a problem with the assimilation of a strange woman into the court; rather it is another *woman*, specifically his mother, who is threatened by the female outsider. Wary of a woman whose social status, ethnic identity, and religious background she cannot verify, his mother schemes to evict her daughter-in-law from the court, citing in particular her concern for Joïe's lack of genealogy, her lack of a family name. She offers Joïe a very pointed warning:

> Mauvaise garce, a vous qui monte,
> Ne quels voloirs a ce vous donte,
> Que voles compaignier mon fil?
> Vous en seres mise en escil.
> S'il vous avient mais a nul jour,
> Vous en serés arse en un four.
> Or gardés plus ne vous aviegne,
> Se ne voles que max vous viengne. (1823–30)

> [Terrible slut, to whom he goes, and you to whom he gives things, what do you want with the company of my son? You will be put into exile for it. If he ever comes back to you again on another day, you will be burned in a fire. Now watch that he does not come back to you, if you do not want that bad things come to you for it.]

The queen's plot to put her daughter-in-law into exile succeeds, and her threat that the girl will be burned ("arse") aligns the Manekine with sexual excessiveness and deviancy. The mother-in-law's censure uses an intertextual reference to King Henry's soliloquy, in which he burned with desire for his daughter ("art de l'etincele"). The intertext aligns Joïe's refusal of patrilineal identity with the deviancy of her father's burning desire, and therefore casts women who try to step outside the bounds of narrating the self through family as deviant. Using words like "garce" and "art," the mother-in-law's speech equates Joïe's form of sexuality (foreign) with the aberrance of her own father's lust (incestuous).

The term "mauvaise garce" ("terrible slut") in the mother-in-law's speech further conflates ideas of foreignness with class and sexual excessiveness.[42] The sexual othering of a foreign queen is common; in this instance, however, it is the decision and judgment of another *woman* – rather than the king's barons or subjects – that punish a foreigner for her perceived differences and her unwillingness to place herself within a narrative about submission and exchange.[43] Here, then, the mother-in-law censures the Manchotte (as she is sometimes known without her hand) for her unwillingness to link her father's family's story to her new husband's lineage, suggesting that women who seek to alter men's narration – the story of patriarchy – are to be punished. That is, if genealogy can be conceptualized as a kind of narration of the story of patriarchy, women who seek to alter this narrative are castigated.

The mother-in-law's attempt to burn the "mauvaise garce" for her foreign/deviant sexuality resonates with the punishment of women's sexual transgressions in contemporary canon law. Gratian's *Decretum*, written in Latin in 1250 (but soon thereafter translated into Old French), constructs incest as something that must explicitly punish women. Gratian moves beyond Aquinas's argument that incest prohibits the circulation of women to focus instead on incest as a crime that affects not only its perpetrator but its victim too, one that sullies the story of patriarchy.[44] In Gratian's terms, the incest victim herself is "soiled," thereby making her an unacceptable partner in a later marriage.[45] He proposes that both the victim and the perpetrator must be punished, but the victim becomes doubly castigated, first by the act of incestuous rape itself, and then by the further prohibition that he or she may not marry. According to Gratian, the incest victim has no name, thus preventing marriage and taking her out of the economy of exchange between men:

> Il ne loist a nul crestien a prandre a fame cele qui a eu mari de som proper lignage, ou qui a esté soillie d'aucun incest, quar celle asamblee est abominable devant Dieu et devant touz bons hommes. Et nos lisons que li saint pere establierent que cil qui sont en incest, n'ont nul non de mariage.[46]

> [It is not befitting for a Christian to take as wife she who had for a husband someone of his own lineage, or who had been soiled by any incest, because this assembly is abominable before God and before all good men. And we read that the holy fathers established that those who are in incest have no marriage name.]

Joïe not only refuses the narrative of patriarchy, but she also responds to a medieval culture where even the victims of incest are soiled and have no "I" from which to narrate their family story. In this culture, incest victims are unable to place themselves within the narrative of genealogy, because they cannot lay claim to a familial name. The two girls, then, work out new identities for themselves as they love westwards and into western courts, transgressing not only the story of patriarchy, but also the normative prohibition against their reintegration into society by marriage (elaborated here by Gratian) after the threat of incest endured in their eastern fathers' courts. In essence, they dare to rename themselves, speaking from a new "I" derived from their identities as western queens and mothers.

Writing the story of western nobility depends, in these romances, as deeply upon women working within its plotlines as upon the pens of the men who author them. It comes as no surprise, then, that women must be recuperated into the folds of patriarchy, that their stories must become a place to narrate the exchange of empire and lineage. The endings of the romances predictably reincorporate women back into the economy of exchange, recuperating them from their position outside of narrative. This moment of recuperation is also the moment where the kinds of exchange previously impossible within the incest romances – the exchanges between east and west, facilitated by a woman and her story of cross-cultural marriage – can begin.

In *La Manekine*, Joïe is reunited with her family, and she is subsequently reunited with and forgives her father. The moment of forgiveness begets narrative, and it also begets lineage. When Joïe forgives, she simultaneously acknowledges the story of her lineage, and accepts the articulation of a hybridized genealogy:

Tuit cil s'entramerent d'amor.
Et la roïne eut puis enfans
Pluiseurs, si com je sui lisans;
Deus filles eurent et trois fix,
Envers qui Dix fu mout bontix.
Car les filles furent roïnes
Et tousjours vers Dieu enterines,
Et li troi malle furent roy,
Puis essaucierent bien la loy.
Ensi com j'ai dit se continrent
En bien, tant c'a bonne fin vinrent. (8513–28)

[And the queen had several children afterwards, as I understand it; two daughters and three sons, to whom God was very bountiful. Because the daughters were queens and always turned towards God. And the three males were kings who exercised well the laws of the land. So as I have said they continued on and went until they met a good end.]

These last few lines of *La Manekine* offer a relatively stereotypical view of womanhood within the narrative of patriarchy. The reattachment of the hand by the magical advent of a sturgeon (who had swallowed it when Joïe cut it off and threw it into a river) can be read as a symbolic re-masculation of the father, an acceptance of the father's name and of Joïe's own circulation in a system of patriarchy between men – that is, after she has modified the story he wished to tell by mutilating his eastern masculinity. Ultimately, it is Joïe – rather than the men – whose choices consistently favouring western exogamy over eastern endogamy condemn and foreclose eastern masculinity. In these romances of cross-cultural exchange, masculinity is tied up not only in relative geographies, but also in the work of women's desires.

The reiteration of this scene in the latter text *La Belle Hélène de Constantinople* may offer some insights into the intentions of *La Manekine*. Like Joïe, Hélène accepts to have her hand reattached after some twenty years without it, and it is at the moment of reattachment that she meets her father. King Henry is both forgiven and then marginalized by the importance accorded to the work of Hélène's sons (read: exogamy) in reattaching her to the structures of patriarchy (15399–402; 15439–46). What is perhaps most telling, though, is how *La Belle Hélène* insists on depicting the westerners (i.e., Hélène, Henry, and their children, specifically the twins Martin and Brise/Bras) at the very end of the poem:

De Dieu le createur qui ne fault ne ne ment
Fu Martins archevesque de Tours parfaitement,
Et regna dedens Tours et vesqui longement.
Et Brisses Engleterre maintint, le casement,
Et si fu empereres de Gresse propement
Et de Constantinoble, moult tient grant tenement.
Mes sains Brisses, ses fieux, n'y vault tenir noient,
Ains vint servir son oncle a Tours devotement.
Depuis fu archevesque, se l'isotire ne ment.
Mes ly romans n'en fait chy plus racontement;
Chy endroit finera men livre leigent;
Jhesus veulle warder de mal et de tourment
Tous cheux qui a l'oïr ont eut esbatement. (15526–38)

[By God the creator, who never lies nor does wrong, was Martin made archbishop of Tours, and reigned within Tours and lived long. And Brises held England in his domain, and so he was also the emperor of Greece and of Constantinople, and he directed them well. Saint Brise, his son, did not want to hold onto them, and he went to serve his uncle at Tours devotedly, and was afterwards made archbishop, if the story does not lie. But the book does not recount any more information, and here I will finish off my book; Jesus please guard from evil and torment all those who have listened to it.]

Unlike its earlier model, the latter text elaborates on the social positioning of the characters *after* Hélène's body and family have been reassembled. In particular, Hélène's western children, Brise and Martin, take over political and ecclesiastical control of Byzantium, once again colonizing Byzantium with western practices. The end rhyme of "tourment" and "esbatement" leaves the reader with a sense that Hélène's incredible travails are somehow justified, or at least assuaged, by her children's success in ruling over her father's Byzantine domain. The "esbatement" imagines that Hélène's excruciating journey moves the impetus of empire away from the Byzantines and squarely into the centre of western courts.

The passage also recuperates her struggle for western exogamy as exemplary, in a narrative that many have read as akin to a hagiographical triumph of west over east.[47] Though their paths and reasons diverge, the women in *Cligès, Floire et Blancheflor, Le Roman de la Manekine,* and *La Belle Hélène de Constantinople* all rewrite the narrative of east-west relations by imagining women to negotiate the value attributed to their lovers through their active decisions about loving, spurning their eastern fathers' embraces in favour of anonymity, love, and peace in the arms of western rulers and within the walls of western courts.

When considered in the context of Franco-Byzantine affairs of the early fourteenth century, the elaboration and amplification of women's roles in shaping eastern masculinities in *La Manekine* and *La Belle Hélène* begins to make more sense. In 1265, about thirty-five years after the authoring of *La Manekine,* and at least fifty years before the authoring of *La Belle Hélène,* a Byzantine force led by Michael VIII Paleologus reclaimed their capital city from the Frankish colonizers, and the slow destruction of the Frankish (mostly Norman) colonial empire began. By the late thirteenth century, the Byzantines had begun a revival of interest in their own literary history, and they were beginning, once again, to flourish as an independent entity, slowly regaining what had been taken from them in the Fourth Crusade. In the same period, the Frankish families who had controlled Byzantium were in decline. It was not until 1341 that civil war brought Byzantium to the brink of destruction and ultimately opened the path for the Turkish invaders whose mid-fifteenth-century invasion would bring the Byzantine Empire to a close.

La Belle Hélène de Constantinople, then, is most likely written during a time period of Frankish frustration with and elimination from access to Byzantium. It is in this context that the ideological conquest of Byzantium by Hélène's two children, and most of all her repulsion by Byzantine wayward masculinity, must be understood. This later rewriting of the handless girl story offers a pointed message about the defeat of Byzantium, and of an incestuous Byzantine father, by western men but staged through the choices of eastern women, both as wife and as mother. Incest becomes a thematic motif to differentiate the self (the noble French audience addressed by the romance) from the other (the deviant and sullied eastern men over which women's choices bring victory) in a historical time of increasing conflict and disarray throughout the crusader colonies, in a time in which the hybridity of the colonies threatened to undermine the western families who ran them.

While the severing of the hand and the incest threat took both Hélène and Joïe out of the economy of circulation between men, their reinsertion into that economy, their recuperation at the end of the story offers, on several levels, a story about a politicized and moralized migration of all things east towards the west. First, the fathers of Hélène and Joïe, maddened with lust for their daughters for thirty years, have spent so much time looking for the girls that they have neither remarried nor produced any other children. Their incestuous lust has precluded the successful reproduction of another eastern ruler, and the throne reverts to their daughters' male children, thereby replacing an eastern ruler with a western one. Incest becomes a trope that names deviant masculinity, situates it geopolitically, and simultaneously represses its further reproduction. Second, from the moment that the women are made whole again, from the symbolic reattachment of the hand, they are suddenly able to tell the story of their backgrounds, their persecution, their wanderings, and their trials; before this moment, their children have no access to the Byzantine throne, and they have no reason to wander waywardly over Europe. It is a moment in which speech – narration of one's life – creates a personal history that melds into familial conquest, and it is accomplished through women's narratives. Finally, the amplification and translation in the last few lines of *La Belle Hélène* point to the ways that *translatio* is caught up in disseminating empire and, specifically, how women's access to translating ideas of culture or transmitting familial power are limited to their access to a familial, patriarchal identity. *Translatio* itself is caught up in the movement of ideas between men, and even if women like Fénice, Blancheflor, Hélène, or even Joïe know how to manipulate that knowledge system in ways that are empowering, their stories are not likely to be heard unless they are put into the context of a paternally named "I," one through which their children have access to a lineage of power.

In the end, Hélène's and Joie's refusal of the narrative of eastern patriarchy – their refusal of their fathers – metonymizes a larger social preoccupation with a thirteenth-century turn towards the west and its own narratives of importance. At stake, then, in reading *Le Roman de la Manekine* and *La Belle Hélène de Constantinople* is understanding not only the role of deviant, marginal masculinities in redefining the centre of western nobility, but also the critical role that women play in assigning value to masculinity in relation to different geographic contexts. Incest, in the end, becomes a way to balance the interests of cross-cultural exchange and reproduction during a time of Mediterranean dynastic empire building.

4 Rewriting Mediterranean Gender and Power in *Floriant et Florete*

As we have seen, twelfth-century romances such as *Cligès* and *Floire et Blancheflor* explore the connections between Mediterranean exoticism and the genealogy of French nobility. By the thirteenth century, however, Old French romances reimagine the Frankish nobility as glorious not for its relationship to a genealogy articulated through a Mediterranean past, but for its mastery of the Mediterranean present. In particular, one old French romance, *Floriant et Florete,* explores a fundamentally medieval and Celtic hero, King Arthur, as an archetype for negotiating Mediterranean politics in thirteenth-century Sicily. Unlike earlier romances, which alluded to the power of the Greek myths – from Trojan prowess to Byzantine splendours – in articulating Frankish glory, *Floriant et Florete* capitalizes on a Mediterraneanized Arthur as the touchpoint for explaining the worth and wealth of western nobility. The romance offers a rich staging of Arthurian myth within a Mediterranean context. *Floriant et Florete,* then, reveals a world in which Byzantium's exoticism and its underlying function of authorizing genealogies of western nobility are changing with the tides of history.

Scholars have tended to dismiss *Floriant et Florete* as a dismal attempt at rewriting and recycling Arthurian material from better-known and often more coherently redacted twelfth-century stories by Chrétien de Troyes (his *Perceval, Lancelot,* and *Yvain* being among the most cited intertexts by scholars such as Keith Busby and Sara Sturm-Maddox).[1] Yet I would argue that the incessant desire to rewrite the twelfth century is in fact the entire point of the romance; perhaps *Floriant et Florete* should be read *exactly* for its reconstruction of thirteenth-century Arthurian nobles *à travers* their encounters with eastern goods, ideas, and peoples. Read from this angle, *Floriant et*

Florete becomes a thirteenth-century revision of the relationship between Frankish households and their relation to eastern goods and stories. In this light, and as we shall see, the romance offers important insights into the changing face of exoticism in the late Middle Ages, and it points to the ways that literary representations of foreign others are linked to highly localized familial concerns relating to literary patronage and manuscript production.[2]

Floriant et Florete begins on the sunny shores of Sicily, a place in between east and west, a place with a long and complicated history of cross-culturalism, production of and trade in exotic goods, and, of course, warmongering in the Mediterranean.[3] Like many other Italian coastal city states, medieval Sicily offered a diverse mix of people, architecture, trading possibilities, and luxurious goods and foods available in few other western medieval ports, and as such offers an ideal staging ground for contact between forces of the east and the west, as in the thirteenth-century Old French *Floriant et Florete*.[4] The narrative opens with Sicilian king Elyadus and his pregnant wife, who is accosted by one of her husband's barons, the seneschal Maragot. Maragot's lust for the queen is so unbearable that he kills Elyadus, and she, in turn, flees the castle, thinking to find safe harbour nearby. She goes into labour in a forest, and while she is asleep after the birth, a fairy named Morgan whisks away her son, named Floriant. Morgan raises the child until he is fifteen and sends him off on a quest to find her brother Arthur and offer him his services, once again beginning a voyage of cross-cultural discovery. Floriant has several adventures that recall in almost word-for-word detail the adventures of many of Chrétien de Troyes's protagonists, but most specifically Perceval. Floriant arrives at Arthur's court, enters into his service, and eventually receives word of his parentage via an enchanted letter from Morgan announcing Floriant's history, Elyadus's treacherous murder, and Maragot's subsequent threat to Floriant's mother and throne.

The manuscript evidence for *Floriant et Florete* suggests that it did not enjoy the popularity of other texts that drew heavily on the principles of *translatio* and *inventio*, such as *Cligès* or the *romans d'antiquité*, and in this sense, the text cannot represent thirteenth-century assumptions about Arthur, Arthurian legends, or even Byzantium. Only one manuscript of *Floriant et Florete* exists, and it is a late thirteenth-century manuscript preserved in the New York Public Library (De Ricci 122). Though of course it is possible that other manuscripts of this text existed at some point, the manuscript suggests that the romance did not enjoy the popularity of Chrétien's Arthuriana, *Floire et Blancheflor*, or *La Manekine*, all of which exist in several copies and versions, sometimes in several languages.[5] Furthermore, as this manuscript is bound alone in a seventeenth-century binding, it offers no contextualized reading program through which to divine how it might have been read or used, unlike *Floire et Blancheflor* and *Cligès*.

Yet despite the scant codicological context, the text itself is evidence that at least one patron was interested in narrating a Mediterranean Arthurian court. Specifically, there are connections to be made between its commissioning, production, and historical context. The key to understanding these connections is to focus on how the text rewrites the twelfth-century Frankish nobility for a particular thirteenth-century audience in a Burgundian court, to focus on the meaning of its use of *translatio* to elaborate old metaphors for a new context. In *Floriant et Florete*, the Byzantines and the Muslims do not face the crusaders depicted in epics like *La Chanson de Roland* or in historical texts like *La Chanson d'Antioche* – instead, they face a military coalition between King Arthur and Floriant, his most valiant knight.

The Arthur-Floriant (or Cornish-Sicilian) pairing rewrites the Celtic origins of Arthurian renown into a Mediterranean setting. Though some have suggested that this is merely another dull iteration of an essentially Arthurian romance, a closer reading of *Floriant et Florete* suggests that Arthur's influence extends well beyond the shores of the sedentary court life in Cornwall.[6] The most common twelfth-century Old French descriptions of Arthur and his court usually depict him as a king who is keenly interested in stories, and whose martial inclinations are next to none.[7] In Chrétien's *Conte du Graal*, for example, Arthur says:

–Ke, fait li rois, laissiez m'en pais;
Que ja par les oex de ma teste
Ne megerai a si grant feste
Que je cort esforchie tiegne.
Jusque novele a ma cort viegne. (2820–6)

["Kay," the king replied, "Let me be. By the eyes in my head, with such a high court assembled, I have no intention of eating on so great a feast day until some news reaches my court."][8]

The same passage appears almost verbatim in *Floriant et Florete*, as Keith Busby has pointed out.[9]

–Keus, fet li rois, loaissiez m'en pés
Que ja, par Dieu, n'i mengerai
Devant que noveles orrai
Ou de novele ou d'aventure,
Quex qu'ele soit ou bone ou dure. (1546–50)

["Kay," says the king, "leave me in peace. By God I will never eat anything before I hear some news or an adventure, be it good or bad."]

Like Busby, most scholars have read this as a relatively rudimentary example of *translatio*. The wording of the two passages is almost identical, and Arthur is depicted as a strong ruler deeply interested in stories of knightly renown; while *Floriant et Florete* seems to reiterate characteristic descriptions of Arthur as a story lover, the narrative process of *amplificatio* also permits the author to expand on the figure of Arthur, moulding him into a warrior who not only hears of heroic deeds but himself leads men to accomplish them.

Scholars have focused on *Floriant et Florete*'s failure to reimagine the drama of Arthurian struggles to articulate identity (in its borrowings from *Perceval*) and establish knightly renown (in its borrowings from *Perceval* and *Yvain*). Yet perhaps *Floriant et Florete* is *not* trying to mimic a Celtic Arthur, but rather to posit the Arthurian court as an important player in Mediterranean combat, noble genealogy, and cross-cultural marriage. Unlike Chrétien's Arthur, who is the centre of courtly storytelling and whose *knights* are transformed by their experiences in the world in Chrétien's narratives, in *Floriant et Florete*, Arthur *himself* is the one who is transformed by the text of the romance. Through the process of *translatio* he is altered from the *Perceval*esque Arthur who refuses to eat unless he is provided some "news" or a story, to an Arthur fully committed to war.

Translatio permits the author to reimagine Arthur as an active warrior, one who reputedly hungers to conquer the Mediterranean. When Arthur agrees to invade Sicily to expel Maragot and enforce Floriant's rightful claim to the throne, for example, observant merchants imagine him as an invader, an empire-builder bent on depriving them of their natural right to Sicilian territories. The merchants make their way to the Sicilian court to warn Maragot that Arthur is coming, claiming that "li rois Artus / O lui plus de .cm. escus / Tuit te voelent desheriter / Et du Suzille fors jeter" [King Arthur has with him more than one hundred thousand horseman and they all want to disinherit you, and send you far away from Sicily] (2791–4). The Byzantine emperor, Filimenis, later exaggerates this description of Arthur as a conquering warrior in ways that are consistent with the processes of the *translatio*. He amplifies the position of Arthur, expanding him from a conquering warrior to a king whose desires for the Mediterranean are boundless. Filimenis warn his liegemen of Arthur's martial inclinations:

Seignors, fet il, or m'entendez:
Savez que ceste charter dist?
Maragos a moi la tramist
Et si me mande et velt prier
Por Dieu que je li voisse aidier
Encontre le fort roi Artui
Qui grant ost amaine sor lui,
Et s'il le puet desheriter
Tot le mont vorra conquester.
D'autre part se jel vois aidier
Et nos em poommes chacier,
Artus et ciaus qui sont od soi,
Il tenra sa terre de moi
Et si m'en rendra treüage. (2830–43)

["Lords," he says, "now listen to me: Do you know what this charter says? Maragot sent it to me, and so he asks and prays by God that I would be willing to help him against the strong king, Arthur, who is bringing a large army against him, and if he can oust him, *he will want to conquer the whole world*. On the other hand if I wish to help him and we can stave [Arthur] off, he [Maragot] will hold his lands from me, and then he will render me tribute."][10]

Here, Arthur has been rewritten from his twelfth-century representation as a relatively peaceful organizer of courtly society (whose main interests vacillate between watching knights joust before him and listening to tales spun in his court) into a thirteenth-century world conqueror. While many earlier romances depict Arthur as a relatively peaceful man, this description relies on an amplification of his glory and power for a new context, one in which the west is staging a military conquest over the east, much more in keeping with crusader texts than with Arthurian romances. The amplification of Arthur into an itinerant warrior is an integral part of the process of *translatio*, the rewriting that differentiates this thirteenth-century text from its twelfth-century models. It simultaneously reveals what is broadly at stake in the romance, namely, the west's reformulation of east-west relations through both war, and, later, love.[11]

Arthur now stands in for western glory, and he is amplified into a mythic conqueror of the east. Arthur becomes a conqueror (one who "want[s] to conquer the whole world"), offering a sharp reinterpretation of the twelfth-century, docile Arthur who longed for stories. Even though Arthur himself expresses no wish to conquer the world, this is a rare example of Arthur described as a territory-hungry marauder. All of these passages combine to suggest that this *translatio*-based romance is not only, as scholars have already explained, a poor and late rewriting of the Arthurian legend. Rather, *Floriant et Florete* imagines a world in which Arthur and his values programmatically conquer the east. It does so by rewriting the past, by rewriting historically shameful defeats and expulsions from Byzantine lands into a literary conquest over the Byzantine emperor and his family.

In building off of – but significantly altering – earlier models of Arthur and his court, *Floriant et Florete* creates meaning through what Michelle Freeman and Hans-Robert Jauss have theorized as a process of meaning accretion, in which reader understanding is linked to a knowledge of and break with past traditions of Arthurian representations.[12] The new meaning of any translation is necessarily dependent on a double moment for its reader, one of the past and one of the present. The past, in Jauss's formulation, plays the role of adding meaning and depth, through the recognizable accretion of knowledge through time. Yet the present is equally important, for the new socio-political context is crucial to understanding the production and reception – the meaning, even – of transformations any translator has made with the text. *Translatio* therefore necessarily exposes the cultural stakes of the moment of (re)writing. To really gauge the political relations implied by the process of translating a sedentary Arthur into the conqueror of Byzantium and Sicily, one must first understand something of the context of *Floriant et Florete*'s production within a historical moment and under the auspices of a particular court.[13]

Codicology and the Mediterranean Arthur

While the one extant manuscript of *Floriant et Florete* offers few codicological clues to its courtly milieu, the political history of Burgundy may permit us to make informed conjectures as to why and how this romance might reimagine Arthur as a world conqueror and the pre-eminent power not only of the English Channel but also of the Mediterranean. The leaders of Burgundy, Sicily, and Byzantium (the key players in our fictional text) all have deep historical resonance with the kinds of political relations staged in this fictional romance, albeit in very different ways.

The Duchy of Burgundy and its court capital, Dijon, played an important and literal role in the production of the manuscript. As the *Grundriss* points out, the manuscript was composed in a northern Burgundian dialect, far from the Sicily it depicts.[14] Furthermore, though almost all of the narrative action takes place in Sicily, there is little evidence to suggest that it has any roots in Sicilian literary culture, which, as Karla Mallette points out, is deeply tied to Arabic cultural and literary traditions. Contemporary Sicilian literature reflected the island's hybridity of languages and cultural traditions to a much greater extent than *Floriant et Florete*.[15]

Still, the abiding interest in narrating the west's coming to power in Sicily is itself revelatory, and, I would argue, reflects Angevin familial politics contemporary to the composition of *Floriant et Florete*. Anjou was connected to the House of Burgundy in this period, and Anjou itself had a long history in Sicily, which had been a Norman kingdom throughout the twelfth century.[16] Under Roger II, in the late 1100s, it truly prospered; in many ways it was as much a meeting point for east and west as Constantinople ever was. Sicily was populated by Muslims, Orthodox (Byzantine) Christians, and Roman Christians, and Roger II was able to integrate these three main bodies of people into a harmonious and highly skilled workforce whose main export was silk.[17] When Roger II died, his throne was passed first to William the Good, who continued Roger II's dreams of Mediterranean conquest, and in 1185 "seized Durazzo and Thessalonika, and seemed poised to capture Constantinople."[18] After William died without an heir, the throne was to be passed to Roger II's daughter (and William's sister), Constance, who was married to the German emperor Henry of Hohenstaufen; Sicilians and Romans alike preferred Norman rule, and instead they crowned Tancred, an illegitimate heir, their king. In 1191, however, the pope overruled the Sicilians' decision and crowned Constance and her husband as the rulers of Sicily. The crown passed down through the Hohenstaufen dynasty to Conrad (1250–4) and then to Conradin

(1254–8), until Manfred (1258–66) seized the throne from Conradin and was eventually deposed by the Angevins.[19]

Charles I of Anjou, whose rule of Sicily began in 1266, provides the link between Burgundy (the place of manuscript production), Sicily (the country everybody wanted to control), Byzantium (one of the key contenders for Sicily) and the monarchy, all the major players in what may be best read as a fictional commentary on their struggles.[20] Charles I was Count of Anjou, King of Naples and Sicily, and brother to the King of France, Louis IX, as well as to Eudes III, the Duke of Burgundy, who died in 1218; he thus had familial claims to Sicily. Charles became King of Sicily in 1266 and ruled until 1285, married first to Beatrice of Provence, the daughter of Raymond, Count of Provence, and next to Marguerite of Burgundy, his great-great niece. Both families had claims to the former Kingdom of Burgundy, which, by the mid-thirteenth century, was reduced to a county and a duchy, one dependent on the Holy Roman Empire, the other independent; Charles's family, then, would have offered an easy link between the place of manuscript production (northern Burgundy) and the content of the manuscript itself (the conquest of Sicily and the destruction of Byzantine grandeur), which would likely have posited him as militarily victorious and reflected his own political ambitions.

If, as scholars claim, the author was from northeastern Burgundy, he may have been writing in the court of either Hugues IV, Duke of Burgundy (d. 1272), who, while on crusade, claimed the kingdom of Thessalonica for himself; or Robert II, Duke of Burgundy (d. 1306). At the same time, his patron's uncles and cousins would have included two kings of France (Philip III and Philip IV), three cousins who married Burgundian nobility, and several rulers of Sicily, which would offer a plausible explanation for both the subject matter (interactions between the west, Byzantium, and Sicily) and the language of composition (Burgundian Picard dialect) of *Floriant et Florete*.[21]

In any case, it seems probable that the nobles in this area would have been long acquainted with Angevin dreams about Sicily and Byzantium. It thus appears likely that the text may have been written for a Burgundian closely tied to the French (either Norman or Angevin) rulers of Sicily. The connection between the actions of Charles I and the plot of *Floriant et Florete* become clearer if we examine them not only in the context of a comparison between literary characters and historical people, but also in terms of the political goals of Charles I's French household.

Within a year of assuming the throne, it appeared that Charles's ambitions to conquer Byzantium were coming to fruition. He had conquered the Byzantine lands of Corfu and Epirus; he also arranged for the marriage of his daughter to the heir of the throne of Achaia, which brought with it the promise of crusades against Byzantium and strengthened his claim to rule over the lands of Thessalonica, most of the Aegean islands, and one-third of all future conquests.[22] Obsessed with victory over Byzantium, Charles sought to eradicate the Byzantine presence in Sicily, and though in the fictional *Floriant et Florete* Arthur eventually defeated the Byzantines, Charles never could oust his Byzantine opponent, Michael VIII Palaeologus.[23] Though it is unlikely that there is any direct correlation between the fictional Arthur and the historical Charles, the Burgundian struggles to invade and conquer Byzantium offer a plausible historical backdrop for understanding the workings of *translatio* in *Floriant et Florete*, and invite us to consider the force of the Mediterranean – rather than the recycling of Arthuriana – as the central work of the romance.

After the death of Pope Gregory X, Charles felt at last free to invade Byzantium, and in 1280 he made his preparations once again, this time for a land attack. In March 1281, after a winter-long siege of the town of Berat, Charles's army was defeated by Palaeologus.[24] Yet Charles was still not to be dissuaded, and when Martin IV was elected to the papacy later that year, Charles could once again invade. This time, his target was Venice, which quickly submitted and signed a treaty to help invade Constantinople, beginning in 1283. Martin IV then excommunicated Michael VIII Palaeologus, and the invasion looked promising. Charles made the mistake, however, of exploiting his Sicilian subjects, and in preparation for the latest war against Byzantium, he had scoured the countryside for horses, cattle, and food to feed his men on their journey. The Sicilians had had enough, and on Easter Monday 1282 they rose up against him in a bloody night of rebellion, in what is known as the Sicilian Vespers. Charles's grip on Sicily was quickly weakened, his influence forever circumscribed, and Byzantium escaped, relatively unscathed, from his wrath. In short, Charles was historically obsessed with eradicating Byzantine power, but, riddled with military and political defeats, could not rally to achieve his goals, and, unlike our fictional King Arthur, he lost the war.

Several scholars have claimed that *Floriant et Florete* could not have been written before the Sicilian Vespers, reinforcing connections between Charles I as the flailing, failing conqueror of Byzantium, Arthur's difficulties in Sicily, and the process of *translatio* that reimagines and rewrites his historical military defeats into stunning western literary victories over Byzantium. The Angevin obsession with defeating Byzantium is a phenomenon limited to late thirteenth-century politics, one that, when taken with my reading of a *Floriant et Florete* most likely produced in its court, has several implications.

First, it is likely that this romance is written, as the editors to the latest edition claim, in the last quarter of the thirteenth century, rather than in the third quarter of the thirteenth century.[25] The historical advent of the Sicilian Vespers and of Byzantium's defeats of Charles of Anjou offer the picture of an Angevin household that was simultaneously determined to oust the Byzantines from any sort of power, and was continuously thwarted from doing so, and this picture is limited to post-1266, after the Sicilian Vespers.

Second, the double moment of Angevin frustration and determination is, I think, rewritten into a mythicized literary success in the text. The text recuperates western defeats in Sicily and in Byzantium in one fell swoop by having Arthur defeat both the Byzantines and their illegitimate claims to the Sicilian throne via Maragot. In *Floriant et Florete*, Arthur becomes a mythological Mediterranean conqueror, rewritten to accomplish what the Angevins could not: the repression of Sicily and the defeat of Byzantium. Even though Charles of Anjou was unable to roust the Byzantines from their claim over Sicily, the romance rewrites history's ending, offering not only the military but also the sexual defeat of Byzantines by the Arthurian court as he and his vassals conquered territories and women along the way.

Using historical context and manuscript history to frame the rewriting of Arthur in *Floriant et Florete*, then, permits us to better understand Maragot's fears of an Arthur wholly devoted to war, and to understand that *Floriant et Florete* is no mere iteration of earlier romances by Chrétien. Manuscript and cultural context permit us to ask the right questions of the text, to understand not only that one eastern character fears Arthur as a world conqueror (claiming, for example, that "s'il le puet desheriter / tot le mont vorra conquester") but also to consider *why* he might be rewritten in this way. Whether directly reinterpreting Charles I of Anjou as an Arthurian world conqueror, or just pointing to the interest French families expressed in dominating Mediterranean politics of the thirteenth century, read in its manuscript context *Floriant et Florete* becomes a pointed reinterpretation of contemporary cultural problematics.

The expanded vision of western dominance imagined in Arthur reflects a contemporary turn away from the glory of a Greek past. The shift away from Greek dominance accompanies a shift towards defining western European pre-eminence in self-referential ways. The narrative affirms western validity not by its relation to stories of Greekness or genealogies of ancient glory, but rather by its relation to the pre-eminent medieval figure of western kingship, Arthur, whom it imagines as a Mediterranean power figure, wholly independent of the kinds of authenticating ancient Greek genealogies in stories like the *Eneas, Cligès,* and even *Floire et Blancheflor*. As we shall see, this shift is as much dependent on newly revisited thirteenth-century versions of western masculinity (something already alluded to in *La Manekine* and prefigured by *Floriant et Florete's* figure of Arthur-the-world-conqueror) as it is upon women's work in revising cross-cultural connections in the crusader empire.

Women and the Rewriting of the Mediterranean Story of Ravishment

The war that situates Arthur as a world conqueror is resolved in *Floriant et Florete* through the exchange of women between men. We have seen women exchanged between noble households in Greek romances like *Digenis Akritas* to cement cross-border relationships; we have seen Fénice exchanged between the German court and Byzantium as a peace offering designed to guarantee territorial independence; we have seen Blancheflor as the conversion tool designed to recuperate non-Roman Catholic kingdoms into the folds of the Kingdom of Christ through her marriage to and conversion of the pagan Floire; we have also seen Byzantine princesses flee the incestuous embrace of their fathers, marrying instead western rulers. Yet while twelfth-century romance celebrated exoticism, later texts begin to turn away from imagining Byzantium as a site of partnership and exchange, or Greekness as a site of authority from which the western nobility stakes its claims to grandeur and constructs its public self. Old French romances like *Floriant et Florete* and *La Belle Hélène de Constantinople* interrogate the fecundity of relying on eastern sources – from exotic sumptuary goods to storytelling motifs and ancient heroes – for defining the glory of thirteenth-century French-speaking noble families.

In *Floriant et Florete,* the tug of war between east and west is resolved to a great extent by women, though in some unexpected ways.

Peace and harmony, for example, are guaranteed by the act of ravishment, the very act that provoked perhaps the most famous of Greek wars, the Trojan War. Arthur's man, Floriant, seduces and kidnaps the daughter of the Byzantine emperor while Arthur's men are on campaign. Gauvain simultaneously abducts her lady-in-waiting, and the double ravishment initially causes such outrage and shock among the Byzantines that it seems implausible that any reconciliation could be arranged. Filimenis, incensed by his daughter's abduction, requests counsel, and King Jeremy advises him to make peace instead of war, to use his daughter as a tool to secure that peace through marriage rather than bloodshed.

Ravishment becomes a tool for peacemaking, cross-cultural exchange, and empire building. As we have seen in previous chapters, recent scholarship has focused on how the movement of women in medieval Mediterranean literature is often predicated on their ravishment – the illegal and unsanctioned removal of them from one man to another, in which they are in physical danger of being raped.[26] But another way of constructing those movements is to try to understand how they are motivated and who, in a sense, authorizes the ravishment, to look beyond the viewpoint of the father and patriarchy and towards that of the women themselves, to read, so to speak, from their perspective.

In the romances we have considered, women are complicit in their ravishment: they are the ones who not only desire illicitly (i.e., illicitly because it is outside of their families' authorization), but who also actively pursue the possibility of escaping from the paternal locus, seeking redemption in the form of exogamous, cross-cultural marriage. From Digenis's wife, who was so charmed by her courtier that she agreed to run away and hatched a plan to be ravished by him, to Fénice's ravishment from the German court by her would-be lover Cligès, to Floire's ravishment and rescue of Blancheflor within the emir's palace, twelfth- and thirteenth-century literary imaginings of cross-culturalism and exogamy are littered with examples of women who choose to abandon their household of birth. In essence, many Old French romances about east-west relationships are predicated on women's exogamous desire, their love across the border, so to speak.

In *Floriant et Florete*, we might consider calling the relationships between the women and their foreign lovers "cross-cultural love." "Cross-cultural love" may be a way of thinking from the point of view of the women involved, one that allows us to consider their desire separately from their position as objects of exchange between men.[27] In this formulation, love becomes a choice articulated within the confines of patriarchy; it is a choice that *Floriant et Florete* suggests has implications not only for cross-cultural relations, but also for the construction of noble French identity and empire.

Read from the women's perspective in cross-cultural romances, women's desires consistently promulgate exogamous cross-cultural bonds, irrespective of the desires of patriarchy, and often with gross implications for the spread of empire. Digenis's wife loves him and wishes to marry him and so arranges a midnight tryst to run away with him; Fénice loves Cligès and seeks to be closer to him by faking her own death and having her body carried away from her husband to him; Blancheflor does not love the emir and wishes to go home to Floire, who is accused of ravishing her from the emir; even Joïe and Hélène do not love their fathers, as they cut off their ties to patriarchy, and send themselves away to find romance elsewhere. While one could read this as a narrative quest to use women's desires to authorize their exchange, their objectification, or their rape, I would argue that women's love – articulated outside of the framework of exchange on which patriarchy depends, but then legitimized through cross-cultural marriage – inaugurates new pathways of communication and permits the expansion of empire. Women's desires promote unexpected, and initially forbidden, hybridized lineages. In short, rather than authorizing further misogyny, women's cross-cultural love creates a new space for cross-cultural exchange and redefines the edges of western patriarchy and empire, as it shifts political and familial alliances and land inheritance patterns.

Women's desires structure *Floriant et Florete* as much as men's dreams of Mediterranean conquest. If the war of *Floriant et Florete* is predicated on Arthur's empirical dreams, the romance of *Floriant et Florete* is predicated on women's cross-cultural love. When Florete, the Byzantine emperor's daughter, falls for Arthur's liegeman and legitimate heir to the Sicilian throne, Floriant, she agonizes over her illicit desire. Likewise, when Florete's servant, Blanchandine, falls for Gauvain, she bemoans her unlucky choice. The narratological attitude towards these love affairs confirms that the romance lines up with the expectations of patriarchy, for the relationships are described as theft and ravishment, and men bitterly complain when other men abduct their female relatives, their property, without their permission. Yet the romance quietly interrogates the patriarchal reading when it underlines how the exchange of women – something ostensibly authorized and policed by men – is not, in fact, instigated by men at all. The women themselves prove otherwise: they love where they choose to love, and they follow their hearts' desires for the excellent warriors they spy fighting on the battlefield, unlocking the gates of their fathers' castle walls to let their lovers in, opting to love freely beyond their fathers' ken. In doing so, they play the traitor, moving not only beyond the borders of their fathers' households, but beyond the borders of their collective eastern empire, loving westwards and outwards, away from their homelands.

The women's soliloquies cement the connections between cross-cultural love and empire. Florete's long internal debate about Floriant, for example, reveals that she not only loves him but also that she understands that love to be unreasonable, for, as the allegorical figure of Sense points out to her, he is a foreigner, and therefore it is transgressive to love him without her father's approval:

"Vels tu estre amie
A .J. home d'autre contree?
Molt par seroie forcenee!
Dont te vient ore tel corage?
Je croi tu as el cors la rage:
Ja est il de guerre mortel
Contre ton pere, il n'i a el!" (3456–62)

["Do you want to be the lover of a man from another country? You would be crazy to do that! From where did such a desire come to you? I believe that you have folly in your heart: right now this man is in mortal war with your father, that's the way things are!"]

Sens uses the wordplay between the various meanings of "corage" ("feelings," "desire," "will") "cors" ("body," but audibly mistakable for "cors," or "heart") and "rage" ("rage," "passion") to reinforce the various ways that reason forbids women to bind their bodily desires to follow their hearts' passions.[28] The allegorical badinage thus recognizes the contradiction between love – the "rage" at the heart of Florete's internal debate – and paternal authority as an important one. The wordplay also situates women's love across the frontier – but especially across lines of war – as an insensible folly, cementing an even tighter prohibition through the end rhyme of "contree"/"forcenee." In short, Florete's speech reveals that she knows her desires to love across the border undercut her father's military and political wishes; it melds the force of women's cross-cultural love with the politics of empire.

While Florete's love is illicit because it is beyond the borders of her father's empire, for Floriant, their love is a mismatch explicitly because of class. He agonizes that he is not worthy of her because he is only a knight, and has no aristocratic position to complement her story of royalty:

Trop pués haut asseoir t'amor
A la fille a l'empereour.
El ne te daigneroit amer
Ne por son ami reclamer.
Roi ou empereor avra
Tantost com ses peres volra. (3517–22)

[You have placed your love too high in the daughter of the emperor. She will never deign to love you, nor to call you her lover. She will have a king or an emperor as soon as her father wishes.]

In many ways, Floriant's lament could be a stanza in an Occitan *canso* or one of several Old French romances, placing the lady high on a pedestal while fretting about the suitor's own ineligibility; as such neither its themes of class difference nor its subject matter of unrequited love are very revelatory. But contrasting the two lovers' laments shows that the problematics of the nascent relationship between Florete and Floriant are viewed differently by each of them. For Florete, the main concern is that she violates her father's (and therefore her empire's) sovereignty by choosing to love outside his realm of authority. For Floriant, the problem is one of class ("Trop pués haut asseoir t'amour"), and he is wholly unconcerned by the prospect of transgressing another man's personal or national boundaries of property. This is indicative of larger patterns of choice and possibility, where lowly knights can love the lady of their will, permitted they deign to love them back: there are no worries about authority and transgressing boundaries for young men on the make.

For young unmarried women much is at stake, for parental consent seems less than optional. When Floire rhymes the verbs "avra" and "volra," he recognizes that what Florete wants and will have are predicted by her father, who is the subject of these verbs. What will happen to Florete and whom she will have ("avra") are dictated by her father's will. It is his will that makes her into an object he desires to marry off ("volra"). The grammatical underpinnings of these monologues reflect, then, not the tension imposed by crossing nationalized borders, but rather the problematics of gender and choice in patriarchal marriage.

While the love affair is a mottled jumble of romance, belligerent skirmishes over the girls, and prominent displays of lavish eastern luxury goods, perhaps most surprisingly, the romance skims over the cultural and empirical differences separating the lovers, focusing not on the difficulties of loving across lines of war but rather upon the ways the girls' choices pacify and unify the many men involved. Indeed, the girls' cross-cultural love, originally considered an unforgiveable betrayal by their fathers, becomes a way of mollifying otherwise quickly outraged men, bringing them together to create lasting and powerful Mediterranean dynasties in which cross-cultural heirs are imagined to rule not only over Sicily, but also over Byzantium, Hungary, and western territories as well. Women's choices to love across the border change patterns of familial inheritance and dynastic order; their choices recentre the locus of empire around the family, and suggest that cross-cultural love – and women's roles in it – have political, as well as personal, implications.

Marking a shift away from eastern frames of reference in the late thirteenth century, both the masculine and feminine narratives of *Floriant et Florete* reformulate twelfth-century notions of identity, combining gender- and geopolitics to rewrite the relation between authority and empire in the thirteenth century. In particular, both of the narrative reinterpretations suggest a shift away from basing western noble identity on a romanticized Hellenic past and towards self-reflexivity. *Floriant et Florete* resists references to a kind of geneaologized eastern glory as the basis for writing western nobility, figured particularly in the movement from west to east that stages Arthur as a victorious world conqueror. The meaning and invocation of this eastern neighbour – and the ways that women's work in intermarriage mitigates that relationship – are slowly evolving in literature, in tandem with a shift in what it means to be part of a larger Mediterranean nobility.

As relations with Byzantium declined in the thirteenth century, romance, too, began to imagine a new space for theorizing the worth and origins of Frenchness, and that space has less and less interest in tales of eastern origins. By the time *Floriant et Florete* is written, Arthur – and his world-conquering abilities – easily replaces and defeats Byzantines through out-and-out war. But, perhaps more importantly, Arthur also defeats past iterations of himself, like in *Cligès*, in which the glory of his court was established vis-à-vis the splendours of an eastern past.[29] The new model of western masculine noble authority that emerges from the reinterpretation of the Arthur narrative is one that points towards a refashioning of the western nobility as stemming from its own sources of power, property, and luxury products. While Charles I of Anjou, to whom Arthur himself is perhaps but a loose intertextual referent, may not have defeated Byzantium in out-and-out war, the Arthur literature reimagines as the western defender of Sicily and conqueror of Byzantium is one who consolidates the power of the west by winning military and genealogical victories over the east, bringing not only Sicily under western control through martial victories, but ultimately much of the Mediterranean, through not only martial but marriage strategies facilitated by eastern noblewomen themselves.

Throughout twelfth- and thirteenth-century romance, literature imagines women as working to construct a culture of connectivity, working to build ties between households across the taboo boundaries of religion and empire. The exchanges in exoticism we would normally theorize as limited to men's writing, warring, and trading are in many ways facilitated by the ties noblewomen around the Mediterranean choose to make across its seas and around its shores. Romances like *Le Roman de la Manekine* and *Floriant et Florete* suggest that the value of that culture of Mediterranean connectivity declines in tandem with the decline of the relationship between Byzantium, Arab Muslims, and the west, and is coterminous with the rise of Salic law, through which women (and particularly foreign women) are prohibited from positions of power at the very moment that anxiety about cross-cultural marriage and its ability to bind French households to other territories through women emerges as a real political threat to the coherence of the French crown.

While there is much debate among historians about the actual power of the kinds of aristocratic women figured in fiction through characters like Florete or Joïe in the thirteenth century or Enide or Fénice in the twelfth, and while of course literary examples do not indicate a historical reality, this study of literary romances about cross-cultural love affairs and women's work within them suggests that literature, at least, did imagine women's choices to love across lines of culture to have formed and reshaped kin networks and family politics across the Mediterranean.[30] In fact, in all of our romances, women are the ones rewriting men's partnerships in ways that end up reshaping the boundaries of familial empires, translating their old ancestral power structures for a new cultural, linguistic, and geographic context as they marry and move into their new households. Women's actions, and in particular their consent to love across the border, not only ensure patriarchal succession, but also their own isolation from power in the court. Nonetheless, these texts open a space for imagining the influence of foreign wives on court culture, and, by extension, on court politics and on the movement of empire.

Conclusion: Rereading the Intersections of the Mediterranean

> Who will believe [the Latins], in their oath or in their word, who will consider them Christians as they say and maintain? With words they are Christians, the deed is lacking to them.
>
> (*Chronicle of Morea*, v. 772–855)

> The unbaptized races, should they make you an oath, according to the customs which they have and to the law which they adhere to, would receive death rather than commit perjury. But the Romans, who say that they believe in Christ, the more they swear to you and affirm their oaths, the more they plot against you to deceive you, to take of your possessions or to slay you.
>
> (*Chronicle of Morea* v. 1221–60)

The Chronicle of Morea is an early fourteenth-century narrative account of the establishment of the thirteenth-century Frankish crusader state of Morea in what is today the Greek Peloponnesus. Purportedly a historical account of the establishment and governance of a French colony in Greece, the narrative is full of inaccurate historical reporting and confusing dates, participants, and even locations. Quotes like those above, in which Moreots complain bitterly about both the Frankish (called Latin) and the Greek (called Roman) overlords, suggest that empirical expansion, conquest, and governance across lines of culture and religion were anything but transparent or facile. Yet nestled within the narrative – even within its gaping historical holes and its pithy invectives – are clues to the ways that local people experienced and retold the Frankish invasion and subsequent cross-cultural interaction with Greek society. The *Morea*, as a literary document, can tell us not only about the success of one of the first French attempts at colonialism, but also about the problems, failures, and fantasies the Franks and, to a lesser extent, the Venetians may have entertained about colonizing Byzantine society.

The very fact that the *Morea* was the literary product of a hybrid class of nobles in a colonial setting – and that scholars still debate whether it was written first in medieval Greek or in Old French – is a testament to the complications of medieval multiculturalism. The *Morea*'s colonial context fleshes out many of the assumptions made within this study, most importantly that marriage served as a fundamental way of uniting Mediterranean nobility and created pathways in which women were vital actors in the exchange of culture across seemingly irreconcilably different familial, geographic, and cultural structures.[1] Even before the fall of Constantinople in 1204, texts like *The Chronicle of Morea* stage the interactions between Byzantines and westerners to be, at best, complicated. From the conflicting interests of the Byzantine crown to look after the integrity of its holdings and peoples to those of Frankish and Venetian families eager to secure fast and cheap passage to the riches of the Middle East, relations between Byzantium and the west were historically just as complicated – if not even more so – than any of the literary representations we have studied might have imagined. Recent scholarly work on the interactions between what is now eastern and western Europe during the Crusades suggests that, while war over trade routes, broken promises, and conflicting familial interests was the norm, in almost every case, cross-cultural marriage became a space of carefully mediated cultural exchange and felicitous hybridity.[2]

More than any other contemporary account of the Frankish crusader states in Greece, the *Morea* is replete with unabashedly detrimental assessments of the enemy – in short, it is full of ethnic, religious, and cultural invectives. These slurs, while at best pejorative and at worst a kind of medieval xenophobia, offer important insights into on-the-ground beliefs and experiences, and suggest that some of the stereotypes that pepper our romances – like the Greeks giving gifts (and being perfidious liars) and the westerners swearing oaths (and being greedy for gifts and gold) – also course through contemporary historical texts. The *Morea* details a bicultural society that in many ways reflects the concerns of the literature explored here, from grappling with the status of speech and the place of oaths in feudal societies (as in *Cligès*); to portraying westerners' incessant thirst for exotic eastern riches (as in *Floire et Blancheflor* and *Kallimachos*); to slurs of inferior masculinities (as in *La Belle Hélène de Constantinople* and *La Manekine*); to the control of the movement of women and through them, empire (as in *Digenis Akritas* and *Floriant et Florete*). With its shoddy historicism and its popular slurs against both the Frankish overlords and the Greek petty nobility, the *Morea* makes for an interesting literary test of the fecundity of cross-cultural exchange in a time and place of strained and often forced hybridity and melding.

Though written over a hundred years later, the *Morea* begins with the Fourth Crusade's diversion to conquer Constantinople, and while it purports to offer a first-hand account of the sacking of the Byzantine capitol, of course it is unlikely that one author could both cover the Fourth Crusade and an enormous part of the Frankish crusader efforts in the Peloponnesus. After detailing the ways in which the Franks and Venetians divided the plunder and formed administrative units in the new colonies, the narrative spins forward to tackle the difficulties encountered by these men as they attempted to systematize the administration and inheritance of French-speaking rights to lands, revenue, and titles. Nestled in among the pseudo-historical chronicle are snippets of information that point to the daily lives of the nobles living in and vying for Greek lands, and the narrative charts the progress of these colonies in Mistra, Monemvasia, Naphlion, and other Greek territories well into the early fifteenth century. It follows the wars between each major administrator, paying particular attention not only to the overlord, but to the ways that local rulers administered on his behalf, for example in the case of Charles I of Anjou, who nominally reigned over Morea and figured perhaps in the manuscript history of our own *Floriant et Florete*.

The manuscript history of the *Morea* is somewhat complicated and contested by scholars still in the process of cementing its origins, but it is a testament to the narrative's popularity that it exists not only in Medieval Greek and Old French, but also in Italian and Aragonese.[3] It seems likely that the original, which is now lost, may have been composed in a popular (demotic) Medieval Greek and then quickly translated into Old French.[4] One version is written in prose, the other in verse, but what is interesting and what goes beyond the question of narrative primacy is the content – both versions feature full-fledged cultural invectives against both the Frankish invaders and the Greek inhabitants of Achaea. That is, all the versions imagine the confrontation of medieval colonialism to be fraught with despair and distrust, open hostility, military jockeying, and above all, strategic uses of cross-cultural marriage. The muddle of languages only serves to reiterate the argument being made throughout *Exchanges in Exoticism,* namely, that the process of empire building depends on rewriting the Mediterranean nobility as entwined through women's choices in cross-cultural marriage. As such the linguistic indeterminacy is something to be celebrated, and it reveals a historical and codicological example of the kinds of cultural meldings we have supposed underlie our readings throughout this study.

Though it is never acknowledged in the *Morea,* where Frankish and Byzantine nobles are portrayed as keeping strictly separate from one another, one of the most effective and immediate colonial practices the Franks initiated was to marry and reproduce with local landed aristocracy, the Greek *archons.*[5] The programmatic infiltration and co-opting of the Greek noble bloodlines meant that the Franks were immediately incorporated into local social and sanguinary structures, thus opening their greatest channel of influence in a largely unknown cultural setting. The strategy of programmatic intermarriage would prove effective for several generations; most likely the author of the *Morea* would have been just such a child. Intermarriage was not only a literary way of imagining the power of nobility to extend its stretch across the shores of the Mediterranean and well into foreign lands and courts in texts like *La Belle Hélène de Constantinople, Le Roman de la Manekine,* and *Floriant et Florete*; it was an on-the-ground practice in crusader colonies and a means of controlling political alliances between French colonizers and Greek locals.

In a completely fictitious rendering of the marriage between Geoffroy II, lord of Morea, and the daughter of the emperor of Constantinople (himself a Frank, Robert) in 1217, for example, the *Morea* reports that the bride involved gave her own consent to be married off to Geoffroy even while en route under her father's orders to be married to the king of Catalonia. The text insists that she assented to the new match with Geoffroy, and after the nuptials had been celebrated and the rapt reported to the emperor, the ravishment was repaid with Geoffroy's offer to hold his lands in Morea directly from the Frankish emperor of Constantinople, her father.[6] Though historically inaccurate in its minutiae, the text imagines several instances of historical relationships in which feudal domination is secured through cross-cultural marriage. In the *Morea,* it is often daughters – rather than the fathers – who acquiesced first, in many ways resonating with the staging of women's choices to love across the border and irrespective of their fathers in texts like *Floriant et Florete, Cligès,* and *Digenis Akritas.*[7]

For scholars used to thinking about how colonial marriage practices often mediated the power dynamic and influence between colonizer and colonized, this comes as little surprise. Marriage practices – or, in worse circumstances, practices of systematic rape – have been used for millennia to ensure the domination of an invading people over the indigenous population. But that is not exactly the case here; in fact, the *Morea* becomes a literary celebration of hybridity and figures a space from which all the outcomes of exchange we have explored in *Exchanges in Exoticism* come into play in social and political exchanges around the new colony. For all its invectives against Latins and Romans alike, *The Chronicle of Morea* is a celebration of cross-culturalism. But the driving question of *Exchanges in Exoticism* – how gender mediated that exchange – has been little studied by scholars in regard to the literary qualities of *The Chronicle of Morea*, perhaps even less so in the historical area of Achaea.[8]

In one instance, involving that very figure at the heart of my rereading of King Arthur in *Floriant et Florete*, Charles I of Anjou, Charles I's wife is reportedly snubbed by her two sisters because, since her husband has not yet captured Sicily, she is not yet of sufficient rank to sit amongst they who have already been made queens.[9] In another instance, Lady Marguerite of Passava (daughter of Jean II de Neuilly) is snubbed by Prince Guillaume of Morea. The prince refuses to grant her the right to inherit her familial lands in Akova because he ransomed her in prison and she was unable to stake her claim for her lands within the allotted time.[10] In fact, despite repeated legal protestations against the prince, Marguerite was unable to lay claim to her lands until she married a man and *he* then staked a claim through her right to offer them to him as dowry in marriage. The prince acquiesced eventually to transfer the lands to Marguerite's new husband, Nicolas de St-Omer, only by his grace and not by her legal right.

In many ways, the themes that are teased out from reading the colonial endeavour in *The Chronicle of Morea* resonate with my readings of literary representations of cross-culturalism in *Exchanges in Exoticism*. The chronicle showcases colonialism as riddled by a complex web of interrelated families, a hybrid network that must be created in the administration of a crusader state. But what is unique to the area of Morea and to the crusader effort in general, what makes Franco-Byzantine relations a crucial cultural referent for reading literatures of empire during the twelfth through fourteenth centuries, is how they imagine familial extension through the Mediterranean, stretching their genealogical claims across its shores through programmatic marriage and reproduction. In short, the Crusades, and in particular the crusader workings of *in-between* spaces like Byzantium, provide a unique vantage point for examining how marriage helped figure empire and permit the exchange of culture across wide swathes of land and sea in a time period of relatively little globalization and cross-cultural contact.

In thinking of *Cligès* and *Digenis Akritas*, for example, in which marriage between eastern and western families helped secure alliances and solidify borders in ways that resonate with the *Morea*, we see that marriage is imagined as a space where not only men's politics are accomplished through the exchange of women, but women bring their own set of cultural and ideological referents to forge their own political landscapes. Fénice, as an outsider within the Byzantine court, was able to target and identify differences between methods of courtly organization in the west (where the feudal oath of loyalty structured court life) and in the east (where the gift secured loyalty), and applied herself to reform her court in her own ideal, western image, to the advantage of her lover. Not only did she put western ideals into practice in the eastern courtly setting, but she also reinforced her opinion through sterility, allowing her love for Cligès to become a kind of political agenda.

When the *Morea* decries the religious differences between Greeks and Franks, calling each of them variously the "unbaptized hoards" or the "treacherous infidels," as in the epigraphs to this chapter, it imagines religious difference as an on-the-ground impediment to cross-cultural understanding and compromise. The invectives that litter the *Morea* are largely absent from other literary representations of cross-cultural interaction amongst Christians and around the Mediterranean, but in the case of *Floire et Blancheflor* we encounter a couple who struggle with the same issues of religious difference amongst the difficulties of empire within the context of cross-cultural love. Here, however, purely literary stagings of cross-confessional marriages might tell us something more about how to read the slurs peppering other historical narratives: perhaps, in the end, the religious differences are not insurmountable, and become merely a narrative trope in a larger story about the complexities of negotiating with people across the Mediterranean in an attempt to control new territories and gain access to trade routes, mercantile privileges, and the capital to produce the economy of exotic goods staged in texts like *Kallimachos* and *Floire et Blancheflor*. As literature would have it, cross-confessional marriage is certainly a space for religious conversion and the movement of religious empire, but even more than that, it is shown to be a space that opens new pathways to trade, exchange, and the creation of wealth. Moreover, texts like *Floire et Blancheflor* reveal exchanges in exoticism to be the very fabric of narrating nobility, entwining women's politics in cross-cultural marriage with the exchange and consumption of sumptuous goods and the production of stories about the glory of Mediterranean nobility.

By the mid-thirteenth century, when our incest romances make their appearance, the Moreot colonies were at their zenith, having by that point survived several generations of intermarriage and cross-cultural rule. But, if the combination of warfare, trickery, and cultural invective are any indication, peace was elusive and the majority of administrative efforts were spent trying to simply secure the succession of the colonies into hybridized French familial lines, suggesting that the overall preoccupation with the story of French nobility in our literary accounts – that is, with negotiating its place within a Mediterranean genealogy – has a certain historical resonance. Sterility, murder, and war plagued the ruling households of the Peloponnese, and, when coupled with the reproductive infelicity of many of the marriages, the picture that emerges is one in which the hold on the Greek territories was anything but steady, and was only possible by constant buttressing through marriages with the daughters of western families. The struggle against the "Romans," as the Byzantines are known in the *Morea*, was never ending, and, during a time when intermarriage with them in an attempt to secure peace was the standard, and differences between what were originally clearly Byzantine, Champenois, and other Frankish noble family lines were all but effaced, *Le Roman de la Manekine* and *La Belle Hélène de Constantinople* emerge as literary commentaries that establish eastern masculinity as twisted and distorted. This marks a thirteenth-century turn away from founding narratives of aristocracy based on Hellenism towards western narratives of identity seeking primacy over – but not through – Byzantium.

The *Morea*'s depictions of the difficulties of cross-cultural intermarriage resonate perhaps most strongly with *Floriant et Florete*, where real historical skirmishes over the future of the rich lands of Sicily are distorted into a struggle for empire staged through women's choices. Both *The Chronicle of Morea* and *Floriant et Florete* stray far from the actual facts of foreign invasions, uprisings, and eventual western domination of the territory; they reflect instead the difficulties of writing about all the different factions' and families' interests in joining and controlling a hybrid Mediterranean, where intermingling and trade form the very basis of medieval noble identity.

Going back, then, to the introductory example of Maria Argyropoulina and her woeful reception in Orseolo's Venetian court in the tenth century, our readings in exchanges in exoticism help us better theorize the space of her derision by Peter Damian – cross-cultural marriage – as an opportunity for cultural exchange. Through her introduction of new eating technologies and new cultural customs in her new court – through the importation not only of forks, but also of the expectation that her new home would adopt, produce, and use them, that she could reshape its culture and conduct – Maria's trivial trousseau becomes a marker for how marriage offered a unique space for exchange, in ways that underline how women unified the practices and construction of nobility around the Mediterranean.

Even, then, as scholars have recently theorized the Mediterranean as a corrupting sea, or as a space of varied practices closely tied to agricultural and geographic features in micro-climatic zones, readings in Old French and Medieval Greek literature suggest that there may have been several pathways that permitted cultural exchange, trade, and unity on a larger scale. In particular, the complicated and intertwined stories of genealogy and trade, represented through cross-cultural marriage and its effect on an economy of exoticism in texts like *Floire et Blancheflor*, *Digenis Akritas*, and even *Cligès*, suggest that the Mediterranean united people by their access to and desire for figuring their status through exotic, foreign goods, and through families extended through networks of marriage and baptism around its shores.

Women's choices form a backbone for understanding how cross-cultural marriage produced much more than what Gratian called a "special friendship" between men. Rather, cross-cultural marriage becomes a space intimately linked with the work of women in the making and breaking of empire, as they bring their own cultural expectations to bear on their new courts, and sometimes even reformulate men's plans to expand empire. Furthermore, women's choices – even when cloaked under the guise of ravishment, as in *Floriant et Florete*, *Digenis Akritas*, or the incest threat within the handless-girl story – represent the narrative underpinnings of the story of empires solidified through women's commentaries on masculinities. When women choose to love outwards and westwards, they choose to love and reproduce the structures of western empire, even as they sometimes are able to modify them but hardly ever escape them. Reading the exchanges of exoticism permitted by cross-cultural marriage suggests that romance is deeply dependent on the medieval Mediterranean, constructed through cross-cultural exchange with multiple easts in a set of interconnected practices to which women and their work make important contributions, and in which gender cannot be neglected.

Notes

Introduction

1 Nicetas Choniates, *O City of Byzantium: Annals of Niketas Choniates*, 317.
2 As Madden and Queller note, "Although, according to the crusaders' pact, the Great Palace was reserved for the winner of the imperial election, the opportunity to grasp it was too great for Boniface to pass up. The palace's inhabitants included the sister of Philip II of France, Agnes, who had been married to Alexius II, Andronicus I, and Theodore Branas. There was also the daughter of Bela III of Hungary, Margaret, the widow of Isaac II. On the condition that their lives be spared, the palace surrendered immediately to Boniface. Control of both the Great Palace and Margaret, whom he would soon marry, gave Boniface the look of an emperor, if not yet the title.' Donald E. Queller and Thomas F. Madden, *The Fourth Crusade: The Conquest of Constantinople*, 193–4.
3 Cavafy himself, for example, categorized one-third of his poetry under the rubric "Historical Poems," and several of these included poems in which he imagines himself directly in dialogue with important Byzantine rulers, including one which is a particularly scathing assessment of Byzantine imperial historiographer and princess Anna Komnene.
4 Patrick Geary, *The Myth of Nations: The Medieval Origins of Europe*. See also Fernand Braudel, *The Mediterranean and the Mediterranean World in the Age of Philip II*; Peregrine Horden and Nicholas Purcell, *The Corrupting Sea: A Study of Mediterranean History*.
5 For examples of the kinds of work on gender and knowledge in the Middle Ages – and particularly women's contributions – see Lesley Smith and Jane H.M. Taylor, eds., *Women and the Book: Assessing the Visual Evidence*; John Carmi Parsons, "Of Queens, Courts, and Books: Reflections on the Literary Patronage of Thirteenth-Century Plantagenet Queens"; Helen Solterer, *The Master and Minerva: Disputing Women in French Medieval Culture*.

6 Katherine Kong, *Lettering the Self in Medieval and Early Modern France*.

7 Gayle Rubin, "The Traffic in Women: Notes on the Political Economy of Sex."

8 Peter Damian, *Institutio Monialis*, 7.

9 Jonathon Shepard, "Marriages towards the Millenium," in *Byzantium in the Year 1000*, 5–9.

10 Many scholars have already worked on the relation between nation and gender in the Middle Ages, both within French and Byzantine Studies, and from many different perspectives, ranging from literary analysis to historiography to translation theory. I build upon this work to examine the intersections between what we nominally call being "French," "Mediterranean," "Byzantine," and "woman" in the twelfth and thirteenth centuries, to see how women might be redefining or bridging those categories. See Sharon Kinoshita, "Pagans Are Wrong and Christians Are Right: Alterity, Gender, and Nation in the *Chanson de Roland*"; Jeanette M.A. Beer, ed., *Translation Theory and Practice in the Middle Ages*; Liz James, *Women, Men, and Eunuchs: Gender in Byzantium and Empresses and Power in Early Byzantium* and "Goddess, Whore, Wife, or Slave: Will the Real Byzantine Empress Please Stand Up?"; Liz James and Barbara Hill, "Women and Politics in the Byzantine Empire: Imperial Women"; Karma Lochrie, Peggy McCracken, and James A. Schultz, *Constructing Medieval Sexuality*.

11 Constance Brittain Bouchard, *"Those of My Blood": Constructing Noble Families in Medieval Francia*; Georges Duby and Jacques Le Goff, eds., *Famille et parenté dans l'Occident médiéval*.

12 Bhabha writes, "Culture becomes as much an uncomfortable, disturbing practice of survival and supplementarity, between art and politics, past and present, the public and the private, as its resplendent being is a moment of pleasure, enlightenment or liberation. It from such narrative positions in-between cultures and nations, theories and texts, the political, the poetic and painterly, the past and the present, that post-colonial perspective seeks to affirm and extend a new inter-national dimension, both within the margins of the nation-space, and in the boundaries in-between nations and peoples." Homi K. Bhabha, *The Location of Culture*, xi.

13 For other perspectives, including how property was controlled and transmitted among very precise groups of people, see André Burguière, *A History of the Family*; Georges Duby, *Love and Marriage in the Middle Ages*; Duby and Le Goff, *Famille et parenté dans l'Occident médiéval*.

14 Paul Magdalino, "Medieval Constantinople: Built Environment and Urban Development."

15 See in particular the introduction to Constantinople in Devereaux, *Constantinople and the West.*

16 Robert de Clari, *La Conquête de Constantinople*, LXXXI.

17 W.J. Aerts, "*The Chronicle of the Morea* as a Mirror of a Crusaders' State at Work"; Jakob Philipp Fallmerayer, *Geschichte der Halbinsel Morea Während des Mittelalters*; Wolfgang Löhneysen, *Mistra: Griechenlands Schicksal im Mittelalter: Morea unter Franken, Byzantinern u. Osmanen*; Anastasia Stouraiti and Laura Marasso, *Immagini dal mito: la conquista veneziana della Morea (1684–1699).*

18 John Day, "The Levant Trade in the Middle Ages"; Angeliki E. Laiou, "Byzantine Trade with Christians and Muslims and the Crusades" and "Exchange and Trade, Seventh – Twelfth Centuries"; Klaus-Peter Matschke, "Commerce, Trade, Markets, and Money, Thirteenth – Fifteenth Centuries."

19 E. Jane Burns, *Courtly Love Undressed: Reading through Clothes in Medieval French Culture*; Sharon Kinoshita, *Medieval Boundaries: Rethinking Difference in Old French Literature.*

20 Devereaux, *Constantinople and the West in Medieval French Literature*, 20.

21 Noblewomen, however, did receive a very rudimentary education, permitting them not only to read but also to participate in the processes of commissioning manuscripts and serving as patrons of various vernacular literatures. See Susan Groag Bell, "Medieval Women Book Owners: Arbiters of Lay Piety and Ambassadors of Culture"; Helen Solterer, *The Master and Minerva: Disputing Women in French Medieval Culture*; June Hall McCash, ed., *The Cultural Patronage of Medieval Women*; Joan M. Ferrante, *To the Glory of Her Sex: Women's Roles in the Composition of Medieval Texts.*

22 Translation taken from Damian, "Institutio Monialis," PL 145, c. 744c; trans. taken from John Julius Norwich, *A History of Venice*, 60.

23 See, for example, William Prynne's critique of Charles I's French and Catholic queen consort, Henrietta Maria, in his seventeenth-century vitriolic diatribe against his queen, *Histriomastrix.*

24 Patricia Hill Collins, *Black Feminist Thought: Knowledge, Consciousness, and the Politics of Empowerment* and "Learning from the Outsider Within: The Sociological Significance of Black Feminist Thought"; Nancy C.M. Hartsock, "The Feminist Standpoint: Developing the Ground for a Specifically Feminist Historical Materialism"; Sara Ruddick, "Maternal Thinking as a Feminist Standpoint"; Sandra Harding, *Whose Science? Whose Knowledge?*

25 Cynthia H. Enloe, *Bananas, Beaches, and Bases: Making Feminist Sense of International Politics.*

26 Day, "The Levant Trade in the Middle Ages"; Laiou, "Byzantine Trade with Christians and Muslims and the Crusades" and "Exchange and Trade, Seventh – Twelfth Centuries"; Matschke, "Commerce, Trade, Markets, and Money, Thirteenth–Fifteenth Centuries."

27 Braudel, *The Mediterranean and the Mediterranean World in the Age of Philip II*; Horden and Purcell, *The Corrupting Sea: A Study of Mediterranean History*; Geary, *The Myth of Nations: The Medieval Origins of Europe*; Palmira Brummett, "Visions of the Mediterranean: A Classification"; Grant Parker, "Mapping the Mediterranean"; Valeria Finucci, ed., *Mapping the Mediterranean*; Marilyn Joyce Segal Chiat and Kathryn Reyerson, eds., *The Medieval Mediterranean: Cross-Cultural Contacts*; Steven Runciman, *The Sicilian Vespers: A History of the Mediterranean World in the Later Thirteenth Century*.

28 For examples, see María Rosa Menocal, *The Arabic Role in Medieval Literary History: A Forgotten Heritage*; Parsons, "Of Queens, Courts, and Books: Reflections on the Literary Patronage of Thirteenth-Century Plantagenet Queens"; Vincent Barletta, *Covert Gestures: Crypto-Islamic Literature as Cultural Practice in Early Modern Spain*. For background in considering the textuality of multilingualism and culture, see Erich Auerbach, *Literary Language and Its Public in Late Latin Antiquity and in the Middle Ages*.

29 In my call to think of medieval French literature's take on exchange and exoticism around the Mediterranean, I do not wish to insist on any kind of monoglossia, but rather I am interested in looking at the different approaches the different dialects contribute towards the formation of cross-cultural familial structures.

30 Suzanne Fleischman, "Medieval Vernaculars and the Myth of Monoglossia: A Conspiracy of Linguistics and Philology."

31 Karla Mallette, *The Kingdom of Sicily, 1100–1250: A Literary History*, 7.

1. Women and the Making of Mediterranean Identities in *Cligès* and Digenis Akritas

1 Chrétien de Troyes, *Cligès*, ed. Charles Méla, Olivier Collet, and Marie-Claire Gérard-Zai, 5970. Quotations throughout this chapter refer to this edition.

2 The Mediterranean inflection forged through intermarriage was all the more prevalent before the Fourth Lateran Council (1215) relaxed its prohibitions on intermarriage from an unwieldy seven degrees of kin affinity to a mere four, meaning that families that were turning far afield in search of suitable exogamous marriages were suddenly permitted to marry much closer to home. See chapter 4 of Rima Devereaux's *Constantinople and the West*, particularly pp. 75–80, where she enumerates cross-cultural

marriages between Byzantium and the West. See also Pierre Bonte, *Epouser au plus proche: inceste, prohibitions et stratégies matrimoniales autour de la Méditerranée*; Christopher N.L. Brooke, *The Medieval Idea of Marriage*; James A. Brundage, *Sex, Law, and Marriage in the Middle Ages*; Angeliki E. Laiou, ed., *Mariage, amour et parenté à Byzance aux XIe–XIIIe siècles*, vol. 7; Ruth Macrides, "Dynastic Marriages and Political Kinship."

3 Several scholars have examined hybridity in terms of dynastic and economic exchange. See, for example, Sandra Origone, "Marriage Connections between Byzantium and the West in the Age of the Palaiologoi."

4 While Bédier and Paris did individually write and lecture extensively about the impact of medieval literature in forming the modern monolithic French republic, Michelle Warren has shifted our assumptions about Bédier's medievalist nationalism by reading him and his nationalism from within his creole context. She writes that for Bédier, "the Middle Ages become the vanishing point of temporal and spatial ruptures … [France is] an immutable version of the nation that abandons no one." *Creole Medievalism: Colonial France and Joseph Bédier's Middle Ages*, 116. See also Patrick Geary, *The Myth of Nations: The Medieval Origins of Europe*.

5 See, for example, Lisa Lampert-Weissig, *Medieval Literature and Postcolonial Studies*; Kathleen Davis and Nadia Altschul, *Medievalisms in the Postcolonial World: The Idea of "the Medieval Ages" Outside Europe*; Patricia Clare Ingham and Michelle R. Warren, *Postcolonial Moves: Medieval through Modern*.

6 Homi K. Bhabha, *The Location of Culture*.

7 Jonathan Harris, *Byzantium and the Crusades*.

8 Unless otherwise noted, translations of Chrétien de Troyes into English are by Chrétien de Troyes and David Staines, *The Complete Romances of Chrétien de Troyes*.

9 In using the terms "greekness," "Greek," and "Byzantine," I follow the conventions of Old French literature, in which "Greek" (*griegois*) is most often conflated with "Byzantine." From Crusader account to romances to *romans antiques*, Old French literature is remarkably uninterested in treating this difference with any specificity. While of course there are many differences between ancient Greeks, contemporary medieval Greeks, and Byzantines, here I am using the terms in ways that resonate with an Old French literary approach. Greeks and Byzantines, however, referred to themselves as "Romans" because they identified themselves as the true followers of the Roman ecclesiastical tradition; they called the French the "Latins." For more on Greekness and nomenclature, see Alexander Kazhdan, "Latins and Franks in Byzantium: Perception and Reality from the Eleventh to the Twelfth Century."

10 This movement has been denigrated as a narrative distraction by some critics. Howard Bloch, for example, complains that cross-cultural marriage in *Cligès* creates "a general loss of narrative coherence. Plots and subplots are complexly intertwined, innumerable secondary characters share the stage with the principal protagonists, action ranges freely over eastern and western Europe, thus contributing to a general sense of disorientation." *Etymologies and Genealogies: A Literary Anthropology of the French Middle Ages*, 195. However, it is precisely the wide range of geographies and peoples invoked in *Cligès* that are of interest to me, for they offer a reading of romance that intersects with concerns of empire. Other scholars, too, have worked on the Byzantine focus of *Cligès*. See in particular Krijna Nelly Ciggaar, "Encore une fois Chrétien de Troyes et la 'matière byzantine': la révolution des femmes au palais de Constantinople"; Sharon Kinoshita, "The Poetics of *Translatio*: French-Byzantine Relations in Chrétien de Troyes's *Cligès*"; Peggy McCracken, "Love and War in *Cligès*."

11 Keith Busby et al., *Les Manuscrits de Chrétien de Troyes*. For another example of the importance of contextualized manuscript reading, see also John Dagenais, *The Ethics of Reading in Manuscript Culture: Glossing the "Libro de buen amor."*

12 Of course, *Cligès* also exists in several other manuscripts. For a complete overview, see Stewart Gregory and Claude Luttrell, "The Manuscripts of *Cligés*."

13 E. Jane Burns, *Courtly Love Undressed: Reading through Clothes in Medieval French Culture*.

14 See Jonathon Riley-Smith's in-depth studies of the causes and results of crusading in *The First Crusaders, 1095–1131* and "Early Crusaders to the East and the Costs of Crusading, 1095–1130."

15 Paul Magdalino, "Medieval Constantinople: Built Environment and Urban Development"; Krijna Nelly Ciggaar, *Western Travellers to Constantinople*.

16 As Sharon Kinoshita points out in her survey of Old French literature and its relation to its larger world context, "[i]f the prologue [of *Cligès*] makes France the center of the political and cultural world, the body of the romance slyly undercuts this brazenly hegemonic claim in the scattered and apparently gratiuitous mentions of Mediterranean sites." Kinoshita, "Worlding Medieval French," in McDonald and Suleiman, eds., *French Global*, 8–9.

17 *Translatio* involves not only translating, in the modern sense, but also editing and supplementing a text with stories and metaphors better suited for a new cultural, linguistic, and/or historical context. For a fuller explanation of *translatio* and its relationship to the project announced in

the prologue, see Michelle A. Freeman, *The Poetics of Translatio Studii and Conjointure: Chrétien de Troyes's "Cligés"*; Jeanette M.A. Beer and Kenneth Lloyd-Jones, eds., *Translation and the Transmission of Culture Between 1300 and 1600*; Kinoshita, "The Poetics of *Translatio*: French-Byzantine Relations in Chrétien de Troyes's *Cligès*"; Renate Blumenfeld-Kosinski, Luise Von Flotow-Evans, and Daniel Russell, eds., *The Politics of Translation in the Middle Ages and the Renaissance*; Christopher Baswell, "Marvels of Translation and Crises of Transition in the Romances of Antiquity"; Rupert Pickens, "Transmission et *translatio*: mouvement textuel et variance"; Lori Walters, "*Translatio Studii*: Christine de Pizan's Self-Portrayal in Two Lyric Poems and in the *Livre de la mutacion de Fortune*"; Douglas Kelly, "The *Fidus interpres*: Aid or Impediment to Medieval Translation and *Translatio*?"; William Kibler, "Translating Chrétien de Troyes: How Faithful?"; Jeanette M.A. Beer, ed., *Translation Theory and Practice in the Middle Ages*; Antoine Berman, "*Translatio studii* et pouvoir royal."

18 David Shirt, for example, critiques what he feels is an overhistoricization of marriage in *Cligès*. Shirt questions literary critics' attempts to trace Byzantium's influence on Chrétien's material, reminding us that some "critics maintain that the influence of some political scandal such as that arising out of the frustrated attempts by Manuel Komnenos, the Emperor of Constantinople, to marry off his daughter Maria to the eldest son of the Emperor of Germany, Frederick Barbarossa, is detectable." "Cligés – A Twelfth-Century Matrimonial Case-Book," 76. Charles Méla goes even further to assert in the introduction to his edition that "Cligès, le second roman de Chrétien de Troyes, est daté de 1176, pour des raisons d'actualité liées aux intrigues matrimoniales entre l'empereur d'Allemagne et de Constantinople, au plus vif de la lutte du Sacerdoce et de l'Empire, et aux démêlés de Frédéric Barberousse avec son cousin, Henri le Lion, le puissant duc de Saxe et de Bavière." Chrétien de Troyes, *Cligès*, 5.

19 Ciggaar, "Encore une fois Chrétien de Troyes et la 'matière byzantine'." For more on the life of Zoë Porphyrogenita, see Lynda Garland, "'The Eye of the Beholder': Byzantine Imperial Women and Their Public Image from Zoë Porphyrogenita to Euphrosyne Kamaterissa Doukaina (1028–1203)."

20 Cynthia H Enloe, *Bananas, Beaches, and Bases: Making Feminist Sense of International Politics*.

21 While more work remains on the links between Chrétien and Shakespeare, see Thomas Honegger, "'But-þat þou louye me, Sertes y dye fore loue of þe': Towards a Typology of Opening Moves in Courtly Amorous Interaction."

22 Ana-María Holzbacher, "Chrétien de Troyes: Una forma soterrada de misoginia"; Lynn Tarte Ramey, "Representations of Women in Chrétien's *Erec et Enide*: Courtly Literature or Misogyny?"; Z.P. Zaddy, "Chrétien misogyne."

23 While reading *Cligès* from women's perspectives reveals how much literature imagines women to contribute to the ideological work of cultural exchange, part of the work of this chapter is to read from another borderland perspective, to see how Byzantium itself imagines cross-cultural marriage on the frontier to facilitate exchange. *Cligès*, though clearly about the movement of knowledge, goods, and, ultimately, value, from east to west, through Fénice's imperialism coupled with the project of *translatio studii*, is written from the western perspective, with western expectations of what is good (the oath) and what is bad (disloyalty and greed). But part of the project of reconsidering how relations are stretched and maintained precisely by the connections anchoring the French-speaking nobility to their Greekness means reading from within Greek sources themselves, to understand how the past is represented and changed there, and to better understand literary representations of the increasingly Mediterraneanized nobility, and the concerns many kinds of literature express about the conflation of love and politics in border spaces.

24 Most critical work examines the production and reception of *Digenis* within the Byzantine literary tradition, paying particular attention to how it differs from the medieval tendency to reinterpret classical Greek narratives. See Paul Bancourt, "Etude de quelques motifs communs à l'épopée byzantine de *Digenis Akritis* et à *La chanson d'Aiol*"; Roderick Beaton and David Ricks, *Digenes Akrites: New Approaches to Byzantine Heroic Poetry*; Elizabeth Jeffreys and Michael Jeffreys, eds., *Popular Literature in Late Byzantium*; David Ricks, *Byzantine Heroic Poetry*; Barry Baldwin, "The description of Agamemnon in *Digenis Akrites*"; Henri Grégoire et al., Digenis Akritas*: The Byzantine Epic in History and Poetry*; Théologitis Homère-Alexandre, "*Digenis Akritas* et la littérature byzantine: problèmes d'approche"; Elizabeth Jeffreys, Digenis Akritis*: The Grottaferrata and Escorial Versions*.

25 *Digenis* exists in six very unique manuscripts, and scholars have long debated the dating and primacy of them. The two most complete and often-cited manuscripts are the Grottaferrata (Z.α XLIV (444), ff. 1r–773r), a late thirteenth-century manuscript on paper, and copied in southern Italy; and Escorial (Gr. 496 (Ψ.IΩ.22), ff. 139r-185v, 198r–201r), a later, perhaps fifteenth-century, version. There is also a lost Trebizond manuscript: Athens, National Library 1074, ff. 1–189; Thessaloniki, University Library 27, ff. 1–101; and Oxford, Lincoln College 24, ff. 10r–107r. For more detailed information, see the introduction to Elizabeth Jeffrey's edition.

26 It is unlikely that either text was directly influenced by the other, for few western writers or crusaders could read or write Greek in the Middle Ages, there is no evidence that the manuscripts of either texts travelled extensively, and most scholars have not even thought to pair them because they were written so far apart and in such different circumstances. There have, however, been several comparative studies. See Leon Stratikis, "Byzantium and France: The Twelfth-Century Renaissance and the Birth of the Medieval Romance"; Ciggaar, "Encore une fois Chrétien de Troyes et la 'matière byzantine'"; Panagiotis A. Agapitos and Ole Langwitz Smith, *The Study of Medieval Greek Romance: A Reassessment of Recent Work.*

27 I do not refer to the ways in which cultures were mixing through not only the exchange of ideas and warriors, but also genetically in the creation of crusader colonies and newly extended kin networks stretching from western France to Palestine.

28 For more on medieval rape law, especially in Byzantium, see Angeliki Laiou, *Mariage, amour et parenté à Byzance aux XIe–XIIIe siècles* and "Sex, Consent, and Coercion in Byzantium"; Anna Roberts, ed., *Violence against Women in Medieval Texts.*

29 *Digenis Akritis: The Grottaferrata and Escorial Versions*, ed. Elizabeth Jeffreys. See introduction.

30 For general historical contextualization, see Paul Magdalino, "*Digenis Akrites* and Byzantine Literature: The Twelfth-Century Background to the Grottaferrata Version." For diverse treatments of the place of abduction as staged in *Digenis* and within Byzantine society, see Michael Angold, "The Wedding of *Digenis Akrites*: Love and Marriage in Byzantium in the Eleventh and Twelfth Centuries"; Roderick Beaton, *The Medieval Greek Romance*, 60–1; Laiou, "Sex, Consent, and Coercion in Byzantium," 200–3. As Laiou points out, when marriage is involved, interpretation (both legal and textual) must shift towards understanding the abduction as elopement, even if the immediate kin behave as if it were a question of abduction.

31 Kathryn Gravdal, *Ravishing Maidens: Writing Rape in Medieval French Literature and Law.*

32 Digenis himself is in fact a borderland figure in this regard, at once a valiant fighter and a murderous rapist who violates two women (one a fallen maiden abandoned by her lover in a desert oasis, the other an Amazonian warrior) and then goes back after the fact to murder the latter and assuage his guilty conscience. Certainly the rapes have few consequences for Digenis, as his wife forgives him and there are no problematic progeny or injured kinsmen to protest. The women he rapes are both cast-offs from their families in one way or another, and as such do not even have legal recourse, as they were unaccompanied outside of the family home.

It is unclear whether Byzantines themselves would have considered this rape. Since the first woman had already consented to her own rapt and seduction by her erstwhile lover (and was therefore no longer part of her father's household or a virgin), it was not theoretically possible to rape her – she could not claim the status that would permit an accusation of sexual violation. The Amazon was a virgin, but a foreigner and self-empowered, and was not accompanied by other men, so her rape would not violate their claims to her. Yet Digenis himself clearly identifies his acts as immoral, for he burns with shame at both his desire and how he assuaged it, and he even kills the Amazon in order to silence the story of the rape and prevent his own shaming. Whether or not these acts would have constituted rape in the eyes of society, Byzantine law clearly would not have considered these two acts rape. The perplexing and dual-faceted nature of Digenis's attitude towards women is hard for critics to explain; some dismiss its presence as bad scribal work in compiling the various Akritic songs, while others attribute it to a desire to dominate all things on the frontier or see it as a possibility for showcasing the powers of contrition and penance. On the former, see Jeffrey's analysis in the introduction to the critical edition; for the latter, see Sarah Ekdawi, Patricia Fann, and Elli Philokyprou, "Bold Men, Fair Maids and Affronts to Their Sex: The Characterization and Structural Roles of Men and Women in the Escorial *Digenis Akritis*." See also Joelle Beaucamp, "La situation juridique de la femme à Byzance."

33 Anna Comnena, *The Alexiad of Anna Comnena*, 3:146.8. For critical commentary on cultural perceptions of Hellenism, Byzantianism, and nomenclature, see Anthony Kaldellis, *Hellenism in Byzantium: The Transformations of Greek Identity and the Reception of the Classical Tradition*.

34 Ralph J. Hexter, *Equivocal Oaths and Ordeals in Medieval Literature*; Kaldellis, *Hellenism in Byzantium*. See also romances written in Old French, in which a vassal's position at court is inaugurated and affirmed through the oath of loyalty, as in Chrétien de Troyes's *Erec et Enide, Lancelot, Yvain, Perceval,* and *Cligès*.

35 For recent work on medieval masculinities and how they are culturally specific performances of identities, see Jeffrey Jerome Cohen and Bonnie Wheeler, eds., *Becoming Male in the Middle Ages*; D.M. Hadley, ed., *Masculinity in Medieval Europe*; Clare A. Lees, Thelma S. Fenster, and Jo Ann McNamara, eds., *Medieval Masculinities: Regarding Men in the Middle Ages*; Jacqueline Murray, *Conflicted Identities and Multiple Masculinities: Men in the Medieval West*; Ruth Mazo Karras, *From Boys to Men: Formations of Masculinity in Late Medieval Europe*.

36 Bloch, *Etymologies and Genealogies: A Literary Anthropology of the French Middle Ages.*

37 Speech act theory focuses on the ways that speech actually enacts something (like the act of naming a ship, or conferring a noble title) rather than merely reporting something (like describing the ceremony of naming). See J.L. Austin, *How to Do Things with Words;* Shoshana Felman, *Le Scandale du corps parlant: Don Juan avec Austin, ou, la séduction en deux langues;* Judith P. Butler, *Excitable Speech: A Politics of the Performative;* Jacques Derrida, *Limited Inc.*

38 Byzantine courtly administration was very different from western feudal models. Nicholas Oikonomedes writes that "[t]he principal item of expenditure for the state was, of course, salaries, which constituted the means for channeling money to the general public. All senior officials and military commanders, most of the holders of titles of honor, many civil servants, and all army officers when engaged in operations of any kind received a salary (*roga*), great or small, distributed by the emperor or his representative, usually on Palm Sunday and in Holy Week. This handout emphasized the personal relationship between the recipient of the salary and the emperor." Nicolas Oikonomides, "The Role of the Byzantine State in the Economy," 1101. See also Jean-Claude Cheynet, Elisabeth Malamut, and Cécile Morrisson, "Prix et salaires dans les sources byzantines (Xe–XVe siècle)." For more on monetary practices in Byzantine court culture, see Angeliki E. Laiou, ed., *The Economic History of Byzantium;* Henry Maguire, *Byzantine Court Culture from 829 to 1204,* 200.

39 Nicetas Choniates, *O City of Byzantium: Annals of Niketas Choniates;* Michael Psellos, *Chronographie, ou Histoire d'un siècle de Byzance (976–1077);* Anna Comnena, *The Alexiad of the Princess Anna Comnena.*

40 *Le Roman de Thèbes: édition du manuscrit S* (Londres, Brit. Libr., Add. 34114), ed. Francine Mora-Lebrun.

41 Translation mine.

42 The theme is interspersed throughout the *Roman d'Alexandre,* but perhaps best represented in the epilogue, when the narrator comments that "proëce et largesce font bien terre tenir / Ice fist Alixandre essaucier et tehir, / Car il conquist le mont trestout a son plaisir" [Prowess and generosity help govern a country / these are the qualities that helped Alexander mature and expand his empire, / because [through them] he conquered the entire world'] (1635–7). Alexandre de Paris, *Le Roman d'Alexandre,* ed. E.C. Armstrong and Laurence Harf-Lancner.

43 For other approaches to this same topic, and especially for more on the function of the east in this romance, see Ciggaar, "Encore une fois Chrétien

de Troyes et la 'matière byzantine': la révolution des femmes au palais de Constantinople"; Leslie Dunton-Downer, "The Horror of Culture: East-West Incest in Chrétien de Troyes's *Cligès*."

44 Conversely, as Fénice disrupts the role of the good wife, and works pointedly outside of the paradigms of diplomatic negotiation and spousal support theorized by Enloe, her condemnation by Chrétien becomes a condemnation of her husband's inability to read her actions. His control and power over his wife – as metonymy for his household and his empire – are essential to his success as a ruler.

45 Again, in this textual context, "Romans" refers to Byzantines. For more on this nomenclature, see the introduction. The terminology is pointedly politicized, and often full of invective, as here when it refers to embattled borderlands. Krijna Ciggaar, for example, suggests that "[t]he Greeks were often considered to be arrogant and effeminate, the Latins were, in the eyes of the Greeks, uncultured people." Ciggaar, *Western Travellers to Constantinople*, 19.

2. Exchanging Exoticism

1 Portions of this chapter have appeared in an earlier form in a preliminary essay, Megan Moore, "Boundaries and Byzantines in the Old French *Floire et Blancheflor*." I am also grateful for the critique it received at the Newberry Library's Fellows' Seminar in 2009.

2 Though much recent work offers insights into constructions of east(s) in medieval literature, Byzantium and other middle grounds are left largely unexplored. For the latest work on *Floire et Blancheflor*, see Marla Segol, "*Floire et Blancheflor*: Courtly Hagiography or Radical Romance?"; Huguette Clain-Legros, *La Rose et le lys: étude littéraire du Con Floire et -p Blancheflor*; Patricia E. Grieve, *"Floire et Blancheflor" and the European Romance*; Peter Haidu, "Narrative Structure in *Floire et Blancheflor*"; Merton Jerome Hubert, ed., *The Romance of Floire and Blanchefleur: A French Idyllic Poem of the Twelfth Century*; Norris Lacy, "The Flowering (and Misreading) of Romance: *Floire et Blancheflor*."

3 The Mediterranean is extremely important to understanding *Floire et Blancheflor*. Even as the action of the romance moves from an ambiguous pagan court (presumably Muslim Spain) along the Mediterranean to Cairo and back to Hungary, the romance itself calls out to so many Mediterranean themes – trade, exchange, exoticism, all figured through references to Byzantium and other easts – that it becomes clear that thinking of it as a strictly Spanish story simply does not suffice. It must be read for its intertexts to a larger Mediterranean context of trade and heritage.

4 Sharon Kinoshita, *Medieval Boundaries*.
5 E. Jane Burns, *Courtly Love Undressed*, 212. Burns, for example, details the kinds of work women do in creating and exchanging exotic foreign textiles, but her more recent work focuses on production and consumption on either end of the religious divide, for example in Muslim Spain and Christian Europe. While Burns is clearly arguing for a more complex hybridity within the locales of "courtly west" and "mercantile east," such terms themselves can obscure and collapse the variety of religious and cultural identity in these very locales. Cairo, though certainly a location of extraordinary medieval trade, was by no means the only "mercantile east" invoked in medieval texts; often, in fact, the wonders of Constantinople rivalled those of Egypt, particularly in textile manufacturing and consumption.
6 See, for example, Kinoshita's remarkable analysis of *Floire et Blancheflor* in her recent book, *Medieval Boundaries*. Kinoshita points to such an analysis herself, but works within the confines of Islam: "the uncanny physical resemblance between the titular protagonists – one a Saracen prince, the other a Christian slave – [reads] as an allegory for the intense interconnection between medieval Islamic and Latin Christian cultures" (10).
7 There is already a substantial body of scholarship that examines the economic connections between many Mediterranean trading centres. In particular, there is a plethora of recent work in the economic history of the Mediterranean, which focuses on both micro-economies along the seashore and macro-economic studies of the ways the sea impacted all aspects of life around its shores. And of course historians are well aware of trading networks, political contacts, and religious differences with Byzantium. See, for example, Peregrine Horden and Nicholas Purcell, *The Corrupting Sea: A Study of Mediterranean History*; Fernand Braudel, *The Mediterranean and the Mediterranean World in the Age of Philip II*; Gilbert Dagron, "The Urban Economy, Seventh – Twelfth Centuries"; John Day, "The Levant Trade in the Middle Ages"; Angeliki E. Laiou, ed., *The Economic History of Byzantium from the Seventh through the Fifteenth Century* and Laiou, "Exchange and Trade, Seventh–Twelfth Centuries"; Paul Magdalino, "Medieval Constantinople: Built Environment and Urban Development"; Klaus-Peter Matschke, "Commerce, Trade, Markets, and Money, Thirteenth–Fifteenth Centuries"; Cécile Morrisson and Jean-Claude Cheynet, "Prices and Wages in the Byzantine World"; Pierre Toubert, "Byzantium and the Mediterranean Agrarian Civilization."
8 For more on my conceptualization of exoticism, please see the discussion of it in the introduction. I do not mean to invoke concepts of Orientalism

per se, but am interested in ways that the foreign other can be appropriated to construct the noble self.

9 Edward W. Said, *Orientalism*.

10 Dated to between 1150 and 1160 by most critics and recently called by Norris Lacy "one of the earliest of French romances," *Floire et Blancheflor* exists in several manuscripts and two basic versions (an older, so-called aristocratic version and a newer, common version) in French, and it was subsequently translated into medieval Spanish, Middle English, Middle High German, Flemish, Czech, Icelandic, Italian, Norse, Greek, and Yiddish. That the story exists in so many versions and so many copies may testify to its popularity. See Lacy, "The Flowering (and Misreading) of Romance," 19.

11 "Exotic" is of course an anachronistic term for describing wonder in the face of the foreign; it is, however, a sentiment that medieval people seem to have experienced, as detailed in Caroline Walker Bynum, "Wonder." I follow Bynum's lead in using modern terminologies, which, while not used by medievals, help us to formulate reactions to the foreign in the medieval period.

12 The principal edition consulted here is *Le Conte de Floire et Blanchefleur: roman pré-courtois du milieu du XIIe siècle*, ed. Jean-Luc Leclanche; secondary consultations from *Floire et Blancheflor: Edition du ms. 19152 du fonds français avec introduction, notes et glossaire*, ed. Margaret Pelan. Principal translation consulted is Hubert, *The Romance of Floire and Blanchefleur: A French Idyllic Poem of the Twelfth Century*. Translations are mine, unless otherwise indicated.

13 Moore, "Boundaries and Byzantines," 4–5.

14 Perhaps more importantly, the mutability of the court itself – the space it offers Blancheflor's mother to transform and blend into pagan society, and then, later, the mutability of the court's religious practices themselves – suggests that the noble court is inherently a space for change, for transformation. The frame narrative, which seems to clearly delineate between pagans and Christians and to set up their interaction as conflict, instead actually constructs a courtly milieu in which cross-cultural exchange and transformation are the norm.

15 In MS 1447, the so-called popular version, which I discuss later in this chapter, the term "pagan" is interchangeably used with "saracen" and "muslim." The ambiguity is unique to BnF Fr. 375, the oldest manuscript copy, and one which critics have called "aristocratic" for its depiction of the love relationship over military concerns. Though not my purpose here,

it would be interesting to read the evolution of this story in tandem with the deepening historical concerns with the Mediterranean easts as the Crusades progress.

16 Of course there are many other cultural referents underlying the truly Mediterranean flavour of *Floire et Blancheflor*; I am focusing on the ways that Byzantium helps us rethink our often black-and-white readings of encounter and difference in Mediterranean noble milieux. Though beyond the ken of this study, it would be very interesting to explore further the invocation of Hungary within several of the courts and texts in this study. Similarly, medieval Bulgaria's role as a grey space, like that of Byzantium, should also be fully explored in the context of reading western romance.

17 Burns, *Courtly Love Undressed*, 214.

18 Kinoshita, *Medieval Boundaries*, 88–9.

19 One has only to look at the many surviving manuscripts of *Floire et Blancheflor* to see that this story of exotic gift giving and cross-cultural love was indeed very popular; that the story is often paired with other texts interested in Byzantines and Greeks merely underlines the rising popularity of the old classic tales, most clearly depicted in the *romans d'antiquité*, like the *Aeneas*, the *Roman de Troie*, and the *Roman de Thèbes*, also found in BnF Fr. 375. See also footnote 23 for more information.

20 Vincent Barletta argues a similar point that from Seneca onwards, the Greek story of Troy was a foundational genealogical myth that played a fundamental role in articulating the greatness of western noble identity, in particular in Rome. See *Death in Babylon: Alexander the Great and Iberian Empire in the Muslim Orient*, 60–4.

21 Though Terry Nixon argues that the *Roman de Troie*, another Old French tale about this founding narrative, is a story essentially about the foundation of Rome, and that is certainly one way of interpreting it, I am more interested in the general notion of the movement of culture, in the way that the story is deployed, than in the way it tells a story either about Troy or, as Nixon argues, about Rome. "Romance Collections and the Manuscripts of Chrétien de Troyes," 22.

22 Several Old French romances, for example, imagine noble families in medieval France to claim their glory by their genealogical relation to the fabled figure of Aeneas. The Aeneas story, while ostensibly about the mythic feats of the victor at Troy, becomes in the medieval imagination a story of the grandeur of medieval French bloodlines and the basis for their claims to control French land. As Christopher Baswell points out, "the Eneas makes the attachment of land to a new race a central theme, carefully looking

forward … to its extension and link to Trojan blood through Eneas's offspring." *Virgil in Medieval England: Figuring the Aeneid from the Twelfth Century to Chaucer*, 202. A similar argument can be made for the Alexander romance as a foundational story of western noble glory, as pointed out in Barletta's *Death in Babylon*. For historical readings of genealogy, and the actual formation of tenth- through twelfth-century Frankish families, see Constance Brittain Bouchard, *"Those of My Blood": Constructing Noble Families in Medieval Francia*.

23 The Old French manuscripts include BnF Fr. 375, fol 247v–254r – *Floire et Blancheflor, Cligés, Erec, Guillaume d'Angleterre, Blancandrin, Roman de Troie, Amadas et Ydoine*. Dated at 1288, according to the mss.; BnF Fr. 1447 – fol 1r–20v – *Floire et Blancheflor, Berte aus grans pies, Claris et Laris*, dated to first half of the 14th century. BnF Fr. 12562 – fol 69r–89v – *Roman de la dame a la Licorne, Floire et Blancheflor*; 14th and 15th centuries. BnF Fr. 19152 – fol. 193r–205v – 13th century. Vatican – MS Pal. Lat. 1971, fol. 85r–90v – *Amadas et Idoine, Brut, Aspremont, Floire et Blancheflor*. On the history of the poem, see the introduction to Hubert, *"The Romance of Floire and Blanchefleur": A French Idyllic Poem of the Twelfth Century*, especially p. 22.

24 Most scholars agree on a dating of 1288. See: Hans Robert Jauss and Erich Köhler, *Le Roman jusqu'à la fin du XIIIè*.

25 While the composition and subsequent binding of *Floriant et Florete* were about 150 years apart, and while of course we cannot superimpose thirteenth-century viewpoints onto a twelfth-century text, the binding suggests that we consider the text in a much broader Mediterranean context, at the very least, and it is one interpretation of how medieval people might have understood such a text. For more codicological and paleographical evidence, see Keith Busby et al., *Les manuscrits de Chrétien de Troyes*. In particular, see chapter 1, by Terry Nixon, "Romance Collections and the Manuscripts by Chrétien de Troyes," where Nixon argues that larger format codices in which secular texts like *Floire et Blancheflor* and *Cligès* were grouped together "show a new interest in creating larger thematic units of literary works" (19).

26 Ibid., 64. The dating of the manuscript is confusing, mostly because the date given within the manuscript is one that falls between the liturgical years of 1288 and 1289, and the name of the scribe is in conflict with death records from those years. Scholars increasingly point towards MS 375 as a copy of an older manuscript, which Jehan Madot (or Madoc, as Busby et. al argue) might then have copied. It seems likely, whatever the precise dating, that the manuscript was a programmatic attempt to copy an earlier exemplar, in which these texts were already gathered together. This would

only further suggest that one of the ways that medieval audiences understood texts was under a rubric of things about ancient Greece and Rome, and that they did so even earlier than 1288. On scribal history, see also Charles François, "Perrot de Nesle, Jehan Madot, et le Ms. B.N. Fr. 375."

27 And, unless otherwise noted, all of the passages I cite can be found in both versions; I am not arguing for differences in plot, but for differences in codicological framing. I am claiming that codicology can indicate how medieval readers might have approached the thematics of the story, and each manuscript offers a different context for what is essentially very similar material.

28 It is particularly interesting to consider this codex in its thirteenth-century context, for after the fall of Constantinople to the Crusaders in 1204, relations between French-speaking families and Byzantine nobility became understandably very strained. Several Frankish families had both territorial and trading interests in the eastern Latin empire, some even holding crusader colonies there. It is no wonder that thirteenth-century scribes and binders sought to create a grouping of texts with interests in figuring the east, and in particular, with interests in exploring how cross-cultural encounter might permit the exchange of ideas and the transformation of noble identities.

29 See *De Ceremoniis Aulae Byzantinae*, 2;15: 566. Commentary and analysis in Gerard Brett, "The Automata in the Byzantine 'Throne of Solomon'"; Helen C. Evans and William D. Wixom, *The Glory of Byzantium: Art and Culture of the Middle Byzantine Era, A.D. 843–1261*.

30 See J. Douglas Bruce, "Human Automata in Classical Tradition and Mediaeval Romance," 512; Brett, "The Automata in the Byzantine 'Throne of Solomon.'" As Laskarina Bouras has suggested, the Arabs were the only ones writing medieval technical treatises on the actual construction of automata; however, I wish to understand how literary representations associate them with their historical roots in Hellenic culture and what kind of exotic world they are meant to invoke and authorize. Laskarina Bouras, "Dragon Representations on Byzantine Phialae and Their Conduits," 67.

31 Brett, "The Automata in the Byzantine 'Throne of Solomon.'" Brett, too, sees the primacy of Byzantium in the medieval appreciation of automata, claiming that "if further proof were needed that it was the Byzantine automata that influenced the West, it lies in the fact that roaring lions are to be found there in addition to singing birds" (486).

32 Liutprand writes: "Aerea sed deaurata quaedam arbor ante Imperatoris oculos stabat, cujus ramos itidem aereae diversi generis deaurataeque volucres replebant, quae secundum species suas diversarum avium voces

emittebant" (*Antapodis* VI:5, 147). See also the remarks about the Byzantine attempt to impress outsiders with palace machinery made by Angeliki Laiou in her introduction to the volume of the same name, "Writing the Economic History of Byzantium."

33 Paul Aebischer, ed. *Le Voyage de Charlemagne à Jerusalem et à Constantinople.*

34 Translations of Clari are from Edward Stone, *Three Old French Chronicles of the Crusades.*

35 Robert de Clari, *La Conquête de Constantinople*, ed. Jean Dufournet (Paris: Champion, 2004), XC.

36 E. Kriaras, *Byzantina ippotika mythistorhmata, Velthandros*, vv. 243–54.

37 Translations are cited from Gavin Betts, *Three Medieval Greek Romances.*

38 For the Greek version, see Kriaras, *Byzantina ippotika mythistorhmata*, 2. Here I want to stress that there are probably dozens of unedited manuscripts of more contemporary Byzantine romances, fictional narratives, plays, and poems. Panagiotis Agapitos, for example, has suggested to me that these texts run very much in the vein of the recently edited and published texts of *Kallimachos* and *Velthandros*, in that some of them, too, celebrate love quests amid fantastic and luxurious scenery.

39 The Greek narratives I discuss here are most likely from the thirteenth century. There is still much discussion about the actual date of the stories involved; some scholars have suggested to me in personal correspondence that the texts could date from the twelfth or early thirteenth centuries; others find them to be much later. In the English translations of *Velthandros and Chrysandza*, for example, Gavin Betts dates the stories from the late fourteenth century. For recent work on medieval Greek narratives, see Panagiotis A. Agapitos and Ole Langwitz Smith, *The Study of Medieval Greek Romance: A Reassessment of Recent Work.* See also Roderick Beaton, *The Medieval Greek Romance.* Agapitos claims that textual innovations in Byzantine romances might be explained "as a socio-cultural result of a simultaneously progressive and regressive attitude of Orthodox Byzantine society towards its new Islamic and Catholic neighbours, an attitude dictated in different ways by the shock of 1204 and the loss of Constantinople" (51).

40 Charles Antoine Gidel and Wilhelm Wägner, *Medieval Greek Texts: Being a Collection of the Earliest Compositions in Vulgar Greek Prior to the Year 1500.*

41 Lynn Jones and Henry Maguire, "A Description of the Jousts of Manuel I Komnenos." On the use of judicial combat and jousting in Byzantium, see Robert Bartlett, *Trial by Fire and Water: The Medieval Judicial Ordeal;* Michael Angold, "The Interaction of Latins and Byzantines during the Period of the Latin Empire (1204–1261): The Case of the Ordeal."

42 See, for example, W.J. Aerts, "A Byzantine Traveller to One of the Crusader States," 166.

43 Though men's bodies are not the place for writing masculinity or for contesting personal valour, women's bodies are, as usual, *en jeu* and in danger. The world of *Floire et Blancheflor*, for all its ambiguity and gender play, is still ultimately one predicated on the narrative of abduction, on the threat of rape, in the sense that Kathryn Gravdal details in her study *Ravishing Maidens*. What is interesting, however, is that this threat does not permit the articulation of masculinity through physical combat between men, but of nobility predicated on gifts exchanged in cross-cultural trade and encounter.

44 Jane Gilbert, "Boys Will Be ... What? Gender, Sexuality, and Childhood in *Floire et Blancheflor* and *Floris et Lyriope*"; Lacy, "The Flowering (and Misreading) of Romance: *Floire et Blancheflor*"; Karen J. Taylor, ed., *Gender Transgressions: Crossing the Normative Barrier in Old French Literature.*

45 See in particular Burns, *Courtly Love Undressed*; Clain-Legros, *La Rose et le lys*, 31; William Kibler, "Archetypal Imagery in *Floire et Blancheflor*."

46 Kathleen Coyne Kelly, "The Bartering of Blauncheflur in the Middle English *Floris and Blauncheflur*," 110.

47 While the men in *Cligès*, *Yvain*, or *Lancelot* or any of the *romans d'antiquité* do bring some gifts with them, the narrative devotes itself to detailing the ways that men prepare the accoutrements of war: horses, food, armour, shields, swords in almost ritualistic manner. I would read these rituals as part of making or marking knightly masculinity – the external signs of how masculinity is practised and how one becomes the good knight.

48 For a more detailed comparison of Byzantine and western relationships to the gift, see chapter 1.

49 One way to further conceptualize the functions of literary objects like the golden goblet and other goods traded for narrative in *Floire et Blancheflor* is to simultaneously think of how gifts enact relations of power, as when they are political gifts like the sardonyx golden chalice given to the French crusaders in Anna Komnena's *Alexiad*. This formulation of the gift follows Marcel Mauss's notion that the gift entails and requires reciprocal exchange, that it creates relationships of power between the giver and the receiver. See Mauss, *The Gift: the Form and Reason for Exchange in Archaic Societies*. But Anthony Cutler has recently responded to Mauss's theory within the context of Byzantine historiography, and I agree with him both that "purposive and ostensibly precise [Byzantine gift registers] reveal an attitude toward gift giving and gift-recording that is fundamentally economic," rather than inherently symbolic, and that "despite the huge

value imputed to [imperial purple silks], it may well be misleading when dealing with medieval objects to treat them as constituting either economic or symbolic capital." Anthony Cutler, "Gifts and Gift Exchange as Aspects of the Byzantine, Arab, and Related Economies," 258.

50 Ruth Karras argues that there was no one dominant narrative about masculinity, and that many of the masculinities were highly specific to class; here, knightly masculinity is invoked because Floire's departure from his father's court is structured like a quest and invokes the traditional topoi of knighthood, only to later break with them. *From Boys to Men: Formations of Masculinity in Late Medieval Europe*, 3–5.

51 In many ways, the iterations of the innkeeper scenes create a Derridean moment, in which masculinity comes into being through its iterability, as a narrative created through the repetition of exchanges in the exotic between Floire and his hosts. It marks masculinity as ultimately tied to iterability, but that also makes it inherently unstable and subject to negotiation.

52 Burns, *Courtly Love Undressed*, 219.

53 See, for example, pseudo-historical chronicles and fictional texts like *Le Roman de Thèbes: édition du manuscrit S* (Londres, Brit. Libr., Add. 34114), ed. Francine Mora-Lebrun; *Le Pèlerinage de Charlemagne*; Graindor de Douai, *La Chanson d'Antioche*. On wonder, see Bynum, "Wonder."

54 In a description from Anna Comnena, an imperial Byzantine princess and court historian, for example, the Byzantine emperor seeks an alliance with the German emperor in an attempt to stymie Robert's advance on Byzantine territories. In exchange for his co-operation, the German emperor is guaranteed that "[a]s a token of friendship we are sending your Highness together with the other presents a gold pectoral cross inset with pearls and a gold pyx which contains relics of several saints, each of which can be recognized by the card attached to it; a chalice of sardonyx, a crystal goblet, a radiated crown of gold … and some Balm of Mecca" (III: 93). Anna's descriptions point to a moment at which Byzantines leverage westerners' perceptions of the exotic in trade and political manoeuvring. Here her historiography moves away from describing Byzantine treasures, turning towards detailing the ways that emperors leveraged exotic goods (such as the Balm of Mecca or sardonyx chalices) as political capital. In the political realm of the Byzantine court, exotic goods become commercialized through storytelling about them. The exotic thus becomes a marketable quantity that has political and monetary value that the nobility is talking about and exchanging in order to create themselves as powerful noble subjects.

55 On the manuscript tradition, see the introduction in Patricia Grieve, *"Floire et Blancheflor" and the European Romance*. See also Marie-Françoise Alamichel, "Introduction à Floris and Blancheflour" http://www.cema.paris-sorbonne.fr/cema1/Floris_et_BlancheflourIntro.pdf .

56 Richard H. Rouse and Mary A. Rouse, *Manuscripts and Their Makers: Commercial Book Producers in Medieval Paris 1200–1500*, 99–103. Their reading depends in part on the envoi at the end of the piece, which is ten lines long and dedicated to Robert d'Artois, who became the special protector of Blanche de Castille and Marie de Brabant, and whose connection to Tunisia (and hence the Arabian Nights) occurred because of his participation in the Crusades there (103).

57 Ibid., 102. Note that the story is usually attributed to Adenet le Roi, the man shown listening to the female narrator in the illuminations.

58 Ibid., 126.

59 On genealogical patterns, see Bouchard, *"Those of My Blood": Constructing Noble Families in Medieval Francia*; Georges Duby and Jacques Le Goff, eds., *Famille et parenté dans l'Occident médiéval*; R. Howard Bloch, *Etymologies and Genealogies: A Literary Anthropology of the French Middle Ages*; Philippe Ariès et al., *Histoire de la vie privée*.

60 BnF Fr. 1447, fol. 1r.

61 Although historically noblewomen had nurses and other caregivers to help rear their children, there is ample evidence to suggest that they played a key role in overseeing them and often had strong bonds with their children. In her discussion of Adela of Blois, Kimberly LoPrete argues that "affective bonds could be forged between noble spouses or mothers and children, and … aristocratic parents invested in their children, both psychologically and materially. […] A sense of common interest and mutual obligation could be inculcated from childhood in sons as well as daughters." LoPrete, "Adela of Blois as Mother and Countess," 314–15. See also *Les Relations de parenté dans le monde médiéval*; Georges Duby and Jacques Le Goff, "Famille et parenté dans l'Occident médiéval"; Angeliki E. Laiou, ed., *Mariage, amour et parenté à Byzance aux XIe–XIIIe siècles*; Mary Dockray-Miller, *Motherhood and Mothering in Anglo-Saxon England*; John Carmi Parsons and Bonnie Wheeler, eds., *Medieval Mothering*.

62 Chryssi Bourbou and Sandra J. Gavrie-Lok, "Breastfeeding and Weaning Patterns in Byzantine Times: Evidence from Human Remains and Written Sources," 67–73; Avner Giladi, *Infants, Parents and Wet Nurses: Medieval Islamic Views on Breastfeeding and Their Social Implications*; Mary Douglas, *Purity and Danger: An Analysis of the Concepts of Pollution and Taboo*; Peggy

McCracken, *The Curse of Eve, the Wound of the Hero: Blood, Gender, and Medieval Literature.*

63 Chrétien interjects, elaborating that while Enide's cousin "n'ot del celer cure; / bien li reconta l' avanture / tot mot a mot sanz antrelais mes a reconter vos an lais, / por ce que d' enui croist son conte / qui deus foiz une chose conte" (6269–74)[told her the adventure word for word, without omission ... [I] pass over it now, because he who tells a story twice makes his tale now tiresome]. Chrétien de Troyes, *Erec et Enide.*

3. Masculinities and the Geographies of Empire in Thirteenth-Century Incest Romances

1 Thirteenth-century Old French historical sources represented Byzantium in an almost uniquely negative light, in a move that modern historians interpret as an attempt to justify the sacking and burning of one of the most important cities in Christendom by fellow Christians. Some western clergy participating in the initial raids on the city inflamed the western forces by claiming that the Byzantines were worse than the Jews. Innocent III's continual call for peace was suppressed by the clergy and remained unknown to the crusader armies; at the urging of their leaders, the crusaders finally attacked in 1204. For an overview of the political changes affecting Franco-Byzantine relationships and contributing to the fall of Constantinople during the Crusades, see Deno John Geanakoplos, *Byzantium: Church, Society, and Civilization Seen through Contemporary Eyes*; Jonathan Harris, *Byzantium and the Crusades*; Peter Lock, *The Franks in the Aegean, 1204–1500.*

2 In the introduction to the latest edition, Barbara Sargent-Bauer argues for a date of composition around 1280, with manuscripts being produced later. At that point, French interests in Byzantium had been thwarted by the defeat of the Latin Empire in Byzantium in 1261, yet the Frankish interests in their crusader colonies in Morea in the Greek Peloponnese were intact. See Donald MacGillivray Nicol, *The Last Centuries of Byzantium, 1261–1453.*

3 Chrétien de Troyes, *Cligès*, 41–4n.

4 Quotations in this chapter are taken from the following modern editions of the main manuscripts of these texts: *La Belle Hélène de Constantinople: chanson de geste du XIVe siècle*, ed. Claude Roussel; Philippe de Remi, *Le Roman de la Manekine*. English translations are mine, unless otherwise noted.

5 See the following manuscript versions: *La Belle Hélène*: Bibliothèque Municipale d'Arras 766 (followed by the Vie de St Alexis and the Trespas Nostre Dame), Bibliothèque Municipale de Lyon 767 (whose explicit states that it was produced for "Loyse, dame de Crequi, Canapples et de pluisseurs autres terres et seignouries"), BnF Fr. 12482, and Bodleian

Douce 381. Later prose versions of the *Belle Hélène* include Bibliothèque Royale de Bruxelles 9967, BNF Fr.1489, BNF Fr. 19167, BNF Fr. 1489 (with the Mélusine and Pierre de Provence), and BN n.a. Fr. 20592; *Le Roman de la Manekine*: BnF Fr. 1588 (containing *Le Ruihote du Monde*; Baudoin de Condé's *Le Ver de la char*; Philippe de Rémi's *La Manekine*, *Jehan et Blonde* and *Salus d'amour*; Philippe de Beaumanoir; and Sarrasin's *Le Roman du Hen*), and Vatican Fonds Regina Latin MS 1505. On manuscripts, see Paul Verhuyck, "Les manuscrits du poème de *La Belle Hélène de Constantinople*."

6 Kathryn Gravdal, "Confessing Incests: Legal Erasures and Literary Celebrations in Medieval France," 280–3; Constance Brittain Bouchard, *"Those of My Blood": Constructing Noble Families in Medieval Francia*.

7 Other incest narratives include the German *Mai und Beaflor* and *Partonopier und Meliur*; the Old French *Yde et Olive*, *Richars Li Biaus*, *La Fille du compte de Ponthieu*, *Le Roman du comte d'Anjou*, *Lion de Bourges*, the *Tristan*, *La Vie de Saint Grégoire*, *Le Miracle de la fille du roy de Hongrie*, *Emaré*, and *Le Roman de Thèbes*; the Middle English *Gower's Confession Amantis*, Chaucer's introduction to The Man of Law's Tale; and of course biblical stories such as Lot and his daughters, Amnon and Tamar, or Judah and Tamar, and the treatment of incest in Leviticus 18.

8 On confession and family organization, see Gravdal, "Confessing Incests," 283–5.

9 See, for example, J. Douglas Bruce, *Mordred's Incestuous Birth*; M. Victoria Guerin, *The Fall of Kings and Princes: Structure and Destruction in Arthurian Tragedy*.

10 In *Richars Li Biaus*, the *Tristan*, *La Vie de Saint Grégoire*, and *Le Roman de Thèbes*, for example, the protagonists react with abject horror when they are made aware of the incestuous nature of their sexual relationships, for they are not aware that they are related to their lovers. These few "unknowing" incest stories are medieval reinterpretations of the classical Oedipus tale. While there are a few examples of "unknowing" nuclear family incest in medieval French literature, "knowing" nuclear-family incest is more frequent. Claude Roussel, *Conter de geste au XIVe siècle: inspiration folklorique et écriture épique dans "La Belle Hélène de Constantinople"* and "Aspects du père incestueux dans la littérature médiévale."

11 Elizabeth Archibald, "Gold in the Dungheap: Incest Stories and Family Values in the Middle Ages"; Thelma S. Fenster, "Beaumanoir's *La Manekine*: Kin D(r)ead: Incest, Doubling, and Death"; Gravdal, "Confessing Incests"; Roussel, "Aspects du père incestueux dans la littérature médiévale"; Karen J. Taylor, *Gender Transgressions: Crossing the Normative Barrier in Old French Literature*.

12 Leslie Dunton-Downer, however, has looked at the problematics of *Cligès* from within the lens of incest. See "The Horror of Culture: East-West Incest in Chrétien de Troyes's *Cligès*."

13 John Lascaratos and E. Poulakou-Rebelakou, "Child Sexual Abuse: Historical Cases in the Byzantine Empire"; Angeliki E. Laiou, ed., *Mariage, amour et parenté à Byzance aux XIe–XIIIe siècles*; Robin Fox, *The Red Lamp of Incest*; David Herlihy, "Making Sense of Incest: Women and the Marriage Rule of the Early Middle Ages." However, some scholars disagree. See in particular Guerin, *The Fall of Kings and Princes: Structure and Destruction in Arthurian Tragedy*, 15. Archibald also cites incest as a problem in medieval society Elizabeth Archibald, "Incest in Medieval Literature and Society."

14 Other versions include a later Morisco version, "La leyenda de la doncella Carcayona," and even a tale within Cervantes's own *Don Quixote*. See Alan Dundes, "The Psychoanalytic Study of the Grimms' Tales with Special Reference to "The Maiden without Hands"'; Mary Quinn, "Handless Maidens, Modern Texts: A New Reading of Cervantes's 'The Captive's Tale'"; J.N. Lincoln, "The Legend of the Handless Maiden"; Mary Perry, *The Handless Maiden: Moriscos and the Politics of Religion in Early Modern Spain*.

15 J.W. Knedler, "The Girl Without Hands: Latin-American Variants," 314. The tale is so popular that it has been classified as an established folklore motif (type 706) in Atti Aarne, *The Types of the Folktale: A Classification and Bibliography*, 240–1.

16 Roussel, "Aspects du père incestueux dans la littérature médiévale," 48. Roussel writes that "la passion du père pour sa fille n'est le plus souvent perçue que comme la marque d'un désir sexuel deviant." See also Fenster, "Beaumanoir's *La Manekine*: Kin D(r)ead: Incest, Doubling, and Death"; Madeleine Jeay, "Chercher une fille, une épouse. Sexualités déviantes et parcours de rédemption."

17 Ironically, in their attempt to save their kingdom from contamination or dissolution by ties to other outside families, the barons destroy all possibility of succession, for incest discredits not only their king and his masculinity but also his only heir in the process. Henry is consigned to sneaking around in search of his daughter or is otherwise largely absent from the narrative for thousands of lines, only to reappear at the conclusion, when he apologizes to his daughter and cedes all of his land and power to his grandsons, sired by a western king and raised without any knowledge of their heirless eastern grandfather. In short, the plot to produce a new male heir to the eastern throne – the plot to prevent a woman's rule – ends up threatening not only the gender norms of the empire, but also the possibility of reproducing the eastern court and its genealogy at all.

18 All translations, unless otherwise noted, are mine. I consulted, for reference, Irene Gnarra, ed., *Philippe de Remi's "La Manekine": Text, Translation, Commentary*.

19 The King's horror at incest's destruction of his masculinity, the core of his identity, resonates with Julia Kristeva's framing of bodily excrement as the abject: "A wound with blood and pus, or the sickly, acrid smell of sweat, of decay, does not signify death. In the presence of signified death – a flat encephalograph, for instance – I would understand, react, or accept. No, as in true theater, without makeup or masks, refuse and corpses show me what I permanently thrust aside in order to live. These body fluids, this defilement, this shit are what life withstands, hardly and with difficulty, on the part of death. There, I am at the border of my condition as a living being" (3). For more on abjection, see Kristeva's *Powers of Horror: An Essay on Abjection*, 3–8.

20 In another medieval fictional tale about incest, Gautier de Coinci's *De une Noble Fame de Rome*, it is a woman who commits incest with her son and later kills the offspring of their incestuous union. This text, which draws from a theological and Christian point of view (in that it is found in a collection of miracle stories), judges infanticide and incest as abominable crimes that actually pollute the air in which the incest perpetrator walks. She bemoans the transgressions she has committed, claiming "tant sui desmesuree et gloute / ne garc l'eure terre m'engloute. Tant ai fait, lasse, d'ors pechiez / puanz en est et entechiez li airs partout la ou je sui" (445–9) [I am so out of line and gluttonous / and slutty that the whole earth should swallow me up. I have done so much, alas, and now have sinned / that now the air stinks and is infected wherever I am]. In this passage, incest is closely associated with pollution, with the abject rubbish of stinking air; it is a passage that underlines – even though from the point of view of mother-son incest – the degree to which incest and infanticide were reviled by medieval French society, the church, and the law. Indeed, she fears being burned alive or dismembered for her sins, and this punishment is the main preoccupation of the first four hundred verses of this text.

21 Though his text was written slightly after *Le Roman de la Manekine*, it is a good indicator of contemporary spiritual and moral beliefs about incest. Thomas Aquinas, *The Summa Theologica*, ed. Daniel J. Sullivan, and *Summa Theologiae*, ed. Pietro Caramello.

22 Aquinas, *Summa Theologica*, II; 154, 12.

23 Of course, Aquinas's intent is not to document masculinity, but to classify sexual behaviour. Yet, as Vern Bullough asserts, "traditionally masculine activities were ways in which men could define, affirm, and assert their

dominant and even aggressive sexuality" Bullough, "Cross-Dressing and Gender Role Change in the Middle Ages," in Bullough and Brundage, *Handbook of Medieval Sexuality*, 135. That is, sexuality, and the right kind of sexuality were critical to the construction of a socially acceptable masculinity. See also Jeffrey Jerome Cohen and Bonnie Wheeler, eds., *Becoming Male in the Middle Ages*.

24 Aquinas, *Summa Theologica*, II; 154, 12 and 154, 9.

25 In Aquinas's terms, then, and as medievalists have pointed out, the incest perpetrator commits a sin against natural heterosexual procreative acts. Many scholars actually characterize this kind of endogamous lust as deviant, and they do so both in popular terms of sexuality as we know it today, as well as in contemporary medieval theological and legal stances on incest. See Elizabeth Archibald, *Incest and the Medieval Imagination* and "Gold in the Dungheap: Incest Stories and Family Values in the Middle Ages" as well as "Incest in Medieval Literature and Society"; Pierre Bonte, *Epouser au plus proche: inceste, prohibitions et stratégies matrimoniales autour de la Méditerranée*; Jeay, "Chercher une fille, une épouse: Sexualités déviantes et parcours de rédemption"; Anna Roberts, ed., *Violence against Women in Medieval Texts*.

26 Aquinas, *Summa Theologica* II; 154, 12.

27 Claude Lévi-Strauss, *Anthropologie structurale*, 56–60.

28 While Lévi-Strauss's observations remain fundamental to our understanding of incest, feminists such as Judith Butler and Gayle Rubin have pushed these observations further to interrogate how they are based on the interpretation of gender and desire uniquely within the framework of a compulsory heterosexuality; medievalists have refined these critiques to better understand the interface between sexual violence, heterosexual desire, and gender in the Middle Ages. Judith P. Butler, *Gender Trouble*, 75; Gayle Rubin, "The Traffic in Women: Notes on the Political Economy of Sex." For feminist medievalist critiques of incest, see Jutta Eming, "Questions on the Theme of Incest in Courtly Literature"; Archibald, "Incest in Medieval Literature and Society"; W. Arens, *The Original Sin: Incest and Its Meaning*; Bonte, *Epouser au plus proche*; Judith Herman and Lisa Hirschmann, "Father-Daughter Incest"; Huguette Legros, "Parenté naturelle, alliance, parenté spirituelle: De l'inceste à la sainteté"; Megan McLaughlin, "'Abominable Mingling': Father-Daughter Incest and the Law."

29 Mary Douglas, *Purity and Danger: An Analysis of the Concepts of Pollution and Taboo*. Douglas remarks that "where there is no differentiation, there is no defilement" (161).

30 See Barbara N. Sargent-Baur, "Echos de Chrétien de Troyes dans les romans de Philippe de Remi."

31 Of course masculinities are produced along a spectrum of positions of desire. See in particular Shawn F. Tougher, "Images of Effeminate Men: The Case of Byzantine Eunuchs"; Liz James, *Women, Men, and Eunuchs: Gender in Byzantium*; Diane Watt, "Behaving Like a Man? Incest, Lesbian Desire, and Gender Play in *Yde et Olive* and Its Adaptations"; D.M. Hadley, ed., *Masculinity in Medieval Europe*. See also Karma Lochrie, Peggy McCracken, and James A. Schultz, eds., *Constructing Medieval Sexuality*.

32 Jeanette M.A. Beer, ed. *Translation Theory and Practice in the Middle Ages*; Jeanette M.A. Beer and Kenneth Lloyd-Jones, eds., *Translation and the Transmission of Culture Between 1300 and 1600*.

33 For a literary example of this kind of crisis, see Sharon Kinoshita, "Pagans Are Wrong and Christians Are Right: Alterity, Gender, and Nation in the *Chanson de Roland*."

34 Carol J. Harvey, "Philippe de Rémi's *Manekine*: Joïe and Pain"; Linda Marie Rouillard, "Mutilation and Marriage in *La Manekine*."

35 Shoshana Felman explains Jacques Lacan's formulation of nuclear family incest – of the Oedipus complex – in terms of a symbolic castration: "The father (or the father's name), as a symbol of the Law of incest prohibition, stands on the other hand for the first authoritative 'no,' the first social imperative of renunciation, inaugurating, through this castration of the child's original desire, both the necessity of repression and the process of symbolic substitution of objects of desire, which Lacan calls, 'the Symbolic.'" *Jacques Lacan and the Adventure of Insight: Psychoanalysis in Contemporary Culture*, 104.

36 Other scholars agree with this reading, but to my knowledge none of them have intertwined the psychoanalytic model with a postcolonial one, which is why I pursue this reading here. See Archibald, "Gold in the Dungheap: Incest Stories and Family Values in the Middle Ages"; Arens, *The Original Sin: Incest and Its Meaning*; Fenster, "Beaumanoir's *La Manekine*: Kin D(r)ead: Incest, Doubling, and Death"; Carol J. Harvey, "From Incest to Redemption in *La Manekine*"; Anne Laskaya, "The Rhetoric of Incest in the Middle English *Emaré*"; McLaughlin, "'Abominable Mingling': Father-Daughter Incest and the Law."

37 Sharon Kinoshita, in reading Brammimonde's rejection of her Muslim culture when she converts to Christianity, makes the parallel point that "In symbolic terms, the convert is the obverse of the traitor: Bramimonde's baptism, signaling her acceptance both of Christianity and of the feudal Frankish world it entails, sutures the breach opened by Ganelon's

treasonous commerce with Marsile. To this point, Bramimonde has functioned as the site of disruption: denouncing Saracen culture from within, her unruly speech (re)establishes difference between the two barely distinguishable sides." "Pagans Are Wrong and Christians Are Right," 98–9.

38 As Constance Bouchard points out in the introduction to her study of noble lineages, the process of narrating one's lineage was, even in the Middle Ages, a choice, and one that in the end may be read as producing a sort of commentary on the best ways of defining the noble self: "each individual had to decide which ones, out of all the people to whom he or she was related by blood, were the true family members, those to whom one was allied." *"Those of My Blood": Constructing Noble Families in Medieval Francia*, 3.

39 Especially in the sense that Howard Bloch theorizes the relationship between etymology and genealogy – between narration and reproduction. He writes that "early medieval grammar, based upon the principle of etymology, and lineage, predicated upon that of genealogy, participate in a common representational paradigm characterized by linearity, temporality, verticality, fixity, continuity, and the inheritance of semantic and social value." Curiously, Joïe's refusal to narrate her nobility becomes a refusal that interrogates how strictly reproducing the "verticality" and "fixity" of the eastern court structures was limited to men. *Etymologies and Genealogies: A Literary Anthropology of the French Middle Ages*, 93.

40 Roberta L. Krueger, *Women Readers and the Ideology of Gender in Old French Verse Romance*. Simon Gaunt elaborates that romance does not make or "discover women, or femininity, or the individual, it constructs models of them, which need evaluating in their historical context." *Gender and Genre in Medieval French Literature*, 71–3.

41 In fact, in her willingness to part with her father's name and her past identity, in her active choice of life as a Scotswoman in love with the new western king, the Manekine positions herself as the ideal malleable foreign queen consort, one without concerns of religious or cultural difference, one who joyously gives herself over to assimilation and integration, bringing absolutely nothing into her new household. She, then, is the exact opposite of someone like Maria Argyropoulina, who toted her forks along to Venice in her Byzantine coffers, or someone like Fénice, who insists on manipulating her new courtly environment to reflect cross-cultural exchange, rather than cross-cultural conquest.

42 Of course, this plot is not limited to these incest tales; persecution by mothers-in-law is a common theme throughout medieval literature, and in particular it features heavily in Chaucer's Man of Law's Tale and in *Le*

Roman du Conte d'Anjou, which both precede the incest tales I study here. Yet what is of interest to me is that both men and women are implicated in disciplining and punishing women who try to move outside of the realm of patriarchal exchange; here, it is not only the wayward father and his seneschal who have punished Joïe for her independence and for cutting off her hand and thwarting her father's plans, but it is also another woman who is upset by Joïe's unwillingness to reveal her origins.

43 Of course, these kinds of accusations fall in line with a contemporary push to enact Salic law, in which foreign queens – even those who embraced their lineages – were meant to be legally prohibited from using reproduction (motherhood) as a weapon with which to interfere in the politics of the realm. Yet Salic law itself was only invoked towards the end of the fifteenth century to proscribe relationships in what is today known as France. See Gaunt, *Gender and Genre in Medieval French Literature*, 53 and 71–3.

44 Daisy Delogu, *Theorizing the Ideal Sovereign: The Rise of the French Vernacular Royal Biography*, 85–8.

45 For an extensive treatment of the incest taboo, and of pollution and sexuality, see Claude Lévi-Strauss, *Anthropologie structurale*, and Mary Douglas, *Purity and Danger*.

46 Gratian, Decretum, C. 35, Q. 2 & 3, c.10.

47 Harvey, "From Incest to Redemption in *La Manekine*."

4. Rewriting Mediterranean Gender and Power in *Floriant et Florete*

1 Keith Busby points out that there are few dissertations on *Floriant et Florete*, and he himself has made valuable inroads into studying the intertextual references within the romance. Sara Sturm-Maddox has written two articles about *Floriant et Florete*, and like Busby, Sturm-Maddox focuses on the sources of and possible explanations for the intertextual references invoked by the text. Keith Busby, "The Intertextual Coordinates of *Floriant et Florete*," 262. See also Sara Sturm-Maddox, "Arthurian Evasions: The End(s) of Fiction in *Floriant et Florete*," and "The Arthurian Romance in Sicily: *Floriant et Florete*."

2 In this way, the revisionist nature of the romance can be coupled with its dependence on the processes of medieval editing and rewriting in *translatio studii*, a practice which, as Louise von Flotow has pointed out, is always inherently "'political' in some sense, conforming to the context in which it is produced, deliberately transgressing it, reflecting upon it, or aiming at a particular readership in order to convince, seduce or otherwise exert

influence. [...] Texts that reach the public, as well as those never published, are embedded in the social, political and cultural processes of their day." Renate Blumenfeld-Kosinski, Luise Von Flotow-Evans, and Daniel Russell, eds., *The Politics of Translation in the Middle Ages and the Renaissance*. See especially the first chapter, page 9.

3 For more on Sicily, see Karla Mallette, *The Kingdom of Sicily, 1100–1250*; Steven Runciman, *The Sicilian Vespers: A History of the Mediterranean World in the Later Thirteenth Century*; David Abulafia, *The Western Mediterranean Kingdoms 1250–1500*.

4 David Abulafia, *The Two Italies: Economic Relations Between the Norman Kingdom of Sicily and the Northern Communes*; Michele Amari and Carlo Alfonso Nallino, *Storia dei Musulmani di Sicilia*; Ferdinand Chalandon, *Histoire de la domination normande en Italie et en Sicile*.

5 While this means that the conclusions I may draw from this text may not be generally representative of either an era or a genre, it nonetheless means that one author wrote and understood his era and this genre in a certain way, which I will explore here.

6 Busby writes: "In some ways, *Floriant et Florete* is to the corpus of epigonal romances what *Cligès* is to the rest of Chrétien's oeuvre: it is at first sight only marginally Arthurian and set mainly in the Mediterranean; the *merveilleux*, while not entirely absent, is quite understated." Busby, "The Intertextual Coordinates of *Floriant et Florete*," 262.

7 See, for example, depictions of Arthur's court as a site of courtly renown, and of Arthur as a just and fair ruler and a magnanimous king in the following passages from Chrétien's romances: *Erec et Enide* (27–34; 1955–65; 2002–11; 4489–95; 6671–76); *Cligès* (66–71; 416–22; 4887–94); *Le Chevalier au lion* (1–6; 3895–903); *Le Chevalier de la charrette* (6256–61); and *Le Conte du Graal* (833–50; 877–90; 2285–96, 6870–5).

8 Translation quoted in Busby.

9 See Busby, "The Intertextual Coordinates of *Floriant et Florete*," 268–9.

10 Emphasis mine.

11 According to John of Salisbury, a sort of medieval literary theorist, *translatio* involves both a good selection of material and the elaboration, the amplification, of an appropriately chosen metaphor for a new cultural context. See especially "Liber Primus," chapter XXIV of John of Salisbury, *The Metalogicon of John of Salisbury: A Twelfth-Century Defense of the Verbal and Logical Arts of the Trivium*) and *Ioannis Saresberiensis Metalogicon*, ed. Daniel D. McGarry.

12 See Michelle A. Freeman, *The Poetics of Translatio Studii and Conjointure: Chrétien de Troyes's "Cligés"*; and Hans Robert Jauss, *Toward an Aesthetic of Reception*.

13 By political, I mean a power system in which alliances and distributions of power are based on geographic claims to lands, rents, and the production of indentured workers.
14 Hans Robert Jauss and Erich Köhler, *Le Roman jusqu'à la fin du XIIIè*.
15 Mallette, *The Kingdom of Sicily, 1100–1250: A Literary History*.
16 Burgundy played an important part in the production of manuscripts both prior to and after the period discussed. Charles the Bold, the Duke of Burgundy in the late fourteenth century, employed many writers to redact the *romans d'antiquité* and his castle was filled with tapestries from Ghent that depicted "the deeds of Hannibal and Alexander the Great ... [and] the destruction of Troy." Otto Cartellieri, *The Court of Burgundy*, 173.
17 Abulafia, *The Western Mediterranean Kingdoms 1250–1500: The Struggle for Dominion*. See especially chapter 1. Steven Runciman, too, comments that "The most remarkable feature of the Norman government was the success with which it brought harmony to the diverse elements in Sicily. [...] In the course of a raid on Greece, Roger II kidnapped trained silk-weavers to improve the nascent silk-factories in the island. Artists from many countries and traditions were given patronage." *The Sicilian Vespers: A History of the Mediterranean World in the Later Thirteenth Century*, 9.
18 Abulafia, *The Western Mediterranean Kingdoms*, 13.
19 By the thirteenth century, Sicily was almost constantly under attack. Abulafia comments that it was Sicily's wealth and its wonderfully productive agrarian landscape that attracted attackers. "The impression that the former Norman territories were a source of enormous wealth and military resources remained strong in the minds of late medieval conquerors such as the French invaders Charles of Anjou, who was crowned king of Sicily in 1266, and Charles VIII of Valois, who added the Neapolitan crown to that of France in 1494–95." Ibid., 3.
20 As George Ostrogorsky points out, the rise of Charles I of Anjou made the "position of the Byzantine Empire ... extremely precarious" because Charles was not only slowly amalgamating claims to power in a number of territories east of his native Anjou, but also actively pursued military, ecclesiastical, and marriage strategies to defeat Michael VIII Paleologus and the Byzantine Empire. Georgije Ostrogorski, *History of the Byzantine State*, 455.
21 Rita Lejeune suggests that *Floriant et Florete* was written much earlier, in the mid-twelfth century, for a wife of William II, though this has not, for reasons of dating, been a widely accepted viewpoint, and indeed, a careful reading of history suggests a later dating. Rita Lejeune, "Le Rôle littéraire de la famille d'Aliénor d'Aquitaine," 331.
22 John Julius Norwich, *A Short History of Byzantium*, 321.

23 See Donald MacGillivray Nicol, *The Last Centuries of Byzantium, 1261–1453*; and Runciman, *The Sicilian Vespers*.
24 As Norwich, perhaps more sympathetic to Angevin pursuits than many Byzantinists, put it, "to Charles of Anjou ... the events of those few fateful hours brought humiliation and the indefinite postponement of his long-held dream of an empire in the East." Norwich, *A Short History of Byzantium*, 327.
25 One of the reasons that the previous editions were dated earlier is that there were several French invasions of and skirmishes over Sicily, and other editors believed that it was not Charles of Anjou's struggles that were being depicted in the romance, but those of earlier pretenders to the Sicilian throne. See the explanation given by Richard Traschler and Annie Combes in the preface to the latest edition: *Floriant et Florete*, xxiv–xxv.
26 See, for example, Kathryn Gravdal's *Ravishing Maidens*.
27 This is, of course, not to be confused with the kinds of ravishment that are predicated against the wishes and sexual desires of the woman involved, such as the rape of Maximou in *Digenis Akritas*, where Digenis, not content with his martial victory over the Amazon, seeks to complete her humiliation with an unwanted sexual assault.
28 Definitions taken from Algirdas Julien Greimas, *Dictionnaire de l'ancien français: le Moyen Age*. Translations mine.
29 This is not to say that Floire's position as "le chevalier qui la nef mainne," in which he travels around in an incredibly luxurious boat, does not reference the same kinds of eastern exoticism as earlier texts. Rather, I am pointing to the ways that the figurehead of justice and courtly organization in the story – Arthur – is suddenly reimagined as being the cultural centre of the Mediterranean, in ways that do not depend on motifs of Greek or other ancient glory, and rather point to the emerging prominence of western cultural heritage as a way of articulating French-speaking noble glory.
30 Recent work suggests that Sicilian women played an important role in the economy of the island and in the education of its children, perhaps more so than in France. See Clifford R. Backman, *The Decline and Fall of Medieval Sicily: Politics, Religion, and Economy in the Reign of Frederick III, 1296–1337*, 248. Georges Duby, though not a scholar of Sicily, would in general disagree that women had the means to change empires, but his work offers a wealth of examples and sources about women's lives, especially aristocratic women, and especially in France. See *The Knight, the Lady, and the Priest: The Making of Modern Marriage in Medieval France* and *Love and Marriage in the Middle Ages* and *Women of the Twelfth Century*; Georges Duby and Elborg Forster, "Medieval Marriage: Two Models from

Twelfth-Century France"; Georges Duby and Michelle Perrot, *A History of Women in the West.*

Conclusion

1 Teresa Shawcross's recent study of the Morea is replete with detailed analyses of these themes and historical underpinnings. See Clare Teresa M. Shawcross, *The Chronicle of Morea: Historiography in Crusader Greece.* For other studies of *The Chronicle of Morea,* see W.J. Aerts, "*The Chronicle of the Morea* as a Mirror of a Crusaders' State at Work"; W.J. Aerts and Hero Hokwerda, "Lexicon on the *Chronicle of Morea*"; John Schmitt, *The Chronicle of Morea [to Chronikon Tou Moreos]: A History in Political Verse, Relating the Establishment of Feudalism in Greece by the Franks in the Thirteenth Century;* Vincenzo Coronelli and Giovanni Battista Moro, *Memorie istorico-geografiche della Morea riacquistata dall' armi venete.*

2 For general work on Frankish crusader states in Byzantium, see Aerts, "*The Chronicle of the Morea* as a Mirror of a Crusaders' State at Work"; Aneta Ilieva, *Frankish Morea, 1205–1262: Socio-Cultural Interaction between the Franks and the Local Population;* Athina Tarsouli, *Kastra Kai Politeies Tou Morea;* Andrew Jotischky, "Ethnographic Attitudes in the Crusader States: The Franks and the Indigenous Orthodox People"; David Jacoby, "The Encounter of Two Societies: Western Conquerors and Byzantines in the Peloponnesus after the Fourth Crusade"; Sharon E.J. Gerstel, "Art and Identity in the Medieval Morea"; Robert Lee Wolff, ed., *Studies in the Latin Empire of Constantinople;* Kazhdan, "Latins and Franks in Byzantium: Perception and Reality from the Eleventh to the Twelfth Century."

3 The Greek text exists in MS Havniensis 57 in Copenhagen, copied in MS Taurinensis B.II.I (Turin); and BnF Parisinus Graecus 2898 and 2753, and MS Bern 509 Grec. The French text exists in three copies: Royal Library of Belgium 15702, BnF Fr. 2753, and University Library of Bern 509. The Italian *Cronaca di Morea* is a later version of the Turin text, and the *Libro de los fechos et conquistas del principado de la Morea* is a fifteenth-century Aragonese version of the Greek text.

4 Michael Jeffreys, "*The Chronicle of the Morea*: Priority of the Greek Version."

5 Shawcross, *The Chronicle of Morea: Historiography in Crusader Greece,* 21–2.

6 Harold E. Lurier, *Crusaders as Conquerors: The Chronicle of Morea,* 146–8.

7 See, in the Greek version, episodes described on pp. 166, 208, 476–8, 500–2, 550–2. Schmitt, *The Chronicle of Morea [to Chronikon Tou Moreos]: A History in Political Verse, Relating the Establishment of Feudalism in Greece by the Franks in the Thirteenth Century.*

8 For the most recent scholarship, see Aerts, "*The Chronicle of the Morea* as a Mirror of a Crusaders' State at Work"; Shawcross, *The Chronicle of Morea: Historiography in Crusader Greece*; Kristian Molin, *Chronicle of Morea*; Gerstel, "Art and Idenntity in the Medieval Morea"; Erhard Peter Opsahl, *The Hospitallers, Templars, and Teutonic Knights in the Morea after the Fourth Crusade*; Ilieva, *Frankish Morea, 1205–1262: Socio-Cultural Interaction between the Franks and the Local Population*.

9 Lurier, *Crusaders as Conquerors: The Chronicle of Morea*, 244–6.

10 Ibid., 278–82.

Bibliography

Primary Sources Consulted

Alexandre de Paris. *Le Roman d'Alexandre*. Edited by E.C. Armstrong and Laurence Harf-Lancner. Paris: Le Livre de Poche, 1994.

Aquinas, Thomas. *Summa Theologiae*. Edited by Pietro Caramello. Turin: Marietti, 1952.

– *The Summa Theologica*. Edited by Daniel J. Sullivan. Chicago: Encyclopaedia Britannica, 1955.

Choniates, Nicetas. *O City of Byzantium: Annals of Niketas Choniates*. Edited by Harry J. Magoulias. Byzantine Texts in Translation. Detroit: Wayne State University Press, 1984.

Chrétien de Troyes. *Cligès*. Edited by Charles Méla, Olivier Collet, and Marie-Claire Gérard-Zai. Paris: Le Livre de Poche, 1994.

– *Erec et Enide*. Edited by Mario Roques. Paris: Champion, 1952.

– *Le Conte du Graal, ou, Le Roman de Perceval*. Paris: Le Livre de Poche, 1990.

Comnena, Anna. *The Alexiad of Anna Comnena*. Edited by Edgar Robert Ashton Sewter. Baltimore: Penguin Books, 1969.

– *The Alexiad of the Princess Anna Comnena*. Edited by Elizabeth Dawes. London: Routledge and Kegan Paul, 1967.

Coronelli, Vincenzo, and Giovanni Battista Moro. *Memorie istorico-geografiche della Morea riacquistata dall' armi venete, del regno di Negroponte, e degli altri luoghi circonvicini, e di quelli ch' hanno sottomesso nella Dalmacia e nell' Epiro dal principio della guerra intimata al Turco in Costantinopoli 1684 sino all'anno presente 1687…* Venice, 1687.

Damian, Peter. *Institutio Monialis*. Edited by J.-P. Migne. Vol. 145, col. 744. *Patrologiae Cursus Completus, Series Latina*. Paris: Vrayet, 1853.

De Ceremoniis Aulae Byzantinae. Edited by J. Reiske. 2 vols. Bonn: CSHB, 1829.

Digenis Akritis: The Grottaferrata and Escorial Versions. Edited by Elizabeth Jeffreys. Cambridge Medieval Classics: 7. Cambridge: Cambridge University Press, 1998.

Floire et Blancheflor: Edition du Ms. 19152 du fonds français avec introduction, notes et glossaire. Edited by Margaret Pelan. 2nd ed. Paris: Editions Ophrys, 1975.

Floriant et Florete. Edited by Richard Trachsler and Annie Combes. Paris: Champion, 2003.

Gnarra, Irene, ed. *Philippe de Remi's "La Manekine": Text, Translation, Commentary*. New York: Garland, 1988.

Graindor de Douai. *La Chanson d'Antioche*. 2 vols. Edited by Suzanne Duparc-Quioc. Paris: P. Geuthner, 1976.

John of Salisbury. *Ioannis Saresberiensis Metalogicon*. Edited by Daniel D. McGarry, J.B. Hall and K.S.B. Keats-Rohan. Corpus Christianorum. Continuatio Mediaevalis: 98. Turnhout: Typographi Brepols Editores Pontificii, 1991.

– *The Metalogicon of John of Salisbury: A Twelfth-Century Defense of the Verbal and Logical Arts of the Trivium*. Edited by Daniel D. McGarry. Berkeley: University of California Press, 1955.

La Belle Hélène de Constantinople: chanson de geste du XIVe siècle. Edited by Claude Roussel. Geneva: Droz, 1995.

Le Conte de Floire et Blanchefleur: roman pré-courtois du milieu du XIIe siècle. Edited by Jean-Luc Leclanche. Vol. 34, *Traductions des classiques français du Moyen Age*. Paris: H. Champion, 1986.

Le Pèlerinage de Charlemagne. Edited by Glyn Burgess. British Rencesvals Publications. Edinburgh: Société Rencesvals British Branch, 1998.

Le Roman de Thèbes: édition du manuscrit S (Londres, Brit. Libr., Add. 34114). Edited by Francine Mora-Lebrun. Paris: Le Livre de Poche, 1995.

Liutprand of Cremona. *Antapodis*. In *Die Werke Lieudprands von Cremona*. Edited by Joseph Becker. Hannover: Leipzig, 1915.

Molin, Kristian. *Chronicle of Morea*. Ashgate, 2004.

Philippe de Remi. *Le Roman de la Manekine*. Amsterdam, Atlanta: Rodopi, 1999.

Polo, Marco. *The Travels of Marco Polo*. Translated by Ronald Latham. London: Penguin Books, 1958.

Psellos, Michael. *Chronographie, ou histoire d'un siècle de Byzance (976–1077)*. Paris: Les Belles Lettres, 1926.

Robert de Clari. *La Conquête de Constantinople*. Edited by Jean Dufournet. Paris: Champion, 2004.

Schmitt, John, ed. *The Chronicle of Morea: A History in Political Verse, Relating the Establishment of Feudalism in Greece by the Franks in the Thirteenth Century.* Cambridge, MA: Harvard University Press, 1904.

Stone, Edward N. *Three Old French Chronicles of the Crusades.* Seattle: University of Washington Press, 1939.

Secondary Sources Consulted

Aarne, Atti. *The Types of the Folktale: A Classification and Bibliography.* Translated by Stith Thompson. Helsinki: Helsingin Liikekirjapaino Oy, 1961.

Abulafia, David. *The Two Italies: Economic Relations between the Norman Kingdom of Sicily and the Northern Communes.* Cambridge, New York: Cambridge University Press, 1977. http://dx.doi.org/10.1017/CBO9780511560996.

– *The Western Mediterranean Kingdoms 1250–1500: The Struggle for Dominion.* London, New York: Longman, 1997.

Aebischer, Paul, ed. *Le Voyage de Charlemagne à Jerusalem et à Constantinople.* Geneva: Droz, 1965.

Aerts, W.J. "A Byzantine Traveller to One of the Crusader States." In Ciggaar and Teule, *East and West in the Crusader States,* 165–222.

– "*The Chronicle of the Morea* as a Mirror of a Crusaders' State at Work." In Ciggaar and Teule, *East and West in the Crusader States,* 153–62.

– and Hero Hokwerda. "Lexicon on the *Chronicle of Morea.*" Groningen: Forsten, 2002.

Agapitos, Panagiotis A., and Ole Langwitz Smith. *The Study of Medieval Greek Romance: A Reassessment of Recent Work.* Vol. 33, Opuscula Graecolatina. Copenhagen: Museum Tusculanum Press, 1992.

Amari, Michele. *Storia dei Musulmani di Sicilia.* Florence: Le Monier, 1858.

Angold, Michael. "The Interaction of Latins and Byzantines during the Period of the Latin Empire (1204–1261): The Case of the Ordeal." In *Actes du Xve Congrès Intérnational d'études Byzantines,* 1–10. Athens, 1980.

– "The Wedding of Digenis Akrites: Love and Marriage in Byzantium in the Eleventh and Twelfth Centuries." In *Του Α' Διεθνούς Συμποσίου, Ν Καθημερινή Ζωή Στο Β.* Athens: Centre Nationale de la Recherche Scientifique, 1989.

Archibald, Elizabeth. "Gold in the Dungheap: Incest Stories and Family Values in the Middle Ages." *Journal of Family History* 22, no. 2 (1997): 133–49. http://dx.doi.org/10.1177/036319909702200201.

– "Incest in Medieval Literature and Society." *Forum for Modern Language Studies* 25, no. 1 (1989): 1–15. http://ew3dm6nd8c.search.serialssolutions.com/?_char_set=utf8&id=doi:10.1093/fmls/XXV.1.1&sid=libx&genre=article.

– *Incest and the Medieval Imagination*. Oxford: Oxford University Press, 2001. http://dx.doi.org/10.1093/acprof:oso/9780198112099.001.0001.

Arens, W. *The Original Sin: Incest and Its Meaning*. New York: Oxford University Press, 1986.

Ariès, Philippe, et al. *Histoire de la vie privée*. 5 vols, L'univers Historique. Paris: Seuil, 1985.

Auerbach, Erich. *Literary Language and Its Public in Late Latin Antiquity and in the Middle Ages*. Translated by Ralph Manheim. London: Routledge, 1965.

Austin, J.L. *How to Do Things with Words*. Oxford: Clarendon Press, 1975. http://dx.doi.org/10.1093/acprof:oso/9780198245537.001.0001.

Backman, Clifford R. *The Decline and Fall of Medieval Sicily: Politics, Religion, and Economy in the Reign of Frederick III, 1296–1337*. Cambridge: Cambridge University Press, 1995. http://dx.doi.org/10.1017/CBO9780511523090.

Baldwin, Barry. "The Description of Agamemnon in *Digenis Akrites*." *Byzantine and Modern Greek Studies* 12 (1988): 279.

Bancourt, Paul. "Etude de quelques motifs communs à l'épopée Byzantine de *Digenis Akritis* et à *La Chanson d'aiol*." *Romania* 95 (1974): 508–32.

Barletta, Vincent. *Covert Gestures: Crypto-Islamic Literature as Cultural Practice in Early Modern Spain*. Minneapolis: University of Minnesota, 2005.

– *Death in Babylon: Alexander the Great and Iberian Empire in the Muslim Orient*. Chicago: University of Chicago Press, 2010.

Bartlett, Robert. *Trial by Fire and Water: The Medieval Judicial Ordeal*. Oxford: Clarendon Press, 1986.

Baswell, Christopher. "Marvels of Translation and Crises of Transition in the Romances of Antiquity." In *The Cambridge Companion to Medieval Romance*, edited by Roberta L. Krueger, 29–44. Cambridge: Cambridge University Press, 2000. http://dx.doi.org/10.1017/CCOL0521553423.003.

– *Virgil in Medieval England: Figuring the Aeneid from the Twelfth Century to Chaucer*. Cambridge: Cambridge University Press, 2006.

Beaton, Roderick. *The Medieval Greek Romance*. 2nd edition. Edited by London, New York: Routledge, 1996.

Beaton, Roderick, and David Ricks. Digenes Akrites*: New Approaches to Byzantine Heroic Poetry*. Aldershot: Variorum, 1993.

Beaucamp, Joelle. "La Situation juridique de la femme à Byzance." *Cahiers de civilisation médiévale* 20, no. 78 (1977): 145–76. http://dx.doi.org/10.3406/ccmed.1977.3069.

Beer, Jeanette M.A., ed. *Translation Theory and Practice in the Middle Ages*. Kalamazoo, MI: Medieval Institute Publications, 1997.

Beer, Jeanette M.A., and Kenneth Lloyd-Jones, eds. *Translation and the Transmission of Culture between 1300 and 1600*. Kalamazoo, MI: Medieval Institute Publications, 1995.

Bell, Susan Groag. "Medieval Women Book Owners: Arbiters of Lay Piety and Ambassadors of Culture." *Signs* 7, no. 4 (1982): 742–68. http://dx.doi.org/10.1086/493920.

Berman, Antoine. "*Translatio studii* et pouvoir royal." *Poésie* 80 (1997): 190–200.

Betts, Gavin. *Three Medieval Greek Romances*. New York: Garland, 1995.

Bhabha, Homi K. *The Location of Culture*. London, New York: Routledge, 1994.

Bloch, R. Howard. *Etymologies and Genealogies: A Literary Anthropology of the French Middle Ages*. Chicago: University of Chicago Press, 1983.

Blumenfeld-Kosinski, Renate, Luise Von Flotow-Evans, and Daniel Russell, eds. *The Politics of Translation in the Middle Ages and the Renaissance*. Ottawa: University of Ottawa Press, 2001.

Bonte, Pierre. *Epouser au plus proche: inceste, prohibitions et stratégies matrimoniales autour de la Méditerranée*. Paris: Editions de l'Ecole des hautes études en sciences sociales, 1994.

Bouchard, Constance Brittain. *"Those of My Blood": Constructing Noble Families in Medieval Francia*. Philadelphia: University of Pennsylvania Press, 2001.

Bouras, Laskarina. "Dragon Representations on Byzantine Phialae and Their Conduits." *Gesta* 16, no. 2 (1977): 65–8. http://dx.doi.org/10.2307/766731.

Bourbou, Chryssi, and Sandra J. Gavrie-Lok. "Breastfeeding and Weaning Patterns in Byzantine Times: Evidence from Human Remains and Written Sources." In *Becoming Byzantine: Children and Childhood in Byzantium*, edited by Arietta Papaconstantinou and Alice-Mary Talbot, 64–111. Cambridge, MA: Harvard University Press, 2009.

Braudel, Fernand. *The Mediterranean and the Mediterranean World in the Age of Philip II*. 2 vols. Los Angeles, Berkeley: University of California Press, 1996.

Brett, Gerard. "The Automata in the Byzantine 'Throne of Solomon.'" *Speculum* 29, no. 3 (1954): 477–87. http://dx.doi.org/10.2307/2846790.

Brooke, Christopher N. L. *The Medieval Idea of Marriage*. Oxford: Oxford University Press, 1989.

Bruce, J. Douglas. "Human Automata in Classical Tradition and Medieval Romance." *Modern Philology* 10, no. 4 (1913): 511–26. http://dx.doi.org/10.1086/386901.

– "Mordred's Incestuous Birth." In *Medieval Studies in Memory of Gertrude Schoepperle Loomis*, edited by Roger Sherman Loomis, 197–208. New York: Columbia University Press, 1927.

Brummett, Palmira. "Visions of the Mediterranean: A Classification." *Journal of Medieval and Early Modern Studies* 37, no. 1 (2007): 9–55. http://dx.doi.org/10.1215/10829636-2006-009.

Brundage, James A. *Sex, Law, and Marriage in the Middle Ages*. Aldershot, UK: Variorum, 1993.

Bullough, Vern, and James A. Brundage, eds. *Handbook of Medieval Sexuality*. New York: Garland, 2000.

Burguière, André. *A History of the Family*. 2 vols. Cambridge: Polity Press, 1996.

Burns, E. Jane. *Courtly Love Undressed: Reading through Clothes in Medieval French Culture*. Philadelphia: University of Pennsylvania Press, 2002.

Busby, Keith. "The Intertextual Coordinates of *Floriant et Florete*." *French Forum* 20, no. 3 (1995): 261–78.

Busby, Keith, et al., eds. *Les Manuscrits de Chrétien de Troyes*. 2 vols. Amsterdam: Rodopi, 1993.

Butler, Judith P. *Excitable Speech: A Politics of the Performative*. New York: Routledge, 1997.

– *Gender Trouble: Feminism and the Subversion of Identity*. New York: Routledge, 1999.

Bynum, Caroline Walker. "Wonder." *American Historical Review* 102, no. 1 (1997): 1–26. http://dx.doi.org/10.2307/2171264.

Cartellieri, Otto. *The Court of Burgundy*. London: Routledge, 1972.

Chalandon, Ferdinand. *Histoire de la domination normande en Italie et en Sicile*. Paris: Picard, 1907.

Cheynet, Jean-Claude, Elisabeth Malamut, and Cécile Morrisson. "Prix et salaires dans les sources byzantines (Xe–Xve Siècle)." In *Hommes et richesses dans l'empire byzantin*, vol. 2, edited by V. Kravari, J. Lefort, and Cécile Morrisson, 339–74. Paris: P. Lethielleux, 1991.

Chiat, Marilyn Joyce Segal, and Kathryn Reyerson, eds. *The Medieval Mediterranean: Cross-Cultural Contacts*. Vol. 3, Medieval Studies at Minnesota. St Cloud, MN: North Star Press of St Cloud, 1988.

Chrétien de Troyes, and David Staines. *The Complete Romances of Chrétien de Troyes*. Bloomington: Indiana University Press, 1990.

Ciggaar, Krijna Nelly. "Encore une fois Chrétien de Troyes et la 'matière byzantine': la révolution des femmes au palais de Constantinople." *Cahiers de civilisation médiévale* 38, no. 3 (1995): 267–74. http://dx.doi.org/10.3406/ccmed.1995.2622.

– *Western Travellers to Constantinople: The West and Byzantium, 962–1204: Cultural and Political Relations*. Vol. 10, Medieval Mediterranean. Leiden and New York: Brill, 1996.

Ciggaar, Krijna Nelly, and Herman Teule, eds. *East and West in the Crusader States: Contexts, Contacts, Confrontations*. Amsterdam: Peeters Publishers, 2003.

Clain-Legros, Huguette. *La Rose et le lys: étude littéraire du Conte de Floire et Blancheflor*. Vol. 31, *Sénéfiance*. Aix-en-Provence: Université de Provence, CUERMA, 1992.

Cohen, Jeffrey Jerome, ed. *The Postcolonial Middle Ages*. New York: St Martin's Press, 2000. http://dx.doi.org/10.1057/9780230107342.

Cohen, Jeffrey Jerome, and Bonnie Wheeler, eds. *Becoming Male in the Middle Ages*. New York: Garland, 1997.

Collins, Patricia Hill. *Black Feminist Thought: Knowledge, Consciousness, and the Politics of Empowerment*. 2nd ed. New York: Routledge, 2000.

– "Learning from the Outsider Within: The Sociological Significance of Black Feminist Thought." In *Feminist Approaches to Theory and Methodology*, edited by S. Hesse-Bibler, C. Gilmartin, and R. Lydenberg, 155–78. Oxford: Oxford University Press, 1999.

Cutler, Anthony. "Gifts and Gift Exchange as Aspects of the Byzantine, Arab, and Related Economies." *Dumbarton Oaks Papers* 55 (2001): 247–78. http://dx.doi.org/10.2307/1291821.

Dagenais, John. *The Ethics of Reading in Manuscript Culture: Glossing the "Libro de buen amor."* Princeton, NJ: Princeton University Press, 1994.

Dagron, Gilbert. "The Urban Economy, Seventh – Twelfth Centuries." In Laiou, *The Economic History of Byzantium from the Seventh through the Fifteenth Century*, 393–461.

Davis, Kathleen, and Nadia Altschul. *Medievalisms in the Postcolonial World: The Idea of "the Medieval Ages" Outside Europe*. Baltimore: Johns Hopkins University Press, 2009.

Day, John. "The Levant Trade in the Middle Ages." In Laiou, *The Economic History of Byzantium from the Seventh through the Fifteenth Century*, 807–14.

Delogu, Daisy. *Theorizing the Ideal Sovereign: The Rise of the French Vernacular Royal Biography*. Toronto: University of Toronto Press, 2008.

Derrida, Jacques. *Limited Inc*. Evanston, IL: Northwestern University Press, 1988.

Devereaux, Rima. *Constantinople and the West in Medieval French Literature: Renewal and Utopia*. Cambridge: D.S. Brewer, 2012.

Dockray-Miller, Mary. *Motherhood and Mothering in Anglo-Saxon England*. New York: St Martin's Press, 2000. http://dx.doi.org/10.1057/9780312299637.

Douglas, Mary. *Purity and Danger: An Analysis of the Concepts of Pollution and Taboo*. London, New York: Routledge, 2002. http://www.routledge.com/books/details/9780415289955/.

Duby, Georges, and Elborg Forster. "Medieval Marriage: Two Models from Twelfth-Century France." In *Johns Hopkins Symposia in Comparative History no. 11*. Baltimore: Johns Hopkins University Press, 1991.

Duby, Georges. *Love and Marriage in the Middle Ages*. Chicago: University of Chicago Press, 1994.

– *The Knight, the Lady, and the Priest: The Making of Modern Marriage in Medieval France*. 1st American ed. New York: Pantheon Books, 1983.

– *Women of the Twelfth Century*. Chicago: University of Chicago Press, 1997.

Duby, Georges, and Jacques Le Goff, eds. *Famille et parenté dans l'Occident médiéval*, Collection de l'école française de Rome: 30. Rome: École française de Rome, 1977.

Duby, Georges, and Michelle Perrot. *A History of Women in the West*. Cambridge, MA: Belknap Press of Harvard University Press, 1992.

Dundes, Alan. "The Psychoanalytic Study of the Grimms' Tales with Special Reference to 'The Maiden Without Hands.'" *Germanic Review* 62, no. 2 (1987): 50–65. http://dx.doi.org/10.1080/00168890.1987.9934192.

Dunton-Downer, Leslie. "The Horror of Culture: East-West Incest in Chrétien de Troyes's *Cligès*." *New Literary History* 28, no. 2 (1997): 367–81. http://dx.doi.org/10.1353/nlh.1997.0020.

Ekdawi, Sarah, Patricia Fann, and Elli Philokyprou. "Bold Men, Fair Maids and Affronts to Their Sex: The Characterization and Structural Roles of Men and Women in the Escorial *Digenis Akritis*." *Byzantine and Modern Greek Studies* 17 (1993): 25–42.

Ellissen, A., and Alexandros Rizos Rankaves. *Die Franken Im Peloponnes*. 2 vols. Leipzig: Otto Wigand, 1856.

Eming, Jutta. "Questions on the Theme of Incest in Courtly Literature." In *The Court Reconvenes: Courtly Literature across the Disciplines*, edited by Barbara K. Altmann and Carleton W. Carroll, 153–60. Cambridge: Brewer, 2003.

Enloe, Cynthia H. *Bananas, Beaches, and Bases: Making Feminist Sense of International Politics*. London: Pandora Press, 1989.

Evans, Helen C., and William D. Wixom. *The Glory of Byzantium: Art and Culture of the Middle Byzantine Era, A.D. 843–1261*. New York: Metropolitan Museum of Art, 1997.

Fallmerayer, Jakob Philipp. *Geschichte der Halbinsel Morea Während des Mittelalters*. Stuttgart, Tübingen: G. Olms Verlagsbuchhandlung, 1830.

Felman, Shoshana. *Jacques Lacan and the Adventure of Insight: Psychoanalysis in Contemporary Culture*. Cambridge, MA: Harvard University Press, 1987.

– *Le Scandale du corps parlant: Don Juan avec Austin, ou, la séduction en deux langues*. Paris: Seuil, 1980.

Fenster, Thelma S. "Beaumanoir's *La Manekine*: Kin D(r)ead: Incest, Doubling, and Death." *American Imago* 39, no. 1 (1982): 41–58.

Ferrante, Joan M. *To the Glory of Her Sex: Women's Roles in the Composition of Medieval Texts.* Bloomington: University of Indiana Press, 1997.

Finucci, Valeria, ed. *Mapping the Mediterranean.* Vol. 37.1, *The Journal of Medieval and Early Modern Studies.* Durham, NC: Duke University Press, 2007.

Fleischman, Suzanne. "Medieval Vernaculars and the Myth of Monoglossia: A Conspiracy of Linguistics and Philology." In *Literary History and the Challenge of Philology: The Legacy of Erich Auerbach,* edited by Seth Lerer, 92–104. Stanford, CA: Stanford University Press, 1996.

Fox, Robin. *The Red Lamp of Incest.* London: Hutchinson, 1980.

François, Charles. "Perrot de Nesle, Jehan Madot, et le ms. B.n. Fr. 375." *Revue Belge de Philologie et d'Histoire. Belgisch Tijdschrift voor Philologie en Geschiedenis* 41, no. 3 (1963): 761–79. http://dx.doi.org/10.3406/rbph.1963.2473.

Freeman, Michelle A. *The Poetics of Translatio Studii and Conjointure: Chrétien de Troyes's "Cligés."* Vol. 12, French Forum Monographs. Lexington: French Forum, 1979.

Garland, Lynda. "'The Eye of the Beholder': Byzantine Imperial Women and Their Public Image from Zoë Porphyrogenita to Euphrosyne Kamaterissa Doukaina (1028–1203)." *Byzantion* 64 (1994): 19–39.

Gaunt, Simon. *Gender and Genre in Medieval French Literature.* Vol. 53, Cambridge Studies in French. Cambridge: Cambridge University Press, 1995.

Geanakoplos, Deno John. *Byzantium: Church, Society, and Civilization Seen through Contemporary Eyes.* Chicago: University of Chicago Press, 1984.

Geary, Patrick. *The Myth of Nations: The Medieval Origins of Europe.* Princeton, NJ: Princeton University Press, 2003.

Gerstel, Sharon E.J. "Art and Identity in the Medieval Morea." In Laiou and Mottahedeh, *The Crusades from the Perspective of Byzantium and the Muslim World,* 263–85.

Gidel, Charles Antoine. *Medieval Greek Texts: Being a Collection of the Earliest Compositions in Vulgar Greek Prior to the Year 1500.* London: A. Asher, 1870.

Giladi, Avner. *Infants, Parents and Wet Nurses: Medieval Islamic Views on Breastfeeding and Their Social Implications.* Leiden, Boston: Brill, 1999.

Gilbert, Jane. "Boys Will Be ... What? Gender, Sexuality, and Childhood in *Floire et Blancheflor* and *Floris et Lyriope.*" *Exemplaria* 9, no. 1 (1997): 39–61. http://dx.doi.org/10.1179/104125797790606709.

Gravdal, Kathryn. "Confessing Incests: Legal Erasures and Literary Celebrations in Medieval France." *Comparative Literature Studies* 32, no. 2 (1995): 280–95.

– *Ravishing Maidens: Writing Rape in Medieval French Literature and Law*. Philadelphia: University of Pennsylvania Press, 1991.

Grégoire, Henri, et al. *Digenis Akritas: The Byzantine Epic in History and Poetry*. New York: National Herald, 1942.

Gregory, Stewart, and Claude Luttrell. "The Manuscripts of *Cligés*." In *Les Manuscrits de Chrétien de Troyes*, edited by Keith Busby, 67–95. Amsterdam: Rodopoi, 1993.

Grieve, Patricia E. *"Floire et Blancheflor" and the European Romance*. Cambridge: Cambridge University Press, 1997. http://dx.doi.org/10.1017/CBO9780511585470.

Guerin, M. Victoria. *The Fall of Kings and Princes: Structure and Destruction in Arthurian Tragedy*. Stanford, CA: Stanford University Press, 1995.

Hadley, D.M., ed. *Masculinity in Medieval Europe*. London: Longman, 1999.

Haidu, Peter. "Narrative Structure in *Floire et Blancheflor*: A Comparison with Two Romances of Chrétien de Troyes." *Romance Notes* 24, no. 2 (1972): 383–6.

Harding, Sandra. *Whose Science? Whose Knowledge?* Ithaca, NY: Cornell University Press, 1991.

Harris, Jonathan. *Byzantium and the Crusades*. New York, London: Hambledon, 2003.

Hartsock, Nancy C.M. "The Feminist Standpoint: Developing the Ground for a Specifically Feminist Historical Materialism." In *The Feminist Standpoint Theory Reader*, edited by Sandra Harding, 35–53. New York, London: Routledge, 2004.

Harvey, Carol J. "From Incest to Redemption in *La Manekine*." *Romance Quarterly* 44, no. 1 (1997): 3–11. http://dx.doi.org/10.1080/08831159709604179.

– "Philippe de Rémi's *Manekine*: Joïe and Pain." In *Women, the Book and the Worldly*, edited by Lesley Smith and Jane H. M. Taylor, 101–10. Cambridge: Brewer, 1995.

Herlihy, David. "Making Sense of Incest: Women and the Marriage Rule of the Early Middle Ages." In *Women, Family, and Society in Medieval Europe: Historical Essays, 1978–1991*, edited by David Herlihy, 96–109. Berghahn Books, 1995.

Herman, Judith, and Lisa Hirschman. "Father-Daughter Incest." *Signs* 2, no. 4 (1977): 735–56. http://dx.doi.org/10.1086/493408.

Hexter, Ralph J. *Equivocal Oaths and Ordeals in Medieval Literature*. Cambridge, MA: Harvard University Press, 1975.

Hill, Barbara. "The Ideal Imperial Komnenian Woman." *Byzantinische Forschungen* 23 (1996): 7–18.

– *Imperial Women in Byzantium, 1025–1204: Power, Patronage and Ideology*. New York: Longman, 1999.

Holzbacher, Ana-María. "Chrétien de Troyes: Una Forma Soterrada de Misoginia." In *Actas del IX Simposio de la Sociedad Española de Literatura General y Comparada*, edited by Túa Blesa et al., 207. Zaragoza, Spain: Universidad de Zaragoza, 1994.

Homère-Alexandre, Théologitis. "*Digenis Akritas* et la littérature byzantine: problèmes d'approche." *Collection de la Maison de l'Orient méditerranéen ancien. Série littéraire et philosophique* 29, no. 1 (2001): 393–405.

Honegger, Thomas. "'But-þat þou louye me, Sertes y dye fore loue of þe': Towards a Typology of Opening Moves in Courtly Amorous Interaction." *Journal of Historical Pragmatics* 1, no. 1 (2000): 117–50. http://dx.doi.org/10.1075/jhp.1.1.09hon.

Horden, Peregrine, and Nicholas Purcell. *The Corrupting Sea: A Study of Mediterranean History*. Oxford and Malden, MA: Blackwell, 2000.

Hubert, Merton Jerome, ed. *The Romance of Floire and Blanchefleur: A French Idyllic Poem of the Twelfth Century*. Chapel Hill: University of North Carolina Press, 1966.

Ilieva, Aneta. *Frankish Morea, 1205–1262: Socio-Cultural Interaction between the Franks and the Local Population*. Athens: Historical Publications St. D. Basilopoulos, 1991.

Ingham, Patricia Clare, and Michelle R. Warren, eds. *Postcolonial Moves: Medieval through Modern*. New York: Palgrave, 2003. http://dx.doi.org/10.1057/9781403980236.

Jacoby, David. "The Encounter of Two Societies: Western Conquerors and Byzantines in the Peloponnesus after the Fourth Crusade." *American Historical Review* 78, no. 4 (1973): 873–906. http://dx.doi.org/10.2307/1858345.

James, Liz. *Empresses and Power in Early Byzantium*. London: Leicester University Press, 2001.

– "Goddess, Whore, Wife, or Slave: Will the Real Byzantine Empress Please Stand Up?" In *Queens and Queenship in Medieval Europe: Proceedings of a Conference Held at King's College London, April 1995*, edited by Anne J. Duggan, 123–39. London: Boydell Press, 1997.

– *Women, Men, and Eunuchs: Gender in Byzantium*. London, New York: Routledge, 1997.

James, Liz, and Barbara Hill. "Women and Politics in the Byzantine Empire: Imperial Women." In *Women in Medieval Western European Culture*, edited by Linda Elizabeth Mitchell, 157–78. New York: Garland, 1999.

Jauss, Hans Robert. *Toward an Aesthetic of Reception*. Vol. 2, Theory and History of Literature. Minneapolis: University of Minnesota Press, 1982.

Jauss, Hans Robert, and Erich Köhler. *Le Roman jusqu'à la fin du XIIIè*. Edited by Jean Frappier. Vol. IV, *Grundriss Der Romanischen Literaturen Des Mittelalters*. Heidelberg: Universität Konstanz, 1978.

Jeay, Madeleine. "Chercher une fille, une épouse: Sexualités déviantes et parcours de rédemption." *Florilegium* 18, no. 1 (2001): 65–82.

Jeffreys, Elizabeth, and Michael Jeffreys, eds. *Popular Literature in Late Byzantium.* London: Variorum Reprints, 1983.

– "The 'Wild Beast from the West': Immediate Literary Reactions in Byzantium to the Second Crusade." In Laiou and Mottahedeh, *The Crusades from the Perspective of Byzantium and the Muslim World,* 101–16.

Jeffreys, Michael. "*The Chronicle of the Morea*: Priority of the Greek Version." *Byzantinische Zeitschrift* 68, no. 2 (1975): 304–50. http://dx.doi.org/10.1515/byzs.1975.68.2.304.

Jones, Lynn, and Henry Maguire. "A Description of the Jousts of Manuel I Komnenos." *Byzantine and Modern Greek Studies* 26 (2002): 104–48.

Jotischky, Andrew. "Ethnographic Attitudes in the Crusader States: The Franks and the Indigenous Orthodox People." In Ciggaar and Teule, *East and West in the Crusader States,* 1–19.

Kaldellis, Anthony. *Hellenism in Byzantium: The Transformations of Greek Identity and the Reception of the Classical Tradition.* Cambridge: Cambridge University Press, 2009. http://dx.doi.org/10.1017/CBO9780511496356.

Karras, Ruth Mazo. *From Boys to Men: Formations of Masculinity in Late Medieval Europe.* Philadelphia: University of Pennsylvania Press, 2003.

Kazhdan, Alexander. "Latins and Franks in Byzantium: Perception and Reality from the Eleventh to the Twelfth Century." In Laiou and Mottahedeh, *The Crusades from the Perspective of Byzantium and the Muslim World,* 83–100.

Kelly, Douglas. "The *Fidus Interpres*: Aid or Impediment to Medieval Translation and *Translatio*?" In Beer, *Translation Theory and Practice in the Middle Ages,* 47–58.

Kelly, Kathleen Coyne. "The Bartering of Blauncheflur in the Middle English *Floris and Blauncheflur*." *Studies in Philology* 91, no. 2 (1994): 101–10.

Kibler, William. "Archetypal Imagery in *Floire et Blancheflor*." *Romance Quarterly* 35, no. 1 (1988): 11–20. http://dx.doi.org/10.1080/08831157.1988.9932570.

– "Translating Chrétien de Troyes: How Faithful?" In Beer, *Translation Theory and Practice in the Middle Ages,* 255–70.

Kinoshita, Sharon. "'Pagans are wrong and Christians are right': Alterity, Gender, and Nation in the *Chanson de Roland*." *Journal of Medieval and Early Modern Studies* 31, no. 1 (2001): 79–111. http://dx.doi.org/10.1215/10829636-31-1-79.

– "The Poetics of *Translatio*: French-Byzantine Relations in Chrétien de Troyes's *Cligès*." *Exemplaria* 8 (1996): 315–54.

– *Medieval Boundaries: Rethinking Difference in Old French Literature*. Philadelphia: University of Pennsylvania Press, 2006.

–"Worlding Medieval French." In *French Global: A New Approach to Literary History*, edited by Christine McDonald and Susan Suleiman, 3-20. New York: Columbia University Press, 2011.

Knedler, J.W. "The Girl without Hands: Latin-American Variants." *Hispanic Review* 10, no. 4 (1942): 314–24. http://dx.doi.org/10.2307/469898.

Kong, Katherine. *Lettering the Self in Medieval and Early Modern France*. Cambridge: Boydell and Brewer, 2010.

Kriaras, E. *Byzantina Ippotika Mythistorhmata*. Vol. 2, Basikh Bibliothhkh. Athens: Aetos, 1955.

Kristeva, Julia. *Powers of Horror: An Essay on Abjection*. New York: Columbia University Press, 1982.

Krueger, Roberta L. *Women Readers and the Ideology of Gender in Old French Verse Romance*. Cambridge: Cambridge University Press, 2005.

Lacy, Norris. "The Flowering (and Misreading) of Romance: *Floire Et Blancheflor*." *South Central Review* 9, no. 2 (1992): 19–26. http://dx.doi.org/10.2307/3189527.

Laiou, Angeliki E. "Byzantine Trade with Christians and Muslims and the Crusades." In Laiou and Mottahedeh, *The Crusades from the Perspective of Byzantium and the Muslim World*, 157–96.

– ed. *The Economic History of Byzantium from the Seventh through the Fifteenth Century*. Washington, DC: Dumbarton Oaks, 2002.

– "Exchange and Trade, Seventh–Twelfth Centuries." In *The Economic History of Byzantium from the Seventh through the Fifteenth Century*, edited by Angeliki E. Laiou, 697–770. Washington, DC: Dumbarton Oaks, 2002.

– ed. *Mariage, amour et parenté à Byzance aux XIe–XIIIe siècles*. Vol. 7. Paris: De Boccard, 1992.

– "Sex, Consent, and Coercion in Byzantium." In *Consent and Coercion to Sex and Marriage in Ancient and Medieval Societies*, 109–221. Washington, DC: Dumbarton Oaks, 1993.

Laiou, Angeliki E., and Roy P. Mottahedeh, eds. *The Crusades from the Perspective of Byzantium and the Muslim World*. Washington, DC: Dumbarton Oaks, 2001.

Lampert-Weissig, Lisa. *Medieval Literature and Postcolonial Studies*. Edinburgh: Edinburgh University Press, 2010.

Lascaratos, John, and E. Poulakou-Rebelakou. "Child Sexual Abuse: Historical Cases in the Byzantine Empire (324–1453 A.D.)." *Child Abuse & Neglect* 24, no. 8 (Aug 2000): 1085–90. http://dx.doi.org/10.1016/S0145-2134(00)00156-3. Medline:10983818.

Laskaya, Anne. "The Rhetoric of Incest in the Middle English *Emaré*." In *Violence against Women in Medieval Texts*, edited by Anna Roberts, 97–114. Gainesville: University Press of Florida, 1998.

Lees, Clare A., Thelma S. Fenster, and Jo Ann McNamara, eds. *Medieval Masculinities: Regarding Men in the Middle Ages*. Vol. 7, Medieval Cultures. Minneapolis: University of Minnesota Press, 1994.

Legros, Huguette. "Parenté naturelle, alliance, parenté spirituelle: De l'inceste à la sainteté." In *Les Relations de Parenté dans le monde médiéval*, 511–64. Aix-en-Provence: Centre Universitaire d'Etudes et de Recherches Médiévales, 1989.

Lejeune, Rita. "Le Rôle littéraire de la famille d'Aliénor d'Aquitaine." *Cahiers de civilisation médiévale* 1, no. 3 (1958): 319–37. http://dx.doi.org/10.3406/ccmed.1958.1058.

Lévi-Strauss, Claude. *Anthropologie structurale*. Paris: Plon, 1958.

Lincoln, J.N. "The Legend of the Handless Maiden." *Hispanic Review* 4, no. 3 (1936): 277–80. http://dx.doi.org/10.2307/469919.

Lochrie, Karma, Peggy McCracken, and James A. Schultz, eds. *Constructing Medieval Sexuality*. Minneapolis: University of Minnesota Press, 1997.

Lock, Peter. *The Franks in the Aegean, 1204–1500*. New York, London: Longman, 1995.

Löhneysen, Wolfgang. *Mistra: Griechenlands Schicksal im Mittelalter: Morea unter Franken, Byzantinern U. Osmanen*. Munich: Prestel, 1977.

LoPrete, Kimberly. "Adela of Blois as Mother and Countess." In *Medieval Mothering*, edited by Bonnie Wheeler and John Carmi Parsons, 313–33. New York: Garland, 1999.

Lurier, Harold E. *Crusaders as Conquerors: The Chronicle of Morea*. New York: Columbia University Press, 1964.

Macrides, Ruth. "Dynastic Marriages and Political Kinship." In *Byzantine Diplomacy*, edited by Jonathon Shepard and Simon Franklin, 263–80. London: Variorum, 1992.

Magdalino, Paul. "*Digenis Akrites* and Byzantine Literature: The Twelfth-Century Background to the Grottaferrata Version." In *Digenis Akrites: New Approaches to Byzantine Heroic Poetry*, edited by Roderick Beaton and David Ricks, 1–14. London: Variorum, 1993.

– "Medieval Constantinople: Built Environment and Urban Development." In Laiou, *The Economic History of Byzantium from the Seventh through the Fifteenth Century*, 529–37.

Maguire, Henry. *Byzantine Court Culture from 829 to 1204*. Washington, DC: Dumbarton Oaks, 1997.

Mallette, Karla. *The Kingdom of Sicily, 1100–1250: A Literary History*. Philadelphia: University of Pennsylvania Press, 2005.

Matschke, Klaus-Peter. "Commerce, Trade, Markets, and Money, Thirteenth – Fifteenth Centuries." In Laiou, *The Economic History of Byzantium from the Seventh through the Fifteenth Century*, 771–806.

Mauss, Marcel. *The Gift: The Form and Reason for Exchange in Archaic Societies*. London, New York: Routledge, 1990.

McCash, June Hall, ed. *The Cultural Patronage of Medieval Women*. Athens: University of Georgia Press, 1996.

McCracken, Peggy. *The Curse of Eve, the Wound of the Hero: Blood, Gender, and Medieval Literature*. The Middle Ages Series. Philadelphia: University of Pennsylvania Press, 2003.

– *The Romance of Adultery: Queenship and Sexual Transgression in Old French Literature*. The Middle Ages Series. Philadelphia: University of Pennsylvania Press, 1998.

– "Love and War in *Cligés*." *Arthuriana* 18, no. 3 (2008): 6–18.

McLaughlin, Megan. "'Abominable Mingling': Father-Daughter Incest and the Law." *Medieval Feminst Newsletter* 24 (1997): 26–30.

Menocal, María Rosa. *The Arabic Role in Medieval Literary History: A Forgotten Heritage*. Philadelphia: University of Pennsylvania Press, 1987.

Mitchell, Linda Elizabeth. *Women in Medieval Western European Culture*. New York: Garland, 1999.

Moore, Megan. "Boundaries and Byzantines in the Old French *Floire et Blancheflor*." *Dalhousie French Studies* 29 (2007): 3–20.

Morrisson, Cécile, and Jean-Claude Cheynet. "Prices and Wages in the Byzantine World." In Laiou, *The Economic History of Byzantium from the Seventh through the Fifteenth Century*, 815–78.

Murray, Jacqueline. *Conflicted Identities and Multiple Masculinities: Men in the Medieval West*. New York: Garland, 1999.

Nicol, Donald MacGillivray. *The Last Centuries of Byzantium, 1261–1453*. 2nd ed. Cambridge: Cambridge University Press, 1993.

Nixon, Terry. "Romance Collections and the Manuscripts of Chrétien de Troyes." In *Les Manuscrits de Chrétien de Troyes*, edited by Keith Busby et al., 17–25. Amsterdam: Rodopi, 1993.

Norwich, John Julius. *A History of Venice*: New York: Vintage, 1983.

– *A Short History of Byzantium*. 1st American ed. New York: Random House, 1997.

Oikonomides, Nicolas. "The Role of the Byzantine State in the Economy." In Laiou, *The Economic History of Byzantium: From the Seventh through the Fifteenth Century*, 973–1058.

– "Title and Income at the Byzantine Court." In *Byzantine Court Culture from 829 to 1204*, edited by Henry Maguire, 199–215. Washington, DC: Harvard University Press, 1997.

Opsahl, Erhard Peter. "The Hospitallers, Templars, and Teutonic Knights in the Morea after the Fourth Crusade." Ph. diss., University of Wisconsin, 1994. microform.

Origone, Sandra. "Marriage Connections between Byzantium and the West in the Age of the Palaiologoi." In *Intercultural Contacts in the Medieval Mediterranean*, edited by Benjamin Arbel, 226–41. Portland, OR: F. Cass, 1996.

Ostrogorski, Georgije. *History of the Byzantine State*. New Brunswick, NJ: Rutgers University Press, 1969.

Parker, Grant. "Mapping the Mediterranean." *Journal of Medieval and Early Modern Studies* 37, no. 1 (2007): 1–7. http://dx.doi.org/10.1215/10829636-2006-008.

Parsons, John Carmi. "Of Queens, Courts, and Books: Reflections on the Literary Patronage of Thirteenth-Century Plantagenet Queens." In *The Cultural Patronage of Medieval Women*, edited by June Hall McCash, 175–201. Athens: University of Georgia Press, 1996.

Parsons, John Carmi, and Bonnie Wheeler, eds. *Medieval Mothering*. New York: Garland, 1996.

Perry, Mary. *The Handless Maiden: Moriscos and the Politics of Religion in Early Modern Spain*. Princeton, NJ: Princeton University Press, 2005.

Pickens, Rupert. "Transmission et *translatio*: mouvement textuel et variance." *French Forum* 23, no. 2 (1998): 133–45.

Queller, Donald E., and Thomas F. Madden. *The Fourth Crusade: The Conquest of Constantinople*. 2nd ed. Philadelphia: University of Pennsylvania Press, 1997.

Quinn, Mary. "Handless Maidens, Modern Texts: A New Reading of Cervante's 'The Captive's Tale.'" *MLN* 123, no. 2 (2008): 213–29. http://dx.doi.org/10.1353/mln.0.0021.

Ramey, Lynn Tarte. "Representations of Women in Chrétien's *Erec Et Enide*: Courtly Literature or Misogyny?" *Romanic Review* 84, no. 4 (1993): 377–86.

Ricks, David. *Byzantine Heroic Poetry*. Bristol: Bristol Classical Press, 1990.

Riley-Smith, Jonathan. "Early Crusaders to the East and the Costs of Crusading, 1095–1130." In *Cross-Cultural Convergences in the Crusader Period*, edited by Michael Goodich, Sophia Menache and Sylvia Schein, 237–58. New York: Peter Lang Publishing, 1995.

– *The First Crusaders, 1095–1131*. Cambridge and New York: Cambridge University Press, 1997.

Roberts, Anna, ed. *Violence against Women in Medieval Texts*. Gainesville: University Press of Florida, 1998.

Rodd, Rennell. *The Princes of Achaia and the Chronicles of Morea: A Study of Greece in the Middle Ages*. London: E. Arnold, 1907.

Rouillard, Linda Marie. "Mutilation and Marriage in *La Manekine*." *RLA: Romance Languages Annual* 12 (2000): 99–104.

Rouse, Richard H., and Mary A. Rouse. *Manuscripts and Their Makers: Commercial Book Producers in Medieval Paris 1200–1500*. 2 vols. Turnhout: Brepols, 2000.

Roussel, Claude. "Aspects du père incestueux dans la littérature médiévale." In *Amour, mariage, et transgressions au moyen age*, edited by Danielle Buschinger and André Crépin, 47–58. Stuttgart: Druck, 1984.

– *Conter de geste au XIVe siècle: inspiration folklorique et écriture épique dans "La Belle Hélène de Constantinople."* Geneva: Librairie Droz, 1998.

Rubin, Gayle. "The Traffic in Women: Notes on the Political Economy of Sex." In *Toward an Anthropology of Women*, edited by Rayna R. Reiter, 157–210. New York: Monthly Review Press, 1975.

Ruddick, Sara. "Maternal Thinking as a Feminist Standpoint." In *The Feminist Standpoint Theory Reader*, edited by Sandra Harding, 161–6. New York, London: Routledge, 2004.

Runciman, Steven. *The Sicilian Vespers: A History of the Mediterranean World in the Later Thirteenth Century*. Cambridge: Cambridge University Press, 1958.

Said, Edward W. *Orientalism*. 1st ed. New York: Pantheon Books, 1978.

Sargent-Baur, Barbara N. "Echos de Chrétien de Troyes dans les romans de Philippe de Remi." In *Miscellanea Mediaevalia, I–II*, edited by J. Claude Faucon, Alain Labbé and Danielle Quéruel, 1193–201. Paris: Champion, 1998.

Segol, Marla. "*Floire et Blancheflor*: Courtly Hagiography or Radical Romance?" *Alif* 23 (2003): 233–75.

Shawcross, Clare Teresa M. *The Chronicle of Morea: Historiography in Crusader Greece*. Oxford Studies in Byzantium. Oxford, New York: Oxford University Press, 2009.

Shepard, Jonathon. "Marriages towards the Millenium." In *Byzantium in the Year 1000*, edited by Paul Magdalino, 1–34. Leiden: Brill, 2003.

Shirt, David J. "*Cligés*–a Twelfth-Century Matrimonial Case-Book." *Forum for Modern Language Studies* 18, no. 18 (1982): 75–89. http://dx.doi.org/10.1093/fmls/XVIII.1.75.

Smith, Lesley, and Jane H.M. Taylor, eds. *Women and the Book: Assessing the Visual Evidence*. London: British Library, 1997.

Solterer, Helen. *The Master and Minerva: Disputing Women in French Medieval Culture*. Berkeley: University of California Press, 1995.

Staines, David. *The Complete Romances of Chrétien de Troyes*. Bloomington: Indiana University Press, 1990.

Stouraiti, Anastasia, and Laura Marasso. *Immagini dal mito: la conquista veneziana della Morea (1684–1699)*. Venice: Fondazione Scientifica Querini Stampalia, 2001.

Stratikis, Leon. "Byzantium and France: The Twelfth-Century Renaissance and the Birth of the Medieval Romance." PhD diss., University of Tennessee–Knoxville, 1992.

Sturm-Maddox, Sara. "Arthurian Evasions: The End(s) of Fiction in *Floriant et Florete*." In *"Por Le Soie Amisté": Essays in Honor of Norris J. Lacy*, edited by Keith Busby and Catherine M. Jones, 475–89. Amsterdam and Atlanta: Rodopi, 2000.

– "The Arthurian Romance in Sicily: *Floriant et Florete*." In *Conjointure Arthurienne*, edited by Juliette Dor, 95–107. Louvain-la-Neuve: Université Catholique de Louvain, 2000.

Tarsouli, Athina. *Kastra Kai Politeies Tou Morea*: Athinai: Ekdosis Trapezis Emporikis Pisteos, 1971.

Taylor, Karen J. *Gender Transgressions: Crossing the Normative Barrier in Old French Literature*. New York: Garland, 1998.

Théologitis, Homère-Alexandre. "*Digenis Akritas* et la littérature byzantine: problèmes d'approche." *Collection de la Maison de l'Orient méditerranéen ancien. Série littéraire et philosophique* 29, no. 1 (2001): 393–405.

Toubert, Pierre. "Byzantium and the Mediterranean Agrarian Civilization." In Laiou, *The Economic History of Byzantium from the Seventh through the Fifteenth Century*, 377–91.

Tougher, Shawn F. "Images of Effeminate Men: The Case of Byzantine Eunuchs." In *Masculinity in Medieval Europe*, edited by D.M. Hadley, 89–100. London, New York: Longman, 1999.

Verhuyck, Paul. "Les Manuscrits du poème de *La Belle Hélène De Constantinople*." *Studi Francesi* 16 (1972): 314–24.

Walters, Lori. "*Translatio Studii*: Christine de Pizan's Self-Portrayal in Two Lyric Poems and in the *Livre de la mutacion de fortune*." In *Christine de Pizan and Medieval French Lyric*, edited by Earl Jeffrey Richards, 155–67. Gainesville: University Press of Florida, 1998.

Warren, Michelle R. *Creole Medievalism: Colonial France and Joseph Bédier's Middle Ages*. Minneapolis: University of Minnesota Press, 2011.

Watt, Diane. "Behaving Like a Man? Incest, Lesbian Desire, and Gender Play in *Yde et Olive* and its Adaptations." *Comparative Literature* 50, no. 4 (1998): 265–85. http://dx.doi.org/10.2307/1771525.

Whittow, Mark. *The Making of Byzantium, 600–1025*. Irvine: University of California Press, 1996.

Wolff, Robert Lee, ed. *Studies in the Latin Empire of Constantinople*. London: Variorum, 1976.

Zaddy, Z.P. "Chrétien Misogyne." *Marche Romane* 30, no. 3–4 (1980): 301–7.

Index

www.ingramcontent.com/pod-product-compliance
Lightning Source LLC
LaVergne TN
LVHW041113090826
844660LV00061B/879/J

* 9 7 8 1 4 4 2 6 4 4 6 9 4 *